CROSS-COUNTRY

CROSS~COUNTRY

A BOOK OF AUSTRALIAN VERSE

Second Edition

Edited by John Barnes and
Brian McFarlane

Heinemann Educational Australia

Rigby Heinemann
a division of the Octopus Publishing Group Australia Pty Ltd
22 Salmon Street, Port Melbourne, Victoria 3207

Offices in Sydney, Brisbane and Adelaide. Associated companies,
branches and representatives throughout the world.

Cover photograph by Malcolm Cross

Typeset in 10/11 Bembo by Savage Type Pty Ltd, Brisbane
Printed in Singapore by Chong Moh Offset Printing Pte Ltd

National Library of Australia
cataloguing-in-publication data:

Cross-country: a book of Australian verse.

  2nd ed.
  Includes index.
  ISBN 0 85859 493 5.

  1. Australian poetry. I. Barnes, John, 1931–   .
  II. McFarlane, Brian, 1934– .

A821'.308

CONTENTS

PART TWO: SELECTED POEMS

x

INTRODUCTION

'. . . so Cook sailed westabout,
So men write poems in Australia'.
   —KENNETH SLESSOR: 'Five Visions of Captain Cook'

Cross-Country is a selection of Australian poetry written in English since the coming of the Europeans to this continent—since Cook sailed westabout. Until quite recently it would have seemed odd to stress that it is poetry in English which is our concern, since the notion that anything written in a language other than English could be Australian would have been regarded as self-contradictory. A recent anthologist, however, declares that Australian poetry is not two hundred years old but in all probability 40,000 years old. Although the poetry of the Aborigines is becoming more accessible to English-speaking Australians as our knowledge of their culture extends and more of their oral literature is recorded and translated, it is not part of the tradition of poetic writing that has been created in this country over the past two centuries.

Poets from Harpur onwards have been interested in the Aborigines and have on occasions sought to render what they have imagined to be their consciousness. Mostly their efforts, however well-intentioned and sympathetic, have not resulted in impressive poetry. However, a poetic sequence like Les Murray's 'The Buladelah—Taree Holiday Song Cycle' shows how, in the work of a gifted poet who is also a linguist, the forms of Aboriginal song can be creatively employed. In the future we may expect that Australian poetry will start to reflect a deeper and more sensitive awareness of Aboriginal culture—and the cultures of the major migrant communities in our increasingly multicultural society.

However, in *Cross-Country* we have not set out to illustrate contemporary trends or to predict the future of poetry in Australia. Our aim has been to represent the range of achievement in Australian poetry from the perspective of the present. We have sought to distinguish what seem to us the strengths of our poetry while at the same time suggesting its scope and variety. And in pursuing this aim we have departed from the usual form of anthology in which there is a long parade of writers, each represented by only one or two poems. We have not attempted to include

I

every poet who might be considered worthy of notice at the present time, nor have we consciously preferred one kind of poetry over another. Inevitably our choices have been influenced by our personal tastes, but we have tried to avoid mere idiosyncracy; and, certainly, there are several inclusions which are at odds with our individual tastes but which seemed important from the point of view of representativeness. Though poems by young poets writing at present are included, our choice is not intended as a prediction of likely success but, rather, to give some sense of what is being written now.

Anyone who cares to look through previous anthologies of Australian poetry will notice how many writers, much admired in their own day, have now sunk without a trace. As sensibility changes, as new attitudes to poetry are formed, as new poets alter the possibilities of the art for future writers, the sense of what constitutes Australian poetry—its strengths and its limitations—is bound to change. We get a new perspective on the past and we look at the contemporary scene with different expectations. There is a continual process of sifting and re-appraisal. Over the past quarter of a century, a great expansion in literary studies, accompanied by an equally great increase in creativity, in the Australian community has intensified and sharpened discussion. While earlier judgements of the colonial poets have not been much disturbed, there have been some striking shifts in twentieth-century reputations. Hugh McCrae, for instance, has suffered what may well be an irreversible decline, whereas John Shaw Neilson has grown steadily in reputation. Bernard O'Dowd, once regarded as the equal of Brennan, no longer seems a poet who matters in the history of poetry, however interesting he may be in the history of ideas.

O'Dowd's sonnet entitled 'Australia' has, however, survived his decline in reputation. Indeed, a large anthology could easily be compiled of poems in which the theme of Australia and Australian identity is pursued. We did not make our selection on the basis of thematically connected poems, but were nevertheless struck by the recurring need poets have felt to come to some sort of terms with this country, in tones of varying directness. Perhaps those who read this anthology will find it interesting to trace the changing approaches to this theme from the time of Harpur and Kendall to the present day. This was not the only preoccupation that made itself felt as our selection settled: the relationship of Australians to the landscape and the pervasiveness of modern suburban life were two others that emerged very clearly.

In compiling an anthology, we have followed two distinct principles. In PART ONE we have made a selection of poets whose work, it seems to us, constitutes the central tradition of Australian poetry. We do not claim that all the poets here are of equal stature or that they are the only significant poets in the history of Australian literature. It will be obvious that as we have come closer to the present we have found more to admire than in the earlier years—up to, say, the time of Slessor. While this may merely reflect our individual tastes, it is our considered judgment that the level of Australian poetry has risen noticeably over the past half-century. The design of our anthology has the disadvantage that it involves making choices where choice may be very difficult—especially among living poets who may still spring surprises on us—but it has the more-than-compensating advantage that it allows us to present the poets we have chosen more fully than is usually the case in anthologies. To someone who is attempting to see Australian poetry as a whole, *Cross-Country* offers a definition through this selection of poets. Poets such as Paterson and Lawson, whose work is comparatively simple in its concerns and limited in its expressiveness, are included because of their historical role as creators of verse in touch with common speech. At the beginning, Australian poets were confronted with problems of idiom and subject matter, and this anthology, which enables the reader to compare the poetry of Harpur and Kendall with that of such contemporary poets as Dawe, Murray and Porter will, we hope, suggest something of how poets have dealt with these problems. Readers will, of course, make their own judgments of the qualities which the poetry exhibits; our aim in this first section has been to give a just representation of the Australian poetic tradition in English.

In PART TWO, we have followed a different principle of selection. Here we have collected a miscellany of individual poems—from Adam Lindsay Gordon's 'The Sick Stockrider' to Fay Zwicky's 'Kaddish'—to illustrate the range and diversity of Australian poetry. The basis of selection has been interest in the particular poems rather than concern to represent the author. Thus, old 'favourites' like O'Dowd's 'Australia' and Dorthea Mackellar's 'My Country' (reminders that some poems retain a life independent of their authors' reputations) are included along with personal preferences and with poems selected for other reasons. For instance, though we have not set out to represent poetic movements, we have chosen poems with an eye on the preoccupations that can be discerned in the work of the poets represented in PART ONE.

We have assumed that many of our readers will have little prior knowledge of Australian poetry—and, perhaps in some cases, of Australia—and that this book will be their introduction to it. For them in particular, we have included brief biographical, descriptive, and bibliographical notes on the poets in PART ONE.

Cross-Country, then, is composed of two parts which are intended to form a whole. We hope this 'whole' will provide a substantial basis for a serious study of Australian poetry as well as a coherent and stimulating selection for the general reader.

Note to the Second Edition

In this expanded edition we have aimed at giving a fuller representation of the rich diversity of Australian poetry by adding twenty-three poems, by seventeen poets, to PART TWO. Along with poems by contemporary poets, we have added some from the past for which there was no room in the original volume and others, such as those of Ada Cambridge and Lesbia Harford, which we have come to know only recently.

At the request of many readers who have commented appreciatively on the notes in PART ONE, we have added notes—necessarily much briefer and more restricted—on the poets in PART TWO.

PART ONE
Selected Poets

CHARLES HARPUR

(1813–1868)

CHARLES HARPUR is, in the words of Judith Wright, 'Australia's first poet of sustained significance, and in important respects ... also our most interesting nineteenth-century poet'. The son of convicts—both his parents had been transported, his father for highway robbery—he was born at Windsor, New South Wales, where his father, having served his sentence, had become a schoolmaster and parish clerk. By his own account, he had a better education than was available to most of the native-born in the colony at that time. He worked at a variety of occupations, including post-office clerk, farmer, schoolmaster and gold commissioner; and although he was publicly recognized as a poet and enjoyed the friendship and support of such prominent men as N.D. Stenhouse, Australia's first literary patron, he was never able to devote himself to poetry. Harpur thought of himself as an Australian poet and was ambitious to be 'the Bard' of his homeland. At the same time he was a bitter critic of the values he saw in the colony, and penned satiric attacks on politicians with whom he disagreed. His life was clouded by disappointment; a year before his death he wrote that he felt himself to be 'living in a sham age, under a sham Government, and amongst sham friends'. He had difficulty in getting his poetry published in book form, his only substantial publication during his lifetime being *The Bushrangers, a Play in Five Acts and Other Poems* in 1853. 'The Creek of the Four Graves' and 'The Dream by the Fountain' both appeared in this volume. There is still no definitive edition of his poetry. The texts of the poems included in this anthology are taken from Adrian Mitchell's selection (Sun Books, 1973), which is based upon the Harpur manuscripts in the Mitchell Library, Sydney.

A Midsummer Noon in the Australian Forest

Not a sound disturbs the air,
There is quiet everywhere;
Over plains and over woods
What a mighty stillness broods.

Even the grasshoppers keep
Where the coolest shadows sleep;
Even the busy ants are found
Resting in their pebbled mound;
Even the locust clingeth now
In silence to the barky bough:
And over hills and over plains
Quiet, vast and slumbrous, reigns.

Only there's a drowsy humming
From yon warm lagoon slow coming:
'Tis the dragon-hornet—see!
All bedaubed resplendently
With yellow on a tawny ground—
Each rich spot nor square nor round,
But rudely heart-shaped, as it were
The blurred and hasty impress there,
Of a vermiel-crusted seal
Dusted o'er with golden meal:
Only there's a droning where
Yon bright beetle gleams the air—
Gleams it in its droning flight
With a slanting track of light,
Till rising in the sunshine higher,
Its shards flame out like gems on fire.

Every other thing is still,
Save the ever wakeful rill,
Whose cool murmur only throws
A cooler comfort round Repose;
Or some ripple in the sea
Of leafy boughs, where, lazily,
Tired Summer, in her forest bower
Turning with the noontide hour,
Heaves a slumbrous breath, ere she
Once more slumbers peacefully.

O 'tis easeful here to lie
Hidden from Noon's scorching eye,
40   In this grassy cool recess
Musing thus of Quietness.

Aboriginal Death Song

Behold, it is the camp-fire of our Brother!—
But I see only in the ring of its light
A weeping woman with a young child,
And look in vain for the gleam of the tomahawk
That but yesterday was merry in the tree-tops.

The fish-pools of the ancient river
Have lost the shadow of a skilful hand!
The well-known tracks of a fleet-footed hunter
Are fast fading from the grassy hills,
10   And a sure spear of the tribe is broken.

There is a vacant place in the circle of the Seers:
From the consultations of the wise and brave
A bold voice has gone up forever!
And a whoop that late was loud on our border
Is terrible only in the deeds of the past.

The Dream by the Fountain

Thought-weary and sad, I reclined by a Fountain
At the head of a white-cedar shaded ravine,
And the breeze that fell over the high-glooming mountain
Sang a lullaby low as I gazed o'er the Scene.

Long I'd reclined not till slumber came o'er me,
Grateful as balm to a suffering child:
When a lofty-souled Maiden seemed standing before me
With a lyre in her hand—O so sounding and wild!

Bright was her brow, not the morning's brow brighter
10 But her eyes were two midnights of passionate thought;
Light was her motion, the breeze's not lighter,
And her locks were like sunshine and shadow inwrought.

Never before did my bosom inherit
Emotion so thrilling, such exquisite awe!
Never such wonder exalted my spirit
Before, as did now, through the Vision I saw.

Rob'd for the chase like a nymph of Diana,
Her ivory limbs were half given below—
Bare, that the pure breath of heaven might fan her,
20 Bare was her bosom of roseate snow.

Then lifting the lyre, and with every feeling
Sublimed as with love, she awakened the strings:
Bliss followed—and half into being came stealing
The motion and light of angelical wings.

Divine were the measures! Each voice of the wildwood
Seemed gathering head in their musical thrills—
The loud joy of streams in their strong mountain childhood,
The shouting of Echoes that look from the hills:

The moaning of trees all at midnight in motion,
30 When the breezes seem lost in the dark, with a rare
And sweet meaning spirit of human devotion,
All blended and woven together were there!

Ceased then the strain: and as soon as were flowing
Around but the accents that people the wild,
The Lyrist, subdued by her rapture, yet glowing
Adjusted her mantle, approached me, and smiled:

Smiled with a look like the radiance of morning
When flushing the crystal of heaven's serene,
Blent with that darkness of beauty adorning
40 The world when the moon just arising is seen.

And repressing it seemed many louder suggestions,
Calmly she spake;—I arose to my knees,
Expectantly glad, while to quiet my questions,
The wild warbled words that she uttered were these:

'I am the Muse of the evergreen Forest—
I am the Spouse of thy spirit, lone Bard!
Ev'n in the days when thy boyhood thou worest,
Thy pastimes drew on thee my dearest regard.

For I felt thee,—ev'n then, wildly, wondrously musing
50   Of glory and grace by old Hawksbury's side,
Scenes that spread recordless round thee suffusing
With the purple of love—I beheld thee, and sighed.

Sighed—for the fire-robe of Thought had entwined thee,
Betok'ning how much that the happy most dread,
And whence there should follow, howe'er it renowned thee,
What sorrows of heart, and what labors of head!

Sighed—though thy dreams did the more but endear thee—
It seemed of the breeze, or a sigh of thine own!
I would sweep then this lyre, gliding viewlessly near thee,
60   To give thy emotions full measure and tone.

Since, have I tracked thee through dissolute places,
And saw thee with sorrow long herd with the vain;
Lured into error by false-smiling faces—
Chained by dull Fashion though scorning her chain.

Then would I prompt in the still hour of dreaming,
Some thought of thy beautiful Country again;
Of her yet to be famed streams through dark woods far
                                                    gleaming—
Of her bold shores that throb to the beat of the main

Till at last I beheld thee arise in devotion,
70   To shake from thy heart the vile bondage it bore,
And my joy gloried out like a morning-lit ocean,
When thy footfall I heard in the mountains once more!

Listen, rejoined one; I promise thee glory
Such as shall rise like the day-star apart,
To brighten the source of Australia's broad story,
But for this thou must give to the future thy heart!

Be then the Bard of thy Country! O rather,
Should such be thy choice than a monarchy wide!
Lo, 'tis the Land of the grave of thy father!
80   'Tis the cradle of Liberty!—Think, and decide.

Well hast thou chosen.' She ceased. Unreplying,
I gazed, mute with love, on her soul-moulded charms:
Deeper they glowed, her lips trembled,—and sighing
She rushed to my heart, and dissolved in my arms!*

Thus seemed she to pass—and yet something remaining,
Like a separate Soul in my soul seemed to be:
An aching delight—an extension, that paining
My spirit, yet made it more strengthy and free.

90   She passed—but to leave in my brain a reflection,
A fore-visioned blaze of prophetical sway;
While tones that seem gushings of mystic affection,
Flow through me by night and around me by day.

And since, or in cities or solitudes dreary,
Upon the lone hill or more lonely sea-sand,
No matter how few in my wanderings cheer me,
I know that 'tis mine 'mid the Prophets to stand!
No matter how many that blame be anear me,
I feel like a Monarch of Song in the Land!

The Creek of the Four Graves

PART I

I verse a Settler's tale of olden times—
One told me by our sage friend, Egremont;
Who then went forth, meetly equipt, with four
Of his most trusty and adventurous men
Into the wilderness,—went forth to seek
New streams and wider pastures for his fast
Augmenting flocks and herds. On foot were all,
For horses then were beasts of too great price
To be much ventured upon mountain routes,

---

* It has been pointed out to me, that there is some resemblance between this phase
of the Vision and the matter of a passage in Shelley's Alastor. But whatever likeness
there may be, my draught cannot possibly be any copy of his, for the simple but
sufficient reason, that up to the time of its production, and for long after, though I
may have heard of Shelley as a Poet, I had never seen a line of his writings. My
acquaintance with these began as late as in '43 or '44,—namely on the occasion of Mr
Henry Parkes sending me as a present, far into the interior, a copy of Mrs Shelley's
edition of them, in six volumes.

10　　And over wild wolds clouded up with brush,
　　　And cut with marshes, perilously pathless.

　　　So went they forth at dawn: and now the sun
　　　That rose behind them as they journeyed out,
　　　Was firing with his nether rim a range
　　　Of unknown mountains that, like rampires, towered
　　　Full in their front, and his last glances fell
　　　Into the gloomy forest's eastern glades
　　　In golden masses, transiently, or flashed
　　　Down on the windings of a nameless Creek,
20　　That noiseless ran betwixt the pioneers
　　　And those new Apennines;—ran, shaded up
　　　With boughs of the wild willow, hanging mixed
　　　From either bank, or duskily befringed
　　　With upward tapering, feathery swamp-oaks—
　　　The sylvan eyelash always of remote
　　　Australian waters, whether gleaming still
　　　In lake or pool, or bickering along
　　　Between the marges of some eager stream.

　　　Before them, thus extended, wilder grew
30　　The scene each moment—beautifully wilder!
　　　For when the sun was all but sunk below
　　　Those barrier mountains,—in the breeze that o'er
　　　Their rough enormous backs deep fleeced with wood
　　　Came whispering down, the wide upslanting sea
　　　Of fanning leaves in the descending rays
　　　Danced interdazzlingly, as if the trees
　　　That bore them, were all thrilling,—tingling all
　　　Even to the roots for very happiness:
　　　So prompted from within, so sentient, seemed
40　　The bright quick motion—wildly beautiful.

　　　But when the sun had wholly disappeared
　　　Behind those mountains—O what words, what hues
　　　Might paint the wild magnificence of view
　　　That opened westward! Out extending, lo,
　　　The heights rose crowding, with their summits all
　　　Dissolving, as it seemed, and partly lost
　　　In the exceeding radiancy aloft;
　　　And thus transfigured, for awhile they stood
　　　Like a great company of Archeons, crowned
50　　With burning diadems, and tented o'er
　　　With canopies of purple and of gold!

Here halting wearied, now the sun was set,
Our travellers kindled for their first night's camp
The brisk and crackling fire, which also looked
A wilder creature than 'twas elsewhere wont,
Because of the surrounding savageness.
And soon in cannikins the tea was made,
Fragrant and strong; long fresh-sliced rashers then
Impaled on whittled skewers, were deftly broiled
On the live embers, and when done, transferred
To quadrants from an ample damper cut,
Their only trenchers,—soon to be dispatched
With all the savoury morsels they sustained,
By the keen tooth of healthful appetite.
And as they supped, birds of new shape and plume,
And wild strange voice, nestward repairing by,
Oft took their wonder; or betwixt the gaps
In the ascending forest growths they saw
Perched on the bare abutments of those mountains,
Where haply yet some lingering gleam fell through,
The wallaroo* look forth: till eastward all
The view had wasted into formless gloom,
Night's front; and westward, the high massing woods
Steeped in a swart but mellowed Indian beauty—
A deep dusk loveliness,—lay ridged and heaped
Only the more distinctly for their darkness
Against the twilight heaven—a cloudless depth
Yet luminous from the sunset's fading splendor;
And thus awhile, in the lit dusk, they seemed
To hang like mighty pictures of themselves
In the still chambers of some vaster world.

The silent business of their supper done,
The Echoes of the solitary place,
Came as in sylvan wonder wide about
To hear, and imitate tentatively,
Strange voices moulding a strange speech, as then
Within the pleasant purlieus of the fire
Lifted in glee—but to the hushed erelong,
As with the night in kindred darkness came
O'er the adventurers, each and all, some sense—
Some vague-felt intimation from without,
Of danger, lurking in its forest lairs.

60

70

80

90

---

* A kind of large Kangaroo peculiar to the higher and more difficult mountains.

But nerved by habit, and all settled soon
About the well-built fire, whose nimble tongues
Sent up continually a strenuous roar
Of fierce delight, and from their fuming pipes
Full charged and fragrant with the Indian weed,
Drawing rude comfort,—typed without, as 'twere,
By tiny clouds over their several heads
100 Quietly curling upward;—thus disposed
Within the pleasant firelight, grave discourse
Of their peculiar business brought to each
A steadier mood, that reached into the night.

The simple subject to their minds at length
Fully discussed, their couches they prepared
Of rushes, and the long green tresses pulled
Down from the boughs of the wild willows near.
Then four, as pre-arranged, stretched out their limbs
Under the dark arms of the forest trees
110 That mixed aloft, high in the starry air,
In arcs and leafy domes whose crossing curves
And roof-like features,—blurring as they ran
Into some denser intergrowth of sprays,—
Were seen in mass traces out against the clear
Wide gaze of heaven; and trustful of the watch
Kept near them by their thoughtful Master, soon
Drowsing away, forgetful of their toil,
And of the perilous vast wilderness
That lay around them like a spectral world,
120 Slept, breathing deep;—whilst all things there as well
Showed slumbrous,—yea, the circling forest trees,
Their foremost boles carved from a crowded mass
Less visible, by the watchfire's bladed gleams,
As quick and spicular, from the broad red ring
Of its more constant light they ran in spurts
Far out and under the umbrageous dark;
And even the shaded and enormous mountains,
Their bluff brows glooming through the stirless air,
Looked in their quiet solemnly asleep:
130 Yea, thence surveyed, the Universe might have seemed
Coiled in vast rest,—only that one dim cloud,
Diffused and shapen like a mighty spider,
Crept as with scrawling legs along the sky;
And that the stars, in their bright orders, still
Cluster by cluster glowingly revealed
As this slow cloud moved on,—high over all,—
Looked wakeful—yea, looked thoughtful in their peace.

PART II

Meanwhile the cloudless eastern heaven had grown
More and more luminous—and now the Moon
Up from behind a giant hill was seen
Conglobing, till—a mighty mass—she brought
Her under border level with its cone,
As thereon it were resting: when, behold
A wonder! Instantly that cone's whole bulk
Erewhile so dark, seemed inwardly a-glow
With her instilled irradiance; while the trees
That fringed its outline,—their huge statures dwarfed
By distance into brambles, and yet all
Clearly defined against her ample orb,—
Out of its very disc appeared to swell
In shadowy relief, as they had been
All sculptured from its substance as she rose.

Thus o'er that dark height her great orb conglobed,
Till her full light, in silvery sequence still
Cascading forth from ridgy slope to slope,
Like the dropt foldings of a lucent veil,
Chased mass by mass the broken darkness down
Into the dense-brushed valleys, where it crouched,
And shrank, and struggled, like a dragon doubt
Glooming some lonely spirit that doth still
Resist the Truth with obstinate shifts and shows,
Though shining out of heaven, and from defect
Winning a triumph that might else not be.

There standing in his lone watch, Egremont
On all this solemn beauty of the world,
Looked out, yet wakeful; for sweet thoughts of home
And all the sacred charities it held,
Ingathered to his heart, as by some nice
And subtle interfusion that connects
The loved and cherished (then the most, perhaps,
When absent, or when passed, or even when *lost*)
With all serene and beautiful and bright
And lasting things of Nature. So then thought
The musing Egremont: when suddenly—hark!
A bough crackt loudly in a neighboring brake,
And drew at once, as with a 'larum, all
His spirits thitherward in wild surmise.

140

150

160

170

But summoning caution, and back stepping close
Against the shade-side of a bending gum,
180   With a strange horror gathering to his heart,
As if his blood were charged with insect life
And writhed along in clots, he stilled himself,
Listening long and heedfully, with head
Bent forward sideways, till his held breath grew
A pang, and his ears rung. But Silence there
Had recomposed her ruffled wings, and now
Brooded it seemed even stillier than before,
Deep nested in the darkness: so that he
Unmasking from the cold shade, grew erelong
190   More reassured from wishing to be so,
And to muse Memory's suspended mood,
Though with an effort, quietly recurred.

But there again—crack upon crack! And hark!
O Heaven! have Hell's worst fiends burst howling up
Into the death-doom'd world? Or whence, if not
From diabolic rage, could surge a yell
So horrible as that which now affrights
The shuddering dark! Ah! Beings as fell are near!
Yea, Beings, in their dread inherited hate
200   And deadly enmity, as vengeful, come
In vengeance! For behold, from the long grass
And nearer brakes, a semi-belt of stript
And painted Savages divulge at once
Their bounding forms!—full in the flaring light
Thrown outward by the fire, that roused and lapped
The rounding darkness with its ruddy tongues
More fiercely than before,—as though even *it*
Had felt the sudden shock the air recieved
From their dire cries, so terrible to hear!

210   A moment in wild agitation seen
Thus, as they bounded up, on then they came
Closing, with weapons brandished high, and so
Rushed in upon the sleepers! three of whom
But started, and then weltered prone beneath
The first fell blow dealt down on each by three
Of the most stalwart of their pitiless foes!
But One again, and yet again, heaved up—

Up to his knees, under the crushing strokes
Of huge-clubbed nulla-nullas, till his own
220   Warm blood was blinding him! For he was one
Who had with Misery nearly all his days
Lived lonely, and who therefore, in his soul,
Did hunger after hope, and thirst for what
Hope still had promised him,—some taste at least
Of human good however long deferred,
And now he could not, even in dying, loose
His hold on life's poor chances of to-morrow—
Could not but so dispute the terrible fact
Of death, even in Death's presence! Strange it is:
230   Yet oft 'tis seen that Fortune's pampered child
Consents to his untimely power with less
Reluctance, less despair, than does the wretch
Who hath been ever blown about the world
The straw-like sport of Fate's most bitter blasts,
Vagrant and tieless;—ever still in him
The craving spirit thus grieves unto itself:

'I never yet was happy—never yet
Tasted unmixed enjoyment, and I would
Yet pass on the bright Earth that I have loved
240   Some season, though most brief, of happiness;
So should I walk thence forward to my grave,
Wherever in her green maternal breast
It might await me, more than now prepared
To house me in its gloom,—resigned at heart,
Subjected to its certainty and soothed
Even by the consciousness of having shaped
Some personal good in being;—strong myself,
And strengthening others. But to have lived long years
Of wasted breath, because of woe and want,
250   And disappointed hope,—and now, at last,
To die thus desolate, is horrible!'

And feeling thus through many foregone moods
Whose lines had in the temper of his soul
All mixed, and formed *one* habit,—that poor man,
Though the black shadows of untimely death,
Inevitably, under every stroke,
But thickened more and more,—against them still
Upstruggled, nor would cease: until one last
Tremendous blow, dealt down upon his head
260   As if in mercy, gave him to the dust
With all his many woes and frustrate hope.

Struck through with a cold horror, Egremont,
Standing apart,—yea, standing as it were
In marble effigy, saw this, saw all!
And when outthawing from his frozen heart
His blood again rushed tingling—with a leap
Awaking from the ghastly trance which there
Had bound him, as with chill petrific bonds,
He raised from instinct more than conscious thought
270   His death-charged tube, and at that murderous crew
Firing! saw one fall ox-like to the earth;—
Then turned and fled. Fast fled he, but as fast
His deadly foes went thronging on his track!
Fast! for in full pursuit, behind him yelled
Wild men whose wild speech hath no word for *mercy*!
And as he fled, the forest beasts as well,
In general terror, through the brakes a-head
Crashed scattering, or with maddening speed athwart
His course came frequent. On—still on he flies—
280   Flies for dear life! and still behind him hears
Nearer and nearer, the so rapid dig
Of many feet,—nearer and nearer still.

PART III

So went the chase! And now what should he do?
Abruptly turning, the wild Creek lay right
Before him! But no time was there for thought:
So on he kept, and from a bulging rock
That beaked the bank like a bare promontory,
Plunging right forth and shooting feet-first down,
Sunk to his middle in the flashing stream—
290   In which the imaged stars seemed all at once
To burst like rockets into one wide blaze
Of interwrithing light. Then wading through
The ruffled waters, forth he sprang and siezed
A stake-like root that from the opponent bank
Protruded, and round which his earnest fear
Did clench his cold hand like a clamp of steel,
A moment,—till as swiftly thence he swung
His dripping form aloft, and up the dark
O'erjutting ledge went clambering in the blind
300   And breathless haste of one who flies for life:
When in its face—O verily our God
Hath those in his peculiar care for whom
The daily prayers of spotless Womanhood
And helpless Infancy, are offered up!—

When in its face a cavity he felt,
The upper earth of which in one rude mass
Was held fast bound by the enwoven roots
Of two old trees,—and which, beneath the mould,
Just o'er the clammy vacancy below,
310 Twisted and lapped like knotted snakes, and made
A natural loft-work. Under this he crept,
Just as the dark forms of his hunters thronged
The bulging rock whence he before had plunged.

Duskily visible, thereon a space
They paused to mark what bent his course might take
Over the farther bank, thereby intent
To hold upon the chase, which way soe'er
It might incline, more surely. But no form
Amongst the moveless fringe of fern was seen
320 To shoot up from its outline,—up and forth
Into the moonlight that lay bright beyond
In torn and shapeless blocks, amid the boles
And mixing shadows of the taller trees,
All standing now in the keen radiance there
So ghostly still, as in a solemn trance.
But nothing in the silent prospect stirred—
No fugitive apparition in the view
Rose, as they stared in fierce expectancy:
Wherefore they augured that their prey was yet
330 Somewhere between,—and the whole group with that
Plunged forward, till the fretted current boiled
Amongst their crowding trunks from bank to bank;
And searching thus the stream across, and then
Lengthwise, along the ledges,—combing down
Still, as they went, with dripping fingers, cold
And cruel as inquisitive, each clump
Of long flagged swamp-grass where it flourished high,—
The whole dark line passed slowly, man by man,
Athwart the cavity—so fearfully near,
340 That as they waded by the Fugitive
Felt the strong odor of their wetted skins
Pass with them, trailing as their bodies moved
Stealthily on,—coming with each, and going.

But their keen search was keen in vain. And now
Those wild men marvelled,—till, in consultation,
There grouped in dark knots standing in the stream
That glimmered past them, moaning as it went,
His vanishment, so passing strange it seemed,

They coupled with the mystery of some crude
350   Old fable of their race; and fear-struck all,
And silent, then withdrew. And when the sound
Of their receeding steps had from his ear
Died off, as back to the stormed Camp again
They hurried to despoil the yet warm dead,
Our Friend slid forth, and springing up the bank,
Renewed his flight, nor rested from it, till
He gained the welcoming shelter of his Home.

Return we for a moment to the scene
Of recent death. There the late flaring fire
360   Now smouldered, for its brands were strewn about,
And four stark corpses plundered to the skin
And brutally mutilated, seemed to stare
With frozen eyeballs up into the pale
Round visage of the Moon,. who, high in heaven,
With all her stars, in golden bevies, gazed
As peacefully down as on a bridal there
Of the warm Living—not, alas! on them
Who kept in ghastly silence through the night
Untimely spousals with a desert death.

370   O God! and thus this lovely world hath been
Accursed for ever by the bloody deeds
Of its prime Creature—Man. Erring or wise,
Savage or civilised, still hath he made
This glorious residence, the Earth, a Hell
Of wrong and robbery and untimely death!
Some dread Intelligence opposed to Good
Did, of a surety, over all the earth
Spread out from Eden—or it were not so!

For see the bright beholding Moon, and all
380   The radiant Host of Heaven, evince no touch
Of sympathy with Man's wild violence;—
Only evince in their calm course, their part
In that original unity of Love,
Which, like the soul that dwelleth in a harp,
Under God's hand, in the beginning, chimed
The sabbath concord of the Universe;
And look on a gay clique of maidens, met
In village tryst, and interwhirling all
In glad Arcadian dances on the green—
390   Or on a hermit, in his vigils long,
Seen kneeling at the doorway of his cell—
Or on a monster battle-field where lie

In sweltering heaps, the dead and dying both,
On the cold gory ground,—as they that night
Looked in bright peace, down on the doomful Forest.

Afterwards there, for many changeful years,
Within a glade that sloped into the bank
Of that wild mountain Creek—midway within,
In partial record of a terrible hour
400   Of human agony and loss extreme,
Four grassy mounds stretched lengthwise side by side,
Startled the wanderer;—four long grassy mounds
Bestrewn with leaves, and withered spraylets, stript
By the loud wintry wingéd gales that roamed
Those solitudes, from the old trees which there
Moaned the same leafy dirges that had caught
The heed of dying Ages: these were all;
And thence the place was long by travellers called
The Creek of the Four Graves. Such was the Tale
410   Egremont told us of the wild old times.

HENRY KENDALL

(1839–1882)

HENRY KENDALL was born in a slab hut on a property near the present township of Milton on the south coast of New South Wales. From the beginning his life was wretched—his parents were periodic alcoholics and his father was gaoled for forgery—but despite the family poverty and little schooling he developed a taste for literature; and, as his poetry reveals, the beauty of the country scenery of his childhood made a lasting impression. His first poem appeared in print just before his twentieth birthday, and by 1862 he had published his first collection, *Poems and Songs*, and had gained the friendship of Harpur whom he acknowledged as the first Australian poet. With patronage Kendall obtained government clerical positions in Sydney, but his life was seldom free of debt, and an attempt to support himself and family by journalism in Melbourne in 1869–70 led to his collapse into alcoholism and nervous depression. By 1875 he had sufficiently recovered his health, working as a storekeeper and accountant in the Gosford district, to be able to provide a home for his family. By 1881 he had gained a well paid but onerous government post, Inspector of Forests, but his health deteriorated under the strain, and he died of consumption in Sydney the following year. In his own time Kendall, who wrote the letters 'N.A.P.' (Native Australian Poet) after his name, was much praised for his description of Australian scenery, but later generations of critics have been struck by his literariness and his reliance upon an English frame of reference. Of the poems in this collection, 'The Muse of Australia' is from *Poems and Songs* (1862); 'Prefatory Sonnets', 'The Last of his Tribe', 'Bell-Birds' and 'September in Australia' from *Leaves From the Australian Forests* (1869). 'Bill the Bullock Driver', one of the earliest attempts to represent bush types, was written in 1876 and included in *Songs from the Mountains* (1881). The definitive edition of Kendall's poetry is *The Poetical Works of Henry Kendall* edited by T.T. Reed (1966). An especially interesting selection of Kendall's poetry is that made by Leonie Kramer and A.D. Hope (Sun Books, 1973) to illustrate Hope's view that Kendall's narrative poetry is superior to his lyrics.

The Muse of Australia

Where the pines with the eagles are nestled in rifts,
And the torrent leaps down to the surges,
I have followed her, clambering over the clifts,
By the chasms and moon-haunted verges.
I know she is fair as the angels are fair,
For have I not caught a faint glimpse of her there;
A glimpse of her face, and her glittering hair,
    And a hand with the Harp of Australia?

I never can reach you, to hear the sweet voice
So full with the music of fountains!
Oh! when will you meet with that soul of your choice,
Who will lead you down here from the mountains?—
A lyre-bird lit on a shimmering space;
It dazzled mine eyes, and I turned from the place,
And wept in the dark for a glorious face,
    And a hand with the Harp of Australia!

Prefatory Sonnets

I

I purposed once to take my pen and write
   Not songs like some tormented and awry
   With Passion, but a cunning harmony
Of words and music caught from glen and height,
And lucid colours born of woodland light,
   And shining places where the sea-streams lie;
But this was when the heat of youth glowed white,
   And since I've put the faded purpose by.
I have no faultless fruits to offer you
   Who read this book; but certain syllables
   Herein are borrowed from unfooted dells
And secret hollows dear to noontide dew;
And these at least, though far between and few,
   May catch the sense like subtle forest spells.

II

So take these kindly, even though there be
   Some notes that unto other lyres belong:
   Stray echoes from the elder sons of Song;

And think how from its neighbouring, native sea
The pensive shell doth borrow melody.
20   I would not do the lordly masters wrong,
        By filching fair words from the shining throng
Whose music haunts me, as the wind a tree!
        Lo, when a stranger, in soft Syrian glooms
Shot through with sunset, treads the cedar dells,
And hears the breezy ring of elfin bells
        Far down by where the white-haired cataract booms,
He, faint with sweetness caught from forest smells,
        Bears thence, unwitting, plunder of perfumes.

The Last of His Tribe

He crouches, and buries his face on his knees,
And hides in the dark of his hair;
For he cannot look up to the storm-smitten trees,
Or think of the loneliness there—
Of the loss and the loneliness there.

The wallaroos grope through the tufts of the grass,
And turn to their coverts for fear;
But he sits in the ashes and lets them pass
Where the boomerangs sleep with the spear—
10   With the nullah, the sling, and the spear.

Uloola, behold him! The thunder that breaks
On the tops of the rocks with the rain,
And the wind which drives up with the salt of the lakes,
Have made him a hunter again—
A hunter and fisher again.

For his eyes have been full with a smouldering thought;
But he dreams of the hunts of yore,
And of foes that he sought, and of fights that he fought
With those who will battle no more—
20   Who will go to the battle no more.

It is well that the water which tumbles and fills
Goes moaning and moaning along;
For an echo rolls out from the sides of the hills,
And he starts at a wonderful song—
At the sound of a wonderful song.

And he sees through the rents of the scattering fogs
The corroboree warlike and grim,
And the lubra who sat by the fire on the logs,
To watch, like a mourner, for him—
Like a mother and mourner for him.

30

Will he go in his sleep from these desolate lands,
Like a chief, to the rest of his race,
With the honey-voiced woman who beckons and stands,
And gleams like a dream in his face—
Like a marvellous dream in his face?

Bell-Birds

By channels of coolness the echoes are calling,
And down the dim gorges I hear the creek falling:
It lives in the mountain where moss and the sedges
Touch with their beauty the banks and the ledges.
Through breaks of the cedar and sycamore bowers
Struggles the light that is love to the flowers;
And, softer than slumber, and sweeter than singing,
The notes of the bell-birds are running and ringing.

The silver-voiced bell-birds, the darlings of daytime!
They sing in September their songs of the May-time;
When shadows wax strong, and the thunder-bolts hurtle,
They hide with their fear in the leaves of the myrtle;
When rain and the sunbeams shine mingled together,
They start up like fairies that follow fair weather;
And straightway the hues of their feathers unfolden
Are the green and the purple, the blue and the golden.

10

October, the maiden of bright yellow tresses,
Loiters for love in these cool wildernesses;
Loiters, knee-deep, in the grasses, to listen,
Where dripping rocks gleam and the leafy pools glisten:
Then is the time when the water-moons splendid
Break with their gold, and are scattered or blended
Over the creeks, till the woodlands have warning
Of songs of the bell-bird and wings of the Morning.

20

Welcome as waters unkissed by the summers
Are the voices of bell-birds to thirsty far-comers.
When fiery December sets foot in the forest,

And the need of the wayfarer presses the sorest,
Pent in the ridges for ever and ever
30   The bell-birds direct him to spring and to river,
With ring and with ripple, like runnels whose torrents
Are toned by the pebbles and leaves in the currents.

Often I sit, looking back to a childhood,
Mixt with the sights and the sounds of the wildwood,
Longing for power and the sweetness to fashion,
Lyrics with beats like the heart-beats of Passion;—
Songs interwoven of lights and of laughters
Borrowed from bell-birds in far forest-rafters;
So I might keep in the city and alleys
40   The beauty and strength of the deep mountain valleys:
Charming to slumber the pain of my losses
With glimpses of creeks and a vision of mosses.

September in Australia

Grey Winter hath gone, like a wearisome guest,
    And, behold, for repayment,
September comes in with the wind of the West,
    And the Spring in her raiment!
The ways of the frost have been filled of the flowers
    While the forest discovers
Wild wings with the halo of hyaline hours,
    And a music of lovers.

September, the maid with the swift, silver feet!
10   She glides, and she graces
The valleys of coolness, the slopes of the heat,
    With her blossomy traces.
Sweet month with a mouth that is made of a rose,
    She lightens and lingers
In spots where the harp of the evening glows,
    Attuned by her fingers.

The stream from its home in the hollow hill slips
    In a darling old fashion;
And the day goeth down with a song on its lips,
20   Whose key-note is passion.
Far out in the fierce bitter front of the sea,
    I stand and remember
Dead things that were brothers and sisters of thee,
    Resplendent September.

The West, when it blows at the fall of the noon,
   And beats on the beaches,
Is filled with a tender and tremulous tune
   That touches and teaches:
The stories of Youth, of the burden of Time,
30   And the death of Devotion,
Come back with the wind, and are themes of the rhyme,
   In the waves of the ocean.

We, having a secret to others unknown,
   In the cool mountain-mosses,
May whisper together, September, alone
   Of our loves and our losses.
One word for her beauty, and one for the grace
   She gave to the hours;
And then we may kiss her, and suffer her face
40   To sleep with the flowers.

High places that knew of the gold and the white
   On the forehead of Morning,
Now darken and quake, and the steps of the Night
   Are heavy with warning!
Her voice in the distance is lofty and loud,
   Through the echoing gorges;
She hath hidden her eyes in a mantle of cloud,
   And her feet in the surges!

On the tops of the hills; on the turreted cones—
50   Chief temples of thunder—
The gale, like a ghost, in the middle watch moans,
   Gliding over and under.
The sea, flying white through the rack and the rain,
   Leapeth wild at the forelands;
And the plover, whose cry is like passion with pain,
   Complains in the moorlands.

O, season of changes—of shadow and shine—
   September the splendid!
My song hath no music to mingle with thine,
60   And its burden is ended:
But thou, being born of the winds and the sun,
   By mountain, by river,
May lighten and listen, and loiter and run,
   With thy voices for ever.

Bill the Bullock Driver

The leaders of millions—the lords of the lands
  Who sway the wide world with their will,
And shake the great globe with the strength of their hands,
  Flash past us—unnoticed by Bill.

The elders of Science who measure the spheres,
  And weigh the vast bulk of the sun—
Who see the grand lights beyond *aeons* of years,
  Are less than a bullock to *one*.

The singers that sweeten all time with their song—
10 Pure voices that make us forget
Humanity's drama of marvellous wrong,
  To Bill are as mysteries yet.

By thunders of battle and nations uphurled,
  Bill's sympathies never were stirred:
The helmsmen who stand at the wheel of the world
  By him are unknown and unheard.

What trouble has Bill for the ruin of lands,
  Or the quarrels of temple and throne,
So long as the whip that he holds in his hands,
20 And the team that he drives, are his own?

As straight and as sound as a slab without crack,
  Our Bill is a king in his way:
Though he camps by the side of a shingle track,
  And sleeps on the bed of his dray.

A whiplash to him is as dear as a rose
  Would be to a delicate maid:
He carries his darlings wherever he goes
  In a pocket-book tattered and frayed.

The joy of a bard when he happens to write
30 A song like the song of his dream
Is nothing at all to our hero's delight
  In the pluck and the strength of his team.

For the kings of the earth—for the faces august
  Of princes, the millions may shout:
To Bill as he lumbers along in the dust,
  A bullock's the grandest thing out.

His fourfooted friends are the friends of his choice—
　　No lover is Bill of your dames;
But the cattle that turn at the sound of his voice
40　　Have the sweetest of features and names.

A father's chief joy is a favourite son
　　When he reaches some eminent goal;
But the pride of Bill's heart is the hairy-legged one
　　That pulls with a will at the pole.

His dray is no living, responsible thing,
　　But he gives it the gender of life;
And, seeing his fancy is free in the wing,
　　It suits him as well as a wife.

He thrives like an Arab. Between the two wheels
50　　Is his bedroom, where, lying up-curled,
He thinks for himself like a sultan, and feels
　　That his home is the best in the world.

For, even though cattle like subjects will break
　　At times from the yoke and the band,
Bill knows how to act when his rule is at stake,
　　And is therefore a lord of the land.

Of course he must dream; but be sure that his dreams,
　　If happy, must compass—alas!—
Fat bullocks at feed by improbable streams,
60　　Knee-deep in improbable grass.

No poet is Bill; for the visions of night
　　To him are as visions of day;
And the pipe that in sleep he endeavours to light
　　Is the pipe that he smokes on the dray.

To the mighty, magnificent temples of God
　　In the hearts of the dominant hills
Bill's eyes are as blind as the fire-blackened clod
　　That burns far away from the rills.

Through beautiful, bountiful forests that screen
70　　A marvel of blossoms from heat—
Whose lights are the mellow and golden, and green—
　　Bill walks with irreverent feet.

The manifold splendours of mountain and wood
    By Bill like nonentities slip:
He loves the black myrtle because it is good
    As a handle to lash to his whip.

And thus through the world, with a swing in his tread,
    Our hero self-satisfied goes;
With his cabbage-tree hat on the back of his head,
80   And the string of it under his nose.

Poor bullocky Bill! In the circles select
    Of the scholars he hasn't a place;
But he walks like a *man* with his forehead erect,
    And he looks at God's day in the face.

For, rough as he seems, he would shudder to wrong
    A dog with the loss of a hair;
And the angels of shine and superlative song
    See his heart and the deity there.

Few know him indeed; but the beauty that glows
90   In the forest is loveliness still;
And Providence helping the life of the rose
    Is a Friend and a Father to Bill.

A.B. PATERSON

(1864–1941)

ANDREW BARTON PATERSON was born near Orange in New
South Wales, where his father leased a sheep and cattle
station. Educated at Sydney Grammar School, he qualified
as a solicitor and practised law in Sydney for some years.
His later experiences included being a journalist and war
correspondent (at the time of the Boer War), station-
owner and editor. Much of his verse was published under
the pen-name of 'The Banjo' (a reference to a favourite
horse). 'Clancy of the Overflow', on its first publication
(in the *Bulletin* in 1889), was praised by the novelist Rolf
Boldrewood as 'the best bush ballad since Gordon'. His
first—and best—collection, *The Man From Snowy River*
(1895), was remarkably popular and established his reputa-
tion as the leading Australian balladist. He collected and
edited a volume entitled *Old Bush Songs* (1905) as well as
publishing several volumes of his own verse, novels, short
stories and reminiscences. Although critical opinion does
not rate Paterson's poetry highly, as the author of 'Clancy
of the Overflow', 'The Man From Snowy River' and
'Waltzing Matilda' (which has become an unofficial
national song), he holds an unchallenged place in the
popular view of Australian culture.

The Man From Snowy River

There was movement at the station, for the word had
    passed around
  That the colt from old Regret had got away,
And had joined the wild bush horses—he was worth a
    thousand pound,
  So all the cracks had gathered to the fray.
All the tried and noted riders from the stations near and far
  Had mustered at the homestead overnight,
For the bushmen love hard riding where the wild bush
    horses are,
  And the stock-horse snuffs the battle with delight.

There was Harrison, who made his pile when Pardon won
    the cup,
  The old man with his hair as white as snow;
But few could ride beside him when his blood was fairly
    up—
  He would go wherever horse and man could go.
And Clancy of the Overflow came down to lend a hand,
  No better horseman ever held the reins;
For never horse could throw him while the saddle-girths
    would stand—
  He learnt to ride while droving on the plains.

And one was there, a stripling on a small and weedy beast;
  He was something like a racehorse undersized,
With a touch of Timor pony—three parts thoroughbred at
    least—
  And such as are by mountain horsemen prized.
He was hard and tough and wiry—just the sort that won't
    say die—
  There was courage in his quick impatient tread;
And he bore the badge of gameness in his bright and fiery
    eye,
  And the proud and lofty carriage of his head.

But still so slight and weedy, one would doubt his power
    to stay,
  And the old man said, 'That horse will never do
For a long and tiring gallop—lad, you'd better stop away,
  Those hills are far too rough for such as you.'
So he waited, sad and wistful—only Clancy stood his
    friend—

  10
  20
  30
  40

'I think we ought to let him come,' he said;
  'I warrant he'll be with us when he's wanted at the end,
    For both his horse and he are mountain bred.

'He hails from Snowy River, up by Kosciusko's side,
    Where the hills are twice as steep and twice as rough;
  Where a horse's hoofs strike firelight from the flint stones
    every stride,
      The man that holds his own is good enough.
  And the Snowy River riders on the mountains make their
50   home,
      Where the river runs those giant hills between;
  I have seen full many horsemen since I first commenced to
    roam,
      But nowhere yet such horsemen have I seen.'

So he went; they found the horses by the big mimosa
    clump,
    They raced away towards the mountain's brow,
  And the old man gave his orders, 'Boys, go at them from
    the jump,
60   No use to try for fancy riding now.
  And, Clancy, you must wheel them, try and wheel them
    to the right.
      Ride boldly, lad, and never fear the spills,
  For never yet was rider that could keep the mob in sight,
      If once they gain the shelter of those hills.'

So Clancy rode to wheel them—he was racing on the wing
    Where the best and boldest riders take their place,
  And he raced his stock-horse past them, and he made the
    ranges ring
70   With the stockwhip, as he met them face to face.
  Then they halted for a moment, while he swung the
    dreaded lash,
      But they saw their well-loved mountain full in view,
  And they charged beneath the stockwhip with a sharp and
    sudden dash,
      And off into the mountain scrub they flew.

Then fast the horsemen followed, where the gorges deep
    and black
      Resounded to the thunder of their tread,
80 And the stockwhips woke the echoes, and they fiercely
    answered back
      From cliffs and crags that beetled overhead.

And upward, ever upward, the wild horses held their way,
  Where mountain ash and kurrajong grew wide;
And the old man muttered fiercely, 'We may bid the mob
    good day,
  No man can hold them down the other side.'

When they reached the mountain's summit, even Clancy
    took a pull—
  It well might make the boldest hold their breath;
The wild hop scrub grew thickly, and the hidden ground
    was full
  Of wombat holes, and any slip was death.
But the man from Snowy River let the pony have his head,
  And he swung his stockwhip round and gave a cheer,
And he raced him down the mountain like a torrent down
    its bed,
  While the others stood and watched in very fear.

He sent the flint-stones flying, but the pony kept his feet,
  He cleared the fallen timber in his stride,
And the man from Snowy River never shifted in his seat—
  It was grand to see that mountain horseman ride.
Through the stringy barks and saplings, on the rough and
    broken ground,
  Down the hillside at a racing pace he went;
And he never drew the bridle till he landed safe and sound
  At the bottom of that terrible descent.

He was right among the horses as they climbed the farther
    hill,
  And the watchers on the mountain, standing mute,
Saw him ply the stockwhip fiercely; he was right among
    them still,
  As he raced across the clearing in pursuit.
Then they lost him for a moment, where two mountain
    gullies met
  In the ranges—but a final glimpse reveals
On a dim and distant hillside the wild horses racing yet,
  With the man from Snowy River at their heels.

And he ran them single-handed till their sides were white
    with foam;
  He followed like a bloodhound on their track,
Till they halted, cowed and beaten; then he turned their
    heads for home,
  And alone and unassisted brought them back.

But his hardy mountain pony he could scarcely raise a trot,
　　He was blood from hip to shoulder from the spur;
But his pluck was still undaunted, and his courage fiery
　　hot,
　　For never yet was mountain horse a cur.

130　And down by Kosciusko, where the pine-clad ridges raise
　　Their torn and rugged battlements on high,
Where the air is clear as crystal, and the white stars fairly
　　blaze
　　At midnight in the cold and frosty sky,
And where around the Overflow the reed-beds sweep and
　　sway
　　To the breezes, and the rolling plains are wide,
The Man from Snowy River is a household word today,
　　And the stockmen tell the story of his ride.

Clancy of the Overflow

I had written him a letter which I had, for want of better
　　Knowledge, sent to where I met him down the Lachlan
　　years ago;
He was shearing when I knew him, so I sent the letter to
　　him,
　　Just on spec, addressed as follows, 'Clancy, of The
　　Overflow'.

And an answer came directed in a writing unexpected
　　　(And I think the same was written with a thumb-nail
10　　　dipped in tar);
'Twas his shearing mate who wrote it, and *verbatim* I will
　　quote it:
　　'Clancy's gone to Queensland droving, and we don't
　　know where he are.'

In my wild erratic fancy visions come to me of Clancy
　　Gone a-droving 'down the Cooper' where the Western
　　drovers go;
As the stock are slowly stringing, Clancy rides behind
　　them singing,
20　　For the drover's life has pleasures that the townsfolk
　　never know.

And the bush has friends to meet him, and their kindly
    voices greet him
    In the murmur of the breezes and the river on its bars,
And he sees the vision splendid of the sunlit plains
    extended,
    And at night the wondrous glory of the everlasting stars.

I am sitting in my dingy little office, where a stingy
    Ray of sunlight struggles feebly down between the
30   houses tall,
And the foetid air and gritty of the dusty, dirty city,
    Through the open window floating, spreads its foulness
    over all.

And in place of lowing cattle, I can hear the fiendish rattle
    Of the tramways and the buses making hurry down the
    street;
And the language uninviting of the gutter children fighting
    Comes fitfully and faintly through the ceaseless tramp of
    feet.

40 And the hurrying people daunt me, and their pallid faces
    haunt me
    As they shoulder one another in their rush and nervous
    haste,
With their eager eyes and greedy, and their stunted forms
    and weedy,
    For townsfolk have no time to grow, they have no time
    to waste.

And I somehow rather fancy that I'd like to change with
    Clancy,
50   Like to take a turn at droving where the seasons come
    and go,
While he faced the round eternal of the cash-book and the
    journal—
    But I doubt he'd suit the office, Clancy, of The
    Overflow.

Black Swans

As I lie at rest on a patch of clover
In the Western Park when the day is done,
I watch as the wild black swans fly over
With their phalanx turned to the sinking sun;
And I hear the clang of their leader crying
To a lagging mate in the rearward flying,
And they fade away in the darkness dying,
Where the stars are mustering one by one.

O ye wild black swans, 'twere a world of wonder
For a while to join in your westward flight,
With the stars above and the dim earth under,
Through the cooling air of the glorious night.
As we swept along on our pinions winging,
We should catch the chime of a church-bell ringing,
Or the distant note of a torrent singing,
Or the far-off flash of a station light.

From the northern lakes with the reeds and rushes,
Where the hills are clothed with a purple haze,
Where the bell-birds chime and the songs of thrushes
Make music sweet in the jungle maze,
They will hold their course to the westward ever,
Till they reach the banks of the old grey river,
Where the waters wash, and the reed-beds quiver
In the burning heat of the summer days.

O ye strange wild birds, will ye bear a greeting
To the folk that live in that western land?
Then for every sweep of your pinions beating
Ye shall bear a wish to the sunburnt band.
To the stalwart men who are stoutly fighting
With the heat and drought and the dust-storm smiting,
Yet whose life somehow has a strange inviting,
When once to the work they have put their hand.

Facing it yet! O my friend stout-hearted,
What does it matter for rain or shine,
For the hopes deferred and the gain departed?
Nothing could conquer that heart of thine.
And thy health and strength are beyond confessing
As the only joys that are worth possessing.

A.B. PATERSON   39

May the days to come be as rich in blessing
As the days we spent in the auld lang syne.

I would fain go back to the old grey river,
To the old bush days when our hearts were light;
But, alas! those days they have fled for ever,
They are like the swans that have swept from sight.
And I know full well that the strangers' faces
Would meet us now in our dearest places;
For our day is dead and has left no traces
But the thoughts that live in my mind tonight.

There are folk long dead, and our hearts would sicken—
We should grieve for them with a bitter pain;
If the past could live and the dead could quicken,
We then might turn to that life again.
But on lonely nights we should hear them calling,
We should hear their steps on the pathways falling,
We should loathe the life with a hate appalling
In our lonely rides by the ridge and plain.

.   .   .   .   .

In the silent park is a scent of clover,
And the distant roar of the town is dead.
And I hear once more, as the swans fly over,
Their far-off clamour from overhead.
They are flying west, by their instinct guided,
And for man likewise is his fate decided,
And griefs apportioned and joys divided
By a mighty power with a purpose dread.

HENRY LAWSON

(1867–1922)

HENRY LAWSON was born at Grenfell, New South Wales, where his father—a Norwegian sailor who had deserted his ship to join the gold rushes twelve years earlier—was working a gold claim. He had little education, but was encouraged in his ambition to write by his mother—a woman of great strength of personality, who wrote verse and sketches, and founded the first women's magazine in Australia. In his youth Lawson was afflicted with deafness which increased as he grew older, and contributed to his sense of isolation. Introverted and melancholic, he suffered periods of alcoholism and debilitating depression; his marriage was unhappy; and he was seldom free of debt, especially in his later years as his ability to write declined. His first work was published in the Sydney *Bulletin* in 1887: by the time *In the Days When the World was Wide* (a collection of his poetry) and *While the Billy Boils* (a collection of stories and sketches) appeared in 1896, he was being regarded as the foremost Australian writer of his generation. Lawson's most creative work was in the short story; but in the early nineties he emerged, with Paterson, as a leading exemplar of the bush ballad. The poems chosen to represent Lawson in this anthology are all from that period and were included in the second edition of *In the Days When the World was Wide* (1900). 'Up the Country' was first published in the *Bulletin*, 9 July 1892, and drew a verse reply from Paterson, 'In Defence of the Bush' (23 July), to which Lawson responded with a further set of verses, entitled 'The City Bushman' (6 August). This public exchange reveals very clearly how fundamentally they differed in their view of the bush. Only a small proportion of Lawson's poetry—the whole occupies three volumes in Colin Roderick's edition—rises above the level of conventional versifying. However, the early poems in which he writes freshly and with feeling about bush life and values were historically important in creating images of Australian life, and they have retained their appeal.

The Ballad of the Drover

Across the stony ridges,
   Across the rolling plain,
Young Harry Dale, the drover,
   Comes riding home again.
And well his stock-horse bears him,
   And light of heart is he,
And stoutly his old pack-horse
   Is trotting by his knee.

Up Queensland way with cattle
   He travelled regions vast;
And many months have vanished
   Since home-folk saw him last.
He hums a song of someone
   He hopes to marry soon;
And hobble-chains and camp-ware
   Keep jingling to the tune.

Beyond the hazy dado
   Against the lower skies
And yon blue line of ranges
   The homestead station lies.
And thitherward the drover
   Jogs through the lazy noon,
While hobble-chains and camp-ware
   Are jingling to a tune.

An hour has filled the heavens
   With storm-clouds inky black;
At times the lightning trickles
   Around the drover's track;
But Harry pushes onward,
   His horses' strength he tries,
In hope to reach the river
   Before the flood shall rise.

The thunder from above him
   Goes rolling o'er the plain;
And down on thirsty pastures
   In torrents falls the rain.
And every creek and gully
   Sends forth its little flood,
Till the river runs a banker,
   All stained with yellow mud.

10

20

30

40

Now Harry speaks to Rover,
    The best dog on the plains,
And to his hardy horses,
    And strokes their shaggy manes:
'We've breasted bigger rivers
    When floods were at their height,
Nor shall this gutter stop us
    From getting home to-night!'

The thunder growls a warning,
    The ghastly lightnings gleam,
As the drover turns his horses
    To swim the fatal stream.
But O the flood runs stronger
    Than e'er it ran before;
The saddle-horse is failing,
    And only half-way o'er!

When flashes next the lightning,
    The flood's grey breast is blank,
And a cattle dog and pack-horse
    Are struggling up the bank.
But in the lonely homestead
    The girl shall wait in vain—
He'll never pass the stations
    In charge of stock again.

The faithful dog a moment
    Sits panting on the bank,
And then swims through the current
    To where his master sank.
And round and round in circles
    He fights with failing strength,
Till, borne down by the waters,
    The old dog sinks at length.

Across the flooded lowland
    And slopes of sodden loam
The pack-horse struggles onward,
    To take dumb tidings home.
And mud-stained, wet, and weary,
    Through ranges dark goes he;
While hobble-chains and tinware
    Are sounding eerily.

The floods are in the ocean,
  The creeks are clear again,
And now a verdant carpet
  Is stretched across the plain.
But bleaching on the desert
  Or in the river reeds
The bones lie of the bravest
  That wide Australia breeds.

The Roaring Days

The night too quickly passes
  And we are growing old,
So let us fill our glasses
  And toast the Days of Gold;
When finds of wondrous treasure
  Set all the South ablaze,
And you and I were faithful mates
  All through the roaring days!

Then stately ships came sailing
10   From every harbour's mouth,
And sought the land of promise
  That beaconed in the South;
Then southward streamed their streamers
  And swelled their canvas full
To speed the wildest dreamers
  E'er borne in vessel's hull.

Their shining Eldorado,
  Beneath the southern skies,
Was day and night for ever
20   Before their eager eyes.
The brooding bush, awakened,
  Was stirred in wild unrest,
And all the year a human stream
  Went pouring to the West.

The rough bush roads re-echoed
  The bar-room's noisy din,
When troops of stalwart horsemen
  Dismounted at the inn.
And oft the hearty greetings

And hearty clasp of hands
Would tell of sudden meetings
Of friends from other lands.

And when the cheery camp-fire
Explored the bush with gleams,
The camping-grounds were crowded
With caravans of teams;
Then home the jests were driven,
And good old songs were sung,
And choruses were given
The strength of heart and lung.

Oft when the camps were dreaming,
And fires began to pale,
Through rugged ranges gleaming
Swept on the Royal Mail.
Behind six foaming horses,
And lit by flashing lamps,
Old Cobb and Co. in royal state,
Went dashing past the camps.

O who would paint a goldfield,
And paint the picture right,
As we have often seen it
In early morning's light;
The yellow mounds of mullock
With spots of red and white,
The scattered quartz that glistened
Like diamonds in light;

The azure line of ridges,
The bush of darkest green,
The little homes of calico
That dotted all the scene.
The flat straw hats with ribands
That old engravings show:
The dress that still reminds us
Of sailors, long ago.

I hear the fall of timber
From distant flats and fells,
The pealing of the anvils
As clear as little bells,
The rattle of the cradle,

70

The clack of windlass-boles,
The flutter of the crimson flags
Above the golden holes.

Ah, then their hearts were bolder,
And if Dame Fortune frowned
Their swags they'd lightly shoulder
And tramp to other ground.
O they were lion-hearted
Who gave our country birth:
O they were of the stoutest sons
80 From all the lands on earth.

But golden days are vanished,
And altered is the scene;
The diggings are deserted,
The camping-grounds are green;
The flaunting flag of progress
Is in the West unfurled,
The mighty Bush with iron rails
Is tethered to the world.

The Sliprails and the Spur

The colours of the setting sun
Withdrew across the Western land—
He raised the sliprails, one by one,
And shot them home with trembling hand;
Her brown hands clung—her face grew pale—
Ah! quivering chin and eyes that brim!—
One quick, fierce kiss across the rail,
And, 'Good-bye, Mary!' 'Good-bye, Jim!'

O he rides hard to race the pain
10 *Who rides from love, who rides from home;*
But he rides slowly home again,
Whose heart has learnt to love and roam.

A hand upon the horse's mane,
And one foot in the stirrup set,
And, stooping back to kiss again,
With 'Good-bye, Mary! don't you fret!
When I come back'—he laughed for her—

'We do not know how soon 'twill be;
I'll whistle as I round the spur—
20   You let the sliprails down for me.'

She gasped for sudden loss of hope,
    As, with a backward wave to her,
He cantered down the grassy slope
    And swiftly round the dark'ning spur.
Black-pencilled panels standing high,
    And darkness fading into stars,
And blurring fast against the sky,
    A faint white form beside the bars.

And often at the set of sun,
30   In winter bleak and summer brown,
She'd steal across the little run,
    And shyly let the sliprails down,
And listen there when darkness shut
    The nearer spur in silence deep;
And when they called her from the hut
    Steal home and cry herself to sleep.

A great white gate where sliprails were,
    A brick house 'neath the mountain brow,
The 'mad girl' buried by the spur
40   So long ago, forgotten now.

   And he rides hard to dull the pain
      Who rides from one that loves him best;
   And he rides slowly back again
      Whose restless heart must rove for rest.

Middleton's Rouseabout

Tall and freckled and sandy,
    Face of a country lout;
This was the picture of Andy,
    Middleton's Rouseabout.

Type of a coming nation,
    In the land of cattle and sheep,
Worked on Middleton's station,
    'Pound a week and his keep'.

On Middleton's wide dominions
    Plied the stockwhip and shears;
Hadn't any opinions,
    Hadn't any 'idears'.

Swiftly the years went over,
    Liquor and drought prevailed;
Middleton went as a drover
    After his station had failed.

Type of a careless nation,
    Men who are soon played out,
Middleton was:—and his station
    Was bought by the Rouseabout.

Flourishing beard and sandy,
    Tall and solid and stout:
This is the picture of Andy,
    Middleton's Rouseabout.

Now on his own dominions
    Works with his overseers;
Hasn't any opinions,
    Hasn't any idears.

Up the Country

I am back from up the country—very sorry that I went—
Seeking for the Southern poets' land whereon to pitch my
        tent;
I have lost a lot of idols, which were broken on the track,
Burnt a lot of fancy verses, and I'm glad that I am back.
Further out may be the pleasant scenes of which our poets
        boast,
But I think the country's rather more inviting round the
        coast.
Anyway, I'll stay at present at a boarding-house in town,
Drinking beer and lemon-squashes, taking baths and
        cooling down.

'Sunny plains!' Great Scott!—those burning wastes of
        barren soil and sand
With their everlasting fences stretching out across the land!

Desolation where the crow is! Desert where the eagle flies,
Paddocks where the luny bullock starts and stares with
        reddened eyes;
Where, in clouds of dust enveloped, roasted
        bullock-drivers creep
Slowly past the sun-dried shepherd dragged behind his
        crawling sheep.
Stunted peak of granite gleaming, glaring like a molten
        mass
Turned from some infernal furnace on a plain devoid of
        grass.

Miles and miles of thirsty gutters—strings of muddy
        water-holes
In the place of 'shining rivers'—'walled by cliffs and forest
        boles'.
Barren ridges, gullies, ridges! where the everlasting flies—
Fiercer than the plagues of Egypt—swarm about your
        blighted eyes!
Bush! where there is no horizon! where the buried
        bushman sees
Nothing—Nothing! but the sameness of the ragged,
        stunted trees!
Lonely hut where drought's eternal—suffocating
        atmosphere—
Where the God-forgotten hatter dreams of city life and
        beer.

Treacherous tracks that trap the stranger, endless roads
        that gleam and glare,
Dark and evil-looking gullies, hiding secrets here and
        there!
Dull dumb flats and stony rises, where the toiling bullocks
        bake,
And the sinister 'gohanna', and the lizard, and the snake.
Land of day and night—no morning freshness, and no
        afternoon,
When the great white sun in rising brings the summer heat
        in June.
Dismal country for the exile, when the shades begin to fall
From the sad heart-breaking sunset, to the newchum
        worst of all.

Dreary land in rainy weather, with the endless clouds that
        drift
O'er the bushman like a blanket that the Lord will never lift—

Dismal land when it is raining—growl of floods, and, O
the woosh
Of the rain and wind together on the dark bed of the
bush—
Ghastly fires in lonely humpies where the granite rocks are
piled
In the rain-swept wildernesses that are wildest of the wild.

Land where gaunt and haggard women live alone and
work like men,
Till their husbands, gone a-droving, will return to them
again:
Homes of men! if homes had ever such a God-forgotten
place,
Where the wild selector's children fly before a stranger's
face.
Home of tragedy applauded by the dingoes' dismal yell,
Heaven of the shanty-keeper—fitting fiend for such a
hell—
And the wallaroos and wombats, and, of course, the
curlew's call—
And the lone sundowner tramping ever onward through it
all!

I am back from up the country, up the country where I
went
Seeking for the Southern poets' land whereon to pitch my
tent;
I have shattered many idols out along the dusty track,
Burnt a lot of fancy verses—and I'm glad that I am back.
I believe the Southern poets' dream will not be realized
Till the plains are irrigated and the land is humanized.
I intend to stay at present, as I said before, in town
Drinking beer and lemon-squashes, taking baths and
cooling down.

CHRISTOPHER BRENNAN

(1870–1932)

CHRISTOPHER BRENNAN was born in Sydney and lived there all his life, except for two years he spent in Berlin as a postgraduate student. A considerable scholar, Brennan worked at the Public Library following his return from Berlin in 1894 until his appointment as a lecturer in Modern Literature at the University in 1909. He became Associate Professor in German and Comparative Literature in 1920, but his academic career ended abruptly five years later when he was forced to resign because of publicity in the divorce court and the dissatisfaction of the authorities with his attitude towards his academic duties. The full story of Brennan's life, including his unhappy marriage and his descent into poverty and alcoholism, is told by Axel Clark in *Christopher Brennan: A Critical Biography* (1980). Most of his poetry was collected in *Poems* (1914) which he designed to be a *livre composé*; that is, the book was meant to be read not as a gathering of individual poems but as a single poem in which the individual pieces formed part of the whole. The sequence of poems entitled 'The Wanderer'—eight of which had been written by 1902—was the third of the five 'movements' or sections which make up the book. Brennan had no sympathy with the work of popular nationalist writers like Paterson and Lawson ('As far as "national traits" go, I might have made my verse in China'), his ambition as a poet being to write in the manner of the French Symbolists. As he told Mallarmé, whom he regarded as his master, he found in their work, 'a style, to which I feel myself instinctively drawn, as some are drawn towards home'. He had few readers in his lifetime, but since the appearance in 1960 of his collected verse and prose, edited in two volumes by A.R. Chisholm, interest in his work has grown steadily, though his stature as a poet is still a matter of some controversy.

The Wanderer

1902 —

Quoniam cor secretum concupivi
  factus sum vagus inter stellas huius revelationis:
Atque annus peregrinationis meae
  quasi annus ventorum invisibilium.

When window-lamps had dwindled, then I rose
and left the town behind me; and on my way
passing a certain door I stopt, remembering
how once I stood on its threshold, and my life
was offer'd to me, a road how different
from that of the years since gone! and I had but
to rejoin an olden path, once dear, since left.
All night I have walk'd and my heart was deep awake,
remembering ways I dream'd and that I chose,
10   remembering lucidly, and was not sad,
being brimm'd with all the liquid and clear dark
of the night that was not stirr'd with any tide;
for leaves were silent and the road gleam'd pale,
following the ridge, and I was alone with night.
But now I am come among the rougher hills
and grow aware of the sea that somewhere near
is restless; and the flood of night is thinn'd
and stars are whitening. O, what horrible dawn
will bare me the way and crude lumps of the hills
20   and the homeless concave of the day, and bare
the ever-restless, ever-complaining sea?

        *   *   *

Each day I see the long ships coming into port
and the people crowding to their rail, glad of the shore:
because to have been alone with the sea and not to have
    known
of anything happening in any crowded way,
and to have heard no other voice than the crooning sea's
has charmed away the old rancours, and the great winds
have search'd and swept their hearts of the old irksome
    thoughts:
10   so, to their freshen'd gaze, each land smiles a good home.
Why envy I, seeing them made gay to greet the shore?
Surely I do not foolishly desire to go
hither and thither upon the earth and grow weary
with seeing many lands and peoples and the sea:
but if I might, some day, landing I reck not where
have heart to find a welcome and perchance a rest,

I would spread the sail to any wandering wind of the air
this night, when waves are hard and rain blots out the
    land.

          *   *   *

I am driven everywhere from a clinging home,
O autumn eves! and I ween'd that you would yet
have made, when your smouldering dwindled to odorous
    fume,
close room for my heart, where I might crouch and
    dream
of days and ways I had trod, and look with regret
on the darkening homes of men and the window-gleam,
and forget the morrows that threat and the unknown
10   way.
But a bitter wind came out of the yellow-pale west
and my heart is shaken and fill'd with its triumphing cry:
You shall find neither home nor rest; for ever you roam
with stars as they drift and wilful fates of the sky!

          *   *   *

O tame heart, and why are you weary and cannot rest?
here is the hearth with its glow and the roof that forbids
    the rain,
a swept and a garnish'd quiet, a peace: and were you not
    fain
to be gather'd in dusk and comfort and barter away the
    rest?

And is your dream now of riding away from a stricken
    field
10 on a lost and baleful eve, when the world went out in
    rain,
one of some few that rode evermore by the bridle-rein
of a great beloved chief, with high heart never to yield?

Was that you? and you ween you are back in your life of
    old
when you dealt as your pride allow'd and reck'd not of
    other rein?
Nay, tame heart, be not idle: it is but the ancient rain
that minds you of manhood foregone and the perilous
20   joy of the bold.

          *   *   *

Once I could sit by the fire hourlong when the dripping
    eaves
sang cheer to the shelter'd, and listen, and know that the

woods drank full,
and think of the morn that was coming and how the
    freshen'd leaves
would glint in the sun and the dusk beneath would be
    bright and cool.

Now, when I hear, I am cold within: for my mind drifts
    10   wide
where the blessing is shed for naught on the salt waste of
    the sea,
on the valleys that hold no rest and the hills that may not
    abide:
and the fire loses its warmth and my home is far from me.

          *   *   *

How old is my heart, how old, how old is my heart,
and did I ever go forth with song when the morn was
    new?
I seem to have trod on many ways: I seem to have left
I know not how many homes; and to leave each
was still to leave a portion of mine own heart,
of my old heart whose life I had spent to make that home
and all I had was regret, and a memory.
So I sit and muse in this wayside harbour and wait
    10   till I hear the gathering cry of the ancient winds and again
I must up and out and leave the embers of the hearth
to crumble silently into white ash and dust,
and see the road stretch bare and pale before me: again
my garment and my home shall be the enveloping winds
and my heart be fill'd wholly with their old pitiless cry.

          *   *   *

I sorrow for youth—ah, not for its wildness (would that
    were dead!)
but for those soft nests of time that enticed the maiden
    bloom
of delight and tenderness to break in delicate air
—O her eyes in the rosy face that bent over our first babe!
but all that was, and is gone, and shall be all forgotten;
it fades and wanes even now: and who is there cares but I?
and I grieve for my heart that is old and cannot cease from
    10   regret.
Ay, might our harms be haven'd in some deathless heart:
but where have I felt its over-brooding luminous tent
save in those eyes of delight (and ah! that they must
    change)
and of yore in her eyes to whom we ran with our childish
    joy?

O brother! if such there were and each of us might lead each
to lean above the little pools where all our heart
lies spilt and clear and shining along the dusky way,
and dream of one that could save it all and salve our ache!

*   *   *

You, at whose table I have sat, some distant eve
beside the road, and eaten and you pitied me
to be driven an aimless way before the pitiless winds,
how much ye have given and knew not, pitying foolishly!
For not alone the bread I broke, but I tasted too
all your unwitting lives and knew the narrow soul
that bodies it in the landmarks of your fields,
and broods dumbly within your little seasons' round,
where, after sowing, comes the short–lived summer's mirth,
and, after harvesting, the winter's lingering dream,
half memory and regret, half hope, crouching beside
the hearth that is your only centre of life and dream.
And knowing the world how limitless and the way how long,
and the home of man how feeble and builded on the winds,
I have lived your life, that eve, as you might never live
knowing, and pity you, if you should come to know.

*   *   *

I cry to you as I pass your windows in the dusk;

Ye have built you unmysterious homes and ways in the wood
where of old ye went with sudden eyes to the right and left;
and your going was now made safe and your staying comforted,
for the forest edge itself, holding old savagery
in unsearch'd glooms, was your houses' friendly barrier.
And now that the year goes winterward, ye thought to hide
behind your gleaming panes, and where the hearth sings merrily
make cheer with meat and wine, and sleep in the long night,
and the uncared wastes might be a crying unhappiness.
But I, who have come from the outer night, I say to you
the winds are up and terribly will they shake the dry wood:

CHRISTOPHER BRENNAN   55

the woods shall awake, hearing them, shall awake to be
        toss'd and riven,
and make a cry and a parting in your sleep all night
as the wither'd leaves go whirling all night along all
        ways.
And when ye come forth at dawn, uncomforted by sleep,
ye shall stand at amaze, beholding all the ways
        overhidden
with worthless drift of the dead and all your broken
        world:
and ye shall not know whence the winds have come, nor
        shall ye know
whither the yesterdays have fled, or if they were.

*   *   *

Come out, come out, ye souls that serve, why will ye
        die?
or will ye sit and stifle in your prison-homes
dreaming of some master that holds the winds in leash
and the waves of darkness yonder in the gaunt hollow of
        night?
nay, there is none that rules: all is a strife of the winds
and the night shall billow in storm full oft ere all be done.
For this is the hard doom that is laid on all of you,
to be that whereof ye dream, dreaming against your will.
But first ye must travel the many ways, and your
        close-wrapt souls
must be blown thro' with the rain that comes from the
        homeless dark:
for until ye have had care of the wastes there shall be no
        truce
for them nor you, nor home, but ever the ancient feud;
and the soul of man must house the cry of the darkling
        waves
as he follows the ridge above the waters shuddering
        towards night,
and the rains and the winds that roam anhunger'd for
        some heart's warmth.
Go: tho' ye find it bitter, yet must ye be bare
to the wind and the sea and the night and the wail of birds
        in the sky;
go: tho' the going be hard and the goal blinded with rain
yet the staying is a death that is never soften'd with sleep.

*   *   *

Dawns of the world, how I have known you all,
so many, and so varied, and the same!

dawns o'er the timid plains, or in the folds
of the arm'd hills, or by the unsleeping shore;
a chill touch on the chill flesh of the dark
that, shuddering, shrinks from its couch, and leaves
a homeless light, staring, disconsolate,
on the drear world it knows too well, the world
it fled and finds again, its wistful hope
10   unmet by any miracle of night,
that mocks it rather, with its shreds that hang
about the woods and huddled bulks of gloom
that crouch, malicious, in the broken combes,
witness to foulnesses else unreveal'd
that visit earth and violate her dreams
in the lone hours when only evil wakes.

*   *   *

What is there with you and me, that I may not forget
but your white shapes come crowding noiselessly in my
        nights,
making my sleep a flight from a thousand beckoning
        hands?
Was it not enough that your cry dwelt in my waking ears
that now, seeking oblivion, I must yet be haunted
by each black maw of hunger that yawns despairingly
a moment ere its whitening frenzy bury it?
10   O waves of all the seas, would I could give you peace
and find my peace again: for all my peace is fled
and broken and blown along your white delirious crests!

*   *   *

O desolate eves along the way, how oft,
despite your bitterness, was I warm at heart!
not with the glow of remember'd hearths, but warm
with the solitary unquenchable fire that burns
a flameless heat deep in his heart who has come
where the formless winds plunge and exult for aye
among the naked spaces of the world,
far past the circle of the ruddy hearths
and all their memories. Desperate eves,
10   when the wind-bitten hills turn'd violet
along their rims, and the earth huddled her heat
within her niggard bosom, and the dead stones
lay battle-strewn before the iron wind
that, blowing from the chill west, made all its way
a loneliness to yield its triumph room;
yet in that wind a clamour of trumpets rang,
old trumpets, resolute, stark, undauntable,
singing to battle against the eternal foe,

the wronger of this world, and all his powers
in some last fight, foredoom'd disastrous,
upon the final ridges of the world:
a war-worn note, stern fire in the stricken eve,
and fire thro' all my ancient heart, that sprang
towards that last hope of a glory won in defeat,
whence, knowing not sure if such high grace befall
at the end, yet I draw courage to front the way.

*   *   *

The land I came thro' last was dumb with night,
a limbo of defeated glory, a ghost:
for wreck of constellations flicker'd perishing
scarce sustain'd in the mortuary air,
and on the ground and out of livid pools
wreck of old swords and crowns glimmer'd at whiles;
I seem'd at home in some old dream of kingship:
now it is clear grey day and the road is plain,
I am the wanderer of many years
who cannot tell if ever he was king
or if ever kingdoms were: I know I am
the wanderer of the ways of all the worlds,
to whom the sunshine and the rain are one
and one to stay or hasten, because he knows
no ending of the way, no home, no goal,
and phantom night and the grey day alike
withhold the heart where all my dreams and days
might faint in soft fire and delicious death:
and saying this to myself as a simple thing
I feel a peace fall in the heart of the winds
and a clear dusk settle, somewhere, far in me.

20

10

20

JOHN SHAW NEILSON

(1872–1942)

JOHN SHAW NEILSON was born in the country town of
Penola in South Australia, where his father was working as
a labourer. He had little formal education, but the songs
and ballads sung by his Scottish parents, his father's own
verses, and his reading of the Bible and of nineteenth-
century English poets, contributed to his becoming a poet.
His life—which he recalls uncomplainingly in *The Auto-
biography of John Shaw Neilson* (1978)—was one of constant
hardship and near-poverty: as a boy working on a poor
selection his father had taken up in the Little Desert region
of Victoria; and as a man working around the Victorian
countryside at clearing, fencing, timber-cutting, road-
making, and other manual jobs. In 1905 A.G. Stephens,
then literary editor of the *Bulletin*, became interested in
Neilson's work; and until his death in 1933 Stephens was
Neilson's literary adviser and agent and his publisher as
well. Literary admirers, concerned for Neilson's health,
secured him an attendant's post in the Country Roads
Board office in Melbourne in 1928, and he was still
officially employed there at the time of his death. Neilson
was reticent about his private life—he never married—
though he made clear in his talk and in his poetry his
reaction against the doctrines ('Creeds the discoloured') of
his Presbyterian parents. In his later years he suffered
increasingly from defective eyesight, and was dependent
upon others (often other labourers) to write down the
verses he had composed. The precise dating of his poems is

difficult, and it is not always apparent from manuscripts which of the several versions of a poem is meant to be the final one. In this anthology the poems have been printed in the order and in the version in which they appear in A.R. Chisholm's edition, which was first published in 1965. That edition, with Chisholm's highly persuasive interpretation of Neilson as an intuitive symbolist poet, marked the beginning of a much greater appreciation of Neilson's art. There is still no definitive edition of his poetry, some of which is as yet unpublished; but there is a general recognition now that he is an important and original poet.

The Orange Tree

The young girl stood beside me. I
  Saw not what her young eyes could see:
—A light, she said, not of the sky
  Lives somewhere in the Orange Tree.

—Is it, I said, of east or west?
  The heartbeat of a luminous boy
Who with his faltering flute confessed
  Only the edges of his joy?

Was he, I said, borne to the blue
  In a mad escapade of Spring
Ere he could make a fond adieu
  To his love in the blossoming?

—Listen! the young girl said. There calls
  No voice, no music beats on me;
But it is almost sound: it falls
  This evening on the Orange Tree.

—Does he, I said, so fear the Spring
  Ere the white sap too far can climb?
See in the full gold evening
  All happenings of the olden time?

Is he so goaded by the green?
  Does the compulsion of the dew
Make him unknowable but keen
  Asking with beauty of the blue?

—Listen! the young girl said. For all
  Your hapless talk you fail to see
There is a light, a step, a call
  This evening on the Orange Tree.

—Is it, I said, a waste of love
  Imperishably old in pain,
Moving as an affrighted dove
  Under the sunlight or the rain?

Is it a fluttering heart that gave
  Too willingly and was reviled?
Is it the stammering at a grave,
  The last word of a little child?

—Silence! the young girl said. Oh, why,
    Why will you talk to weary me?
  Plague me no longer now, for I
40   Am listening like the Orange Tree.

Love's Coming

Quietly as rosebuds
  Talk to the thin air,
Love came so lightly
  I knew not he was there.

Quietly as lovers
  Creep at the middle moon,
Softly as players tremble
  In the tears of a tune;

Quietly as lilies
10   Their faint vows declare
Came the shy pilgrim:
  I knew not he was there;

Quietly as tears fall
  On a wild sin,
Softly as griefs call
  In a violin;

Without hail or tempest,
  Blue sword or flame,
Love came so lightly
20   I knew not that he came.

Song be Delicate

Let your song be delicate.
  The skies declare
No war—the eyes of lovers
  Wake everywhere.

Let your voice be delicate.
  How faint a thing

Is Love, little Love crying
  Under the Spring.

Let your song be delicate.
  The flowers can hear:
Too well they know the tremble
  Of the hollow year.

Let your voice be delicate.
  The bees are home:
All their day's love is sunken
  Safe in the comb.

Let your song be delicate.
  Sing no loud hymn:
Death is abroad.... Oh, the black season!
  The deep—the dim!

The Crane is My Neighbour

The bird is my neighbour, a whimsical fellow and dim;
There is in the lake a nobility falling on him.

The bird is a noble, he turns to the sky for a theme,
And the ripples are thoughts coming out to the edge of a
  dream.

The bird is both ancient and excellent, sober and wise,
But he never could spend all the love that is sent for his
  eyes.

He bleats no instruction, he is not an arrogant drummer;
His gown is simplicity—blue as the smoke of the summer.

How patient he is as he puts out his wings for the blue!
His eyes are as old as the twilight, and calm as the dew.

The bird is my neighbour, he leaves not a claim for a sigh,
He moves as the guest of the sunlight—he roams in the
  sky.

The bird is a noble, he turns to the sky for a theme,
And the ripples are thoughts coming out to the edge of a
  dream.

JOHN SHAW NEILSON 63

The Gentle Water Bird

(For Mary Gilmore)

In the far days, when every day was long,
Fear was upon me and the fear was strong,
Ere I had learned the recompense of song.

In the dim days I trembled, for I knew
God was above me, always frowning through,
And God was terrible and thunder-blue.

Creeds the discoloured awed my opening mind,
Perils, perplexities—what could I find?—
All the old terror waiting on mankind.

10   Even the gentle flowers of white and cream,
The rainbow with its treasury of dream,
Trembled because of God's ungracious scheme.

And in the night the many stars would say
Dark things unaltered in the light of day:
Fear was upon me even in my play.

There was a lake I loved in gentle rain:
One day there fell a bird, a courtly crane:
Wisely he walked, as one who knows of pain.

Gracious he was and lofty as a king:
20   Silent he was, and yet he seemed to sing
Always of little children and the Spring.

God? Did he know him? It was far he flew....
God was not terrible and thunder-blue:
—It was a gentle water bird I knew.

Pity was in him for the weak and strong,
All who have suffered when the days were long,
And he was deep and gentle as a song.

As a calm soldier in a cloak of grey
He did commune with me for many a day
30   Till the dark fear was lifted far away.

Sober-apparelled, yet he caught the glow:
Always of Heaven would he speak, and low,
And he did tell me where the wishes go.

Kinsfolk of his it was who long before
Came from the mist (and no one knows the shore)
Came with the little children to the door.

Was he less wise than those birds long ago
Who flew from God (He surely willed it so)
Bearing great happiness to all below?

40 Long have I learned that all his speech was true:
I cannot reason it—how far he flew—
God is not terrible nor thunder-blue.

Sometimes, when watching in the white sunshine,
Someone approaches—I can half define
All the calm beauty of that friend of mine.

Nothing of hatred will about him cling:
Silent—how silent—but his heart will sing
Always of little children and the Spring.

The Moon Was Seven Days Down

'Peter!' she said, 'the clock has struck
    At one and two and three;
You sleep so sound, and the lonesome hours
    They seem so black to me.
I suffered long, and I suffered sore:
    —What else can I think upon?
I fear no evil; but, oh!—the moon!
    She is seven days gone.'

'Peter!' she said, 'the night is long:
10   The hours will not go by:
The moon is calm; but she meets her death
    Bitter as women die.
I think too much of the flowers. I dreamed
    I walked in a wedding gown,
Or was it a shroud? The moon! the moon!
    She is seven days down.'

'Woman!' he said, 'my ears could stand
    Much noise when I was young;
But year by year you have wearied me:
20   Can you never stop your tongue?

Here am I, with my broken rest,
　To be up at the break of day:
—So much to do; and the sheep not shorn,
　And the lambs not yet away.'

'Peter!' she said, 'your tongue is rude;
　You have ever spoken so:
My aches and ills, they trouble you not
　This many a year, I know:
You talk of your lambs and sheep and wool:
　—'Tis all that you think upon:
I fear no evil; but, oh! the moon!
　She is seven days gone.'

'Peter!' she said, 'the children went:
　My children would not stay:
By the hard word and the hard work
　You have driven them far away.
I suffered, back in the ten years
　That I never saw a town:
—Oh! the moon is over her full glory!
　She is seven days down!

'Woman!' he said, 'I want my rest.
　'Tis the worst time of the year:
The weeds are thick in the top fallow,
　And the hay will soon be here.
A man is a man, and a child a child:
　From a daughter or a son
Or a man or woman I want no talk
　For anything I have done.'

'Peter!' she said, ''twas told to me,
　Long back, in a happy year,
That I should die in the turning time
　When the wheat was in the ear;
That I should go in a plain coffin
　And lie in a plain gown
When the moon had taken her full glory
　And was seven days down.'

Peter, he rose and lit the lamp
　At the first touch of the day:
His mind was full of the top fallow,
　And the ripening of the hay.

He said, 'She sleeps',—but the second look
  He knew how the dead can stare:
And there came a dance of last beauty
  That none of the living share.

How cool and straight and steady he was:
  He said, 'She seems so young!
Her face is fine—it was always fine—
  But, oh, by God! her tongue!
She always thought as the children thought:
  Her mind was made for a town.'
—And the moon was out in the pale sky:
  She was seven days down.

He sauntered out to the neighbour's place
  As the daylight came in clear:
'The wheat,' he said, 'it is filling well,'
  And he stopped at a heavy ear.
He said, 'A good strong plain coffin
  Is the one I am thinking on.'
—And the moon was over his shoulder:
  She was seven days gone.

The Bard and the Lizard

The lizard leans in to October,
  He walks on the yellow and green,
The world is awake and unsober,
  It knows where the lovers have been:
The wind, like a violoncello,
  Comes up and commands him to sing:
He says to me, 'Courage, good fellow!
  We live by the folly of Spring!'

A fish that the sea cannot swallow,
  A bird that can never yet rise,
A dreamer no dreamer can follow,
  The snake is at home in his eyes.
He tells me the paramount treason,
  His words have the resolute ring:
'Away with the homage to Reason!
  We live by the folly of Spring!'

The leaves are about him; the berry
Is close in the red and the green,
His eyes are too old to be merry,
20   He knows where the lovers have been.
And yet he could never be bitter,
He tells me no sorrowful thing:
'The Autumn is less than a twitter!
We live by the folly of Spring!'

As green as the light on a salad
He leans in the shade of a tree,
He has good breath of a ballad,
    The strength that is down in the sea.
How silent he creeps in the yellow—
30   How silent! and yet can he sing:
He gives me, 'Good morning, good fellow!
We live by the folly of Spring!'

I scent the alarm of the faded
Who love not the light and the play,
I hear the assault of the jaded,
    I hear the intolerant bray.
My friend has the face of a wizard,
He tells me no desolate thing:
I learn from the heart of the lizard,
40   We live by the folly of Spring!

The Sundowner

I know not when this tiresome man
With his shrewd, sable billy-can
And his unwashed Democracy
His boomed-up Pilgrimage began.

Sometimes he wandered far outback
On a precarious Tucker Track;
Sometimes he lacked Necessities
No gentleman would like to lack.

Tall was the grass, I understand,
10 When the old Squatter ruled the land.
Why were the Conquerors kind to him?
Ah, the Wax Matches in his hand!

Where bullockies with oaths intense
Made of the dragged-up trees a fence,
Gambling with scorpions he rolled
His Swag, conspicuous, immense.

In the full splendour of his power
Rarely he touched one mile an hour,
Dawdling at sunset, History says,
For the Pint Pannikin of flour.

Seldom he worked; he was, I fear,
Unreasonably slow and dear;
Little he earned, and that he spent
Deliberately drinking Beer.

Cheerful, sorefooted child of chance,
Swiftly we knew him at a glance;
Boastful and self-compassionate,
Australia's Interstate Romance.

Shall he not live in Robust Rhyme,
Soliloquies and Odes Sublime?
Strictly between ourselves, he was
A rare old Humbug all the time.

In many a Book of Bushland dim
Mopokes shall give him greeting grim;
The old swans pottering in the reeds
Shall pass the time of day to him.

On many a page our Friend shall take
Small sticks his evening fire to make;
Shedding his waistcoat, he shall mix
On its smooth back his Johnny-Cake.

'Mid the dry leaves and silvery bark
Often at nightfall will he park
Close to a homeless creek, and hear
The Bunyip paddling in the dark.

I Spoke to the Violet

Shy one, I said, you can take me away in a breath,
But I like not the coat that you come in—the colour of
    death.

The silence you come with is sweeter to me than a sound,
But I love not the colour—I saw it go into the ground.

And, though you haunt me with all that is health to a
    rhyme,
My thoughts are as old as the naked beginning of Time.

Your scent does encompass all beauty in one loving breath,
But I like not the coat that you come in—the colour of
    death.

The Poor Can Feed the Birds

Ragged, unheeded, stooping, meanly shod,
The poor pass to the pond; not far away
The spires go up to God.

Shyly they come from the unpainted lane;
Coats have they made of old unhappiness
That keeps in every pain.

The rich have fear, perchance their God is dim;
'Tis with the hope of stored-up happiness
They build the spires to Him.

The rich go out in clattering pomp and dare
In the most holy places to insult
The deep Benevolence there.

But 'tis the poor who make the loving words.
Slowly they stoop; it is a sacrament:
The poor can feed the birds.

Old, it is old, this scattering of the bread,
Deep as forgiveness, or the tears that go
Out somewhere to the dead.

The feast of love, the love that is the cure
For all indignities—it reigns, it calls,
It chains us to the pure.

Seldom they speak of God, He is too dim;
So without thought of after happiness
They feed the birds for Him.

The rich men walk not here on the green sod,
But they have builded towers, the timorous
That still go up to God.

Still will the poor go out with loving words;
In the long need, the need for happiness
The poor can feed the birds.

The Smoker Parrot

He has the full moon on his breast,
The moonbeams are about his wing;
He has the colours of a king.
I see him floating unto rest
When all eyes wearily go west,
And the warm winds are quieting.
The moonbeams are about his wing:
He has the full moon on his breast.

KENNETH SLESSOR

(1901 – 1971)

KENNETH SLESSOR was born at Orange, New South Wales. His father was an English-born mining engineer whose work involved his moving around the country. His grandfather, Adolphe Schloesser, had left Germany to take up a professorship at the Royal Academy of Music in London and had married there. The family name was changed at the beginning of the First World War, presumably as a result of the widespread prejudice against things German at that time. On completing his education at Sydney Church of England Grammar School, Slessor chose journalism as a career, and except for a year or so in Melbourne and four years as an Official War Correspondent, spent his adult life in Sydney working on various newspapers. When he retired in 1969 he was the doyen of Sydney journalists and acknowledged as a foremost Australian poet. His first poems were published while he was a teenager, but his total output was comparatively small and his work as a poet was complete before middle age. He stopped writing poetry altogether in 1947. Apart from describing poetry as 'a pleasure out of hell', Slessor had virtually nothing to say about his preoccupations as a poet or the experiences which lay behind his poems. The notes on his poems, which he published in the Sydney *Sun* as a result of the enquiries he received from students asking him to explain allusions and structural intentions, give little away about the feelings he had. These notes are reprinted in his collection of prose, *Bread and Wine* (1970), which also contains his interesting lectures on Australian poetry. From the very first Slessor's poems were technically very assured, and he is rightly regarded as an outstanding craftsman. Of the poems in this anthology, 'Earth-Visitors' and 'The Night-Ride' are from *Earth-Visitors* (1926); 'Five Visions of Captain Cook' from *Cuckooz Country* (1932); and the remainder from *Five Bells* (1939), with the exception of 'Beach Burial' which resulted from Slessor's war experience.

Earth-Visitors

(To N.L.)

There were strange riders once, came gusting down
Cloaked in dark furs, with faces grave and sweet,
And white as air. None knew them, they were strangers—
Princes gone feasting, barons with gipsy eyes
And names that rang like viols—perchance, who knows,
Kings of old Tartary, forgotten, swept from Asia,
Blown on raven chargers across the world,
For ever smiling sadly in their beards
    And stamping abruptly into courtyards at midnight.

10   Post-boys would run, lanterns hang frostily, horses fume,
The strangers wake the Inn. Men, staring outside
Past watery glass, thick panes, could watch them eat,
Dyed with gold vapours in the candleflame,
Clapping their gloves, and stuck with crusted stones,
Their garments foreign, their talk a strange tongue,
    But sweet as pineapple—it was Archdukes, they must
      be.

In daylight, nothing; only their prints remained
Bitten in snow. They'd gone, no one knew where,
20   Or when, or by what road—no one could guess—
None but some sleepy girls, half tangled in dreams,
Mixing up miracle and desire; laughing, at first,
Then staring with bright eyes at their beds, opening their
    lips,
Plucking a crushed gold feather in their fingers,
And laughing again, eyes closed. But one remembered,
Between strange kisses and cambric, in the dark,
That unearthly beard had lifted.... 'Your name, child?'
'Sophia, sir—and what to call your Grace?'
30   Like a bubble of gilt, he had laughed 'Mercury!'

It is long now since great daemons walked on earth,
Staining with wild radiance a country bed,
And leaving only a confusion of sharp dreams
To vex a farm-girl—that, and perhaps a feather,
Some thread of the Cloth of Gold, a scale of metal,
Caught in her hair. The unpastured Gods have gone,
They are above those fiery-coasted clouds
Floating like fins of stone in the burnt air,
And earth is only a troubled thought to them

That sometimes drifts like wind across the bodies
    Of the sky's women.

There is one yet comes knocking in the night,
The drums of sweet conspiracy on the pane,
When darkness has arched his hands over the bush
And Springwood steams with dew, and the stars look
    down
On that one lonely chamber. . . .
She is there suddenly, lit by no torch or moon,
But by the shining of her naked body.
Her breasts are berries broken in snow; her hair
Blows in a gold rain over and over them.
She flings her kisses like warm guineas of love,
    And when she walks, the stars walk with her above.

She knocks. The door swings open, shuts again.
'Your name, child?'
    A thousand birds cry 'Venus!'

The Night-Ride

Gas flaring on the yellow platform; voices running up and
    down;
Milk-tins in cold dented silver; half-awake I stare,
Pull up the blind, blink out—all sounds are drugged;
The slow blowing of passengers asleep;
Engines yawning; water in heavy drips;
Black, sinister travellers, lumbering up the station,
One moment in the window, hooked over bags;
Hurrying, unknown faces—boxes with strange labels—
All groping clumsily to mysterious ends,
Out of the gaslight, dragged by private Fates.
Their echoes die. The dark train shakes and plunges;
Bells cry out; the night-ride starts again.
Soon I shall look out into nothing but blackness,
Pale, windy fields. The old roar and knock of the rails
Melts in the dull fury. Pull down the blind. Sleep. Sleep.
Nothing but grey, rushing rivers of bush outside.
Gaslight and milk-cans. Of Rapptown I recall nothing else.

Five Visions of Captain Cook

I

Cook was a captain of the Admiralty
When sea-captains had the evil eye,
Or should have, what with beating krakens off
And casting nativities of ships;
Cook was a captain of the powder-days
When captains, you might have said, if you had been
Fixed by their glittering stare, half-down the side,
Or gaping at them up companionways,
Were more like warlocks than a humble man—
And men were humble then who gazed at them,
Poor horn-eyed sailors, bullied by devils' fists
Of wind or water, or the want of both,
Childlike and trusting, filled with eager trust—
Cook was a captain of the sailing days
When sea-captains were kings like this,
Not cold executives of company-rules
Cracking their boilers for a dividend
Or bidding their engineers go wink
At bells and telegraphs, so plates would hold
Another pound. Those captains drove their ships
By their own blood, no laws of schoolbook steam,
Till yards were sprung, and masts went overboard—
Daemons in periwigs, doling magic out,
Who read fair alphabets in stars
Where humbler men found but a mess of sparks,
Who steered their crews by mysteries
And strange, half-dreadful sortilege with books,
Used medicines that only gods could know
The sense of, but sailors drank
In simple faith. That was the captain
Cook was when he came to the Coral Sea
And chose a passage into the dark.

How many mariners had made that choice
Paused on the brink of mystery! 'Choose now!'
The winds roared, blowing home, blowing home,
Over the Coral Sea. 'Choose now!' the trades
Cried once to Tasman, throwing him for choice
Their teeth or shoulders, and the Dutchman chose
The wind's way, turning north. 'Choose, Bougainville!'

40 The wind cried once, and Bougainville had heard
The voice of God, calling him prudently
Out of a dead lee shore, and chose the north.
The wind's way. So, too, Cook made choice,
Over the brink, into the devil's mouth,
With four months' food, and sailors wild with dreams
Of English beer, the smoking barns of home.
So Cook made choice, so Cook sailed westabout,
So men write poems in Australia.

II

Flowers turned to stone! Not all the botany
50 Of Joseph Banks, hung pensive in a porthole,
Could find the Latin for this loveliness,
Could put the Barrier Reef in a glass box
Tagged by the horrid Gorgon squint
Of horticulture. Stone turned to flowers
It seemed—you'd snap a crystal twig,
One petal even of the water-garden,
And have it dying like a cherry-bough.

They'd sailed all day outside a coral hedge,
And half the night. Cook sailed at night,
60 Let there be reefs a fathom from the keel
And empty charts. The sailors didn't ask,
Nor Joseph Banks. Who cared? It was the spell
Of Cook that lulled them, bade them turn below,
Kick off their sea-boots, puff themselves to sleep,
Though there were more shoals outside
Than teeth in a shark's head. Cook snored loudest
    himself.

One day, a morning of light airs and calms,
They slid towards a reef that would have knifed
70 Their boards to mash, and murdered every man.
So close it sucked them, one wave shook their keel,
The next blew past the coral. Three officers,
In gilt and buttons, languidly on deck
Pointed their sextants at the sun. One yawned,
One held a pencil, one put eye to lens:
Three very peaceful English mariners
Taking their sights for longitude.
I've never heard
Of sailors aching for the longitude
80 Of shipwrecks before or since. It was the spell

Of Cook did this, the phylacteries of Cook.
Men who ride broomsticks with a mesmerist
Mock the typhoon. So, too, it was with Cook.

III

Two chronometers the captain had,
One by Arnold that ran like mad,
One by Kendal in a walnut case,
Poor devoted creature with a hangdog face.

Arnold always hurried with a crazed click–click
Dancing over Greenwich like a lunatic,
Kendal panted faithfully his watch–dog beat,
Climbing out of Yesterday with sticky little feet.

Arnold choked with appetite to wolf up time,
Madly round the numerals his hands would climb,
His cogs rushed over and his wheels ran miles,
Dragging Captain Cook to the Sandwich Isles.

But Kendal dawdled in the tombstoned past,
With a sentimental prejudice to going fast,
And he thought very often of a haberdasher's door
And a yellow-haired boy who would knock no more.

All through the night-time, clock talked to clock,
In the captain's cabin, tock-tock-tock,
One ticked fast and one ticked slow,
And Time went over them a hundred years ago.

IV

Sometimes the god would fold his wings
And, stone of Caesars turned to flesh,
Talk of the most important things
That serious-minded midshipmen could wish,

Of plantains, and the lack of rum
Or spearing sea-cows—things like this
That hungry schoolboys, five days dumb,
In jolly-boats are wonted to discuss.

What midshipman would pause to mourn
The sun that beat about his ears,
Or curse the tide, if he could horn
His fists by tugging on those lumbering oars?

Let rum-tanned mariners prefer
To hug the weather-side of yards;
'Cats to catch mice' before they purr,
Those were the captain's enigmatic words.

120   Here, in this jolly-boat they graced,
Were food and freedom, wind and storm,
While, fowling-piece across his waist,
Cook mapped the coast, with one eye cocked for game.

V

After the candles had gone out, and those
Who listened had gone out, and a last wave
Of chimney-haloes caked their smoky rings
Like fish-scales on the ceiling, a Yellow Sea
Of swimming circles, the old man,
Old Captain-in-the Corner, drank his rum
With friendly gestures to four chairs. They stood
130   Empty, still warm from haunches, with rubbed nails
And leather glazed, like agéd serving-men
Feeding a king's delight, the sticky, drugged
Sweet agony of habitual anecdotes.
But these, his chairs, could bear an old man's tongue,
Sleep when he slept, be flattering when he woke,
And wink to hear the same eternal name
From lips new-dipped in rum.

'Then Captain Cook,
140   I heard him, told them they could go
If so they chose, but he would get them back,
Dead or alive, he'd have them,'
The old man screeched, half-thinking to hear 'Cook!
Cook again! Cook! It's other cooks he'll need,
Cooks who can bake a dinner out of pence,
That's what he lives on, talks on, half-a-crown
A day, and sits there full of Cook.
Who'd do your cooking now, I'd like to ask,
If someone didn't grind her bones away?
150   But that's the truth, six children and half-a-crown
A day, and a man gone daft with Cook.'

That was his wife,
Elizabeth, a noble wife but brisk,
Who lived in a present full of kitchen-fumes
And had no past. He had not seen her

For seven years, being blind, and that of course
Was why he'd had to strike a deal with chairs,
Not knowing when those who chafed them had gone
　　to sleep
160　Or stolen away. Darkness and empty chairs,
This was the port that Alexander Home
Had come to with his useless cutlass-wounds
And tales of Cook, and half-a-crown a day—
This was the creek he'd run his timbers to,
Where grateful countrymen repaid his wounds
At half-a-crown a day. Too good, too good,
This eloquent offering of birdcages
To gulls, and Greenwich Hospital to Cook,
Britannia's mission to the sea-fowl.

170　It was not blindness picked his flesh away,
Nor want of sight made penny-blank the eyes
Of Captain Home, but that he lived like this
In one place, and gazed elsewhere. His body moved
In Scotland, but his eyes were dazzle-full
Of skies and water farther round the world—
Air soaked with blue, so thick it dripped like snow
On spice-tree boughs, and water diamond-green,
Beaches wind-glittering with crumbs of gilt,
And birds more scarlet than a duchy's seal
180　That had come whistling long ago, and far
Away. His body had gone back,
Here it sat drinking rum in Berwickshire,
But not his eyes—they were left floating there
Half-round the earth, blinking at beaches milked
By suck-mouth tides, foaming with ropes of bubbles
And huge half-moons of surf. Thus it had been
When Cook was carried on a sailor's back,
Vengeance in a cocked hat, to claim his price,
A prince in barter for a longboat.
190　And then the trumpery springs of fate—a stone,
A musket-shot, a round of gunpowder,
And puzzled animals, killing they knew not what
Or why, but killing . . . the surge of goatish flanks
Armoured in feathers, like cruel birds:
Wild, childish faces, killing; a moment seen,
Marines with crimson coats and puffs of smoke
Toppling face-down; and a knife of English iron,
Forged aboard ship, that had been changed for pigs,
Given back to Cook between the shoulder-blades.
200　There he had dropped, and the old floundering sea,

The old, fumbling, witless lover-enemy,
Had taken his breath, last office of salt water.

Cook died. The body of Alexander Home
Flowed round the world and back again, with eyes
Marooned already, and came to English coasts,
The vague ancestral darknesses of home,
Seeing them faintly through a glass of gold,
Dim fog-shapes, ghosted like the ribs of trees
Against his blazing waters and blue air.
210 But soon they faded, and there was nothing left,
Only the sugar-cane and the wild granaries
Of sand, and palm-trees and the flying blood
Of cardinal-birds; and putting out one hand
Tremulously in the direction of the beach,
He felt a chair in Scotland. And sat down.

South Country

After the whey-faced anonymity
Of river-gums and scribbly-gums and bush,
After the rubbing and the hit of brush,
You come to the South Country

As if the argument of trees were done,
The doubts and quarrelling, the plots and pains,
All ended by these clear and gliding planes
Like an abrupt solution.

And over the flat earth of empty farms
10 The monstrous continent of air floats back
Coloured with rotting sunlight and the black,
Bruised flesh of thunderstorms:

Air arched, enormous, pounding the bony ridge,
Ditches and hutches, with a drench of light,
So huge, from such infinities of height,
You walk on the sky's beach

While even the dwindled hills are small and bare,
As if, rebellious, buried, pitiful,
Something below pushed up a knob of skull,
20 Feeling its way to air.

Out of Time

I

I saw Time flowing like the hundred yachts
That fly behind the daylight, foxed with air;
Or piercing, like the quince-bright, bitter slats
Of sun gone thrusting under Harbour's hair.

So Time, the wave, enfolds me in its bed,
Or Time, the bony knife, it runs me through.
'Skulker, take heart,' I thought my own heart said.
'The flood, the blade, go by—Time flows, not you!'

Vilely, continuously, stupidly,
Time takes me, drills me, drives through bone and vein,
So water bends the seaweeds in the sea,
The tide goes over, but the weeds remain.

Time, you must cry farewell, take up the track,
And leave this lovely moment at your back!

II

Time leaves the lovely moment at his back,
Eager to quench and ripen, kiss or kill;
To-morrow begs him, breathless for his lack,
Or beauty dead entreats him to be still.

His fate pursues him; he must open doors,
Or close them, for that pale and faceless host
Without a flag, whose agony implores
Birth, to be flesh, or funeral, to be ghost.

Out of all reckoning, out of dark and light,
Over the edges of dead Nows and Heres,
Blindly and softly, as a mistress might,
He keeps appointments with a million years.

I and the moment laugh, and let him go,
Leaning against his golden undertow.

III

Leaning against the golden undertow,
30   Backward, I saw the birds begin to climb
With bodies hailstone-clear, and shadows flow,
Fixed in a sweet meniscus, out of Time,

Out of the torrent, like the fainter land
Lensed in a bubble's ghostly camera,
The lighted beach, the sharp and china sand,
Glitters and waters and peninsula—

The moment's world, it was; and I was part,
Fleshless and ageless, changeless and made free.
'Fool, would you leave this country?' cried my heart,
40   But I was taken by the suck of sea.

The gulls go down, the body dies and rots,
And Time flows past them like a hundred yachts.

Five Bells

Time that is moved by little fidget wheels
Is not my Time, the flood that does not flow.
Between the double and the single bell
Of a ship's hour, between a round of bells
From the dark warship riding there below,
I have lived many lives, and this one life
Of Joe, long dead, who lives between five bells.

Deep and dissolving verticals of light
Ferry the falls of moonshine down. Five bells
10   Coldly rung out in a machine's voice. Night and water
Pour to one rip of darkness, the Harbour floats
In air, the Cross hangs upside-down in water.

Why do I think of you, dead man, why thieve
These profitless lodgings from the flukes of thought
Anchored in Time? You have gone from earth,
Gone even from the meaning of a name;
Yet something's there, yet something forms its lips
And hits and cries against the ports of space,
Beating their sides to make its fury heard.

20   Are you shouting at me, dead man, squeezing your face
In agonies of speech on speechless panes?
Cry louder, beat the windows, bawl your name!

But I hear nothing, nothing ... only bells,
Five bells, the bumpkin calculus of Time.
Your echoes die, your voice is dowsed by Life,
There's not a mouth can fly the pygmy strait—
Nothing except the memory of some bones
Long shoved away, and sucked away, in mud;
And unimportant things you might have done,
30   Or once I thought you did; but you forgot,
And all have now forgotten—looks and words
And slops of beer; your coat with buttons off,
Your gaunt chin and pricked eye, and raging tales
Of Irish kings and English perfidy,
And dirtier perfidy of publicans
Groaning to God from Darlinghurst.

                                                Five bells.

Then I saw the road, I heard the thunder
Tumble, and felt the talons of the rain
40   The night we came to Moorebank in slab-dark,
So dark you bore no body, had no face,
But a sheer voice that rattled out of air
(As now you'd cry if I could break the glass),
A voice that spoke beside me in the bush,
Loud for a breath or bitten off by wind,
Of Milton, melons, and the Rights of Man,
And blowing flutes, and how Tahitian girls
Are brown and angry-tongued, and Sydney girls
Are white and angry-tongued, or so you'd found.
50   But all I heard was words that didn't join
So Milton became melons, melons girls,
And fifty mouths, it seemed, were out that night,
And in each tree an Ear was bending down,
Or something had just run, gone behind grass,
When, blank and bone-white, like a maniac's thought,
The naphtha-flash of lightning slit the sky,
Knifing the dark with deathly photographs.
There's not so many with so poor a purse
Or fierce a need, must fare by night like that,
60   Five miles in darkness on a country track,
But when you do, that's what you think.

                                                Five bells.

In Melbourne, your appetite had gone,
Your angers too; they had been leeched away
By the soft archery of summer rains
And the sponge-paws of wetness, the slow damp
That stuck the leaves of living, snailed the mind,
And showed your bones, that had been sharp with rage,
The sodden ecstasies of rectitude.
I thought of what you'd written in faint ink,
70   Your journal with the sawn-off lock, that stayed behind
With other things you left, all without use,
All without meaning now, except a sign

That someone had been living who now was dead:
'At Labassa. Room 6 x 8
On top of the tower; because of this, very dark
And cold in winter. Everything has been stowed
Into this room—500 books all shapes
And colours, dealt across the floor
And over sills and on the laps of chairs;
80   Guns, photoes of many differant things
And differant curioes that I obtained. . . .'

In Sydney, by the spent aquarium-flare
Of penny gaslight on pink wallpaper,
We argued about blowing up the world,
But you were living backward, so each night
You crept a moment closer to the breast,
And they were living, all of them, those frames
And shapes of flesh that had perplexed your youth,
And most your father, the old man gone blind,
90   With fingers always round a fiddle's neck,
That graveyard mason whose fair monuments
And tablets cut with dreams of piety
Rest on the bosoms of a thousand men
Staked bone by bone, in quiet astonishment
At cargoes they had never thought to bear,
These funeral-cakes of sweet and sculptured stone.

Where have you gone? The tide is over you,
The turn of midnight water's over you,
As Time is over you, and mystery,
100   And memory, the flood that does not flow.
You have no suburb, like those easier dead
In private berths of dissolution laid—
The tide goes over, the waves ride over you
And let their shadows down like shining hair,

But they are Water; and the sea-pinks bend
Like lilies in your teeth, but they are Weed;
And you are only part of an Idea.
I felt the wet push its black thumb-balls in,
The night you died, I felt your eardrums crack,
110 And the short agony, the longer dream,
The Nothing that was neither long nor short;
But I was bound, and could not go that way,
But I was blind, and could not feel your hand.
If I could find an answer, could only find
Your meaning, or could say why you were here
Who now are gone, what purpose gave you breath
Or seized it back, might I not hear your voice?

I looked out of my window in the dark
At waves with diamond quills and combs of light
120 That arched their mackerel-backs and smacked the sand
In the moon's drench, that straight enormous glaze,
And ships far off asleep, and Harbour-buoys
Tossing their fireballs wearily each to each,
And tried to hear your voice, but all I heard
Was a boat's whistle, and the scraping squeal
Of seabirds' voices far away, and bells,
Five bells. Five bells coldly ringing out.

Five bells.

Beach Burial

Softly and humbly to the Gulf of Arabs
The convoys of dead sailors come;
At night they sway and wander in the waters far under,
But morning rolls them in the foam.

Between the sob and clubbing of the gunfire
Someone, it seems, has time for this,
To pluck them from the shallows and bury them in burrows
And tread the sand upon their nakedness;

And each cross, the driven stake of tidewood,
10 Bears the last signature of men,
Written with such perplexity, with such bewildered pity,
The words choke as they begin—

'*Unknown seaman*'—the ghostly pencil
Wavers and fades, the purple drips,
The breath of the wet season has washed their inscriptions
As blue as drowned men's lips,

Dead seamen, gone in search of the same landfall,
Whether as enemies they fought,
Or fought with us, or neither; the sand joins them together,
20   Enlisted on the other front.

El Alamein.

A.D. HOPE

(b. 1907)

ALEC DERWENT HOPE was born at Cooma, New South Wales, but his earliest memories are of the Macquarie Valley near Campbelltown in Tasmania, to which the family moved when he was three years old. His father was a Presbyterian minister, and several moves to other parishes followed. Hope eventually completed his schooling at Bathurst High School, back in New South Wales. His intention had been to study medicine, but in spite of a further year's study at Fort Street High School in Sydney, which won him a scholarship to university, he was not accepted for medicine and chose Arts instead. On graduating in 1928, he won the same travelling scholarship which had enabled Christopher Brennan to go abroad. After Oxford where he studied English, he returned to New South Wales and took employment as a school teacher. In 1938 he became a lecturer in education at Sydney Teachers College, where James McAuley was one of his students. In 1945 he moved to Melbourne as Senior Lecturer in English at the University, and in 1950 he became Professor of English at the Canberra University College (later incorporated into the Australian National University), where he remained until his retirement. His first poems were not published until the mid-thirties, and his first book, *The Wandering Islands*, did not appear until 1955. By the time his *Collected Poems* appeared in 1970 he was everywhere acknowledged as a major Australian poet. He was at first regarded as being primarily a satirist, but with succeeding volumes he had emerged as a lyrical and meditative poet, capable of an eloquence uncharacteristic of Australian poets. Of the poems by which he is represented here, 'Australia' is the earliest, having been written in 1939. The poems are in chronological order, according to the dates given in the *Collected Poems*, except for 'Hay Fever' which is from *A Late Picking* (1975) and 'Tasmanian Magpies' which is from *Antechinus* (1981). Hope continues to write poetry and has in recent years published a number of scholarly works. He is one of several contemporary Australian poets who command attention as critics, his most important publication being the collection of essays on poetry entitled *The Cave and the Spring* (1965). A later volume, *Native Companions* (1974), which collects his book reviews and includes some autobiographical essays, gives his views on a range of Australian writers. He writes sympathetically of Judith Wright as a fellow poet in the Australian Writers and their Work series (1975).

Australia

A Nation of trees, drab green and desolate grey
In the field uniform of modern wars,
Darkens her hills, those endless, outstretched paws
Of Sphinx demolished or stone lion worn away.

They call her a young country, but they lie:
She is the last of lands, the emptiest,
A woman beyond her change of life, a breast
Still tender but within the womb is dry.

Without songs, architecture, history:
The emotions and superstitions of younger lands,
Her rivers of water drown among inland sands,
The river of her immense stupidity

Floods her monotonous tribes from Cairns to Perth.
In them at last the ultimate men arrive
Whose boast is not: 'we live' but 'we survive',
A type who will inhabit the dying earth.

And her five cities, like five teeming sores,
Each drains her: a vast parasite robber-state
Where second-hand Europeans pullulate
Timidly on the edge of alien shores.

Yet there are some like me turn gladly home
From the lush jungle of modern thought, to find
The Arabian desert of the human mind,
Hoping, if still from the deserts the prophets come,

Such savage and scarlet as no green hills dare
Springs in that waste, some spirit which escapes
The learned doubt, the chatter of cultured apes
Which is called civilization over there.

The Wandering Islands

You cannot build bridges between the wandering islands;
The Mind has no neighbours, and the unteachable heart
Announces its armistice time after time, but spends
Its love to draw them closer and closer apart.

They are not on the chart; they turn indifferent shoulders
On the island-hunters; they are not afraid
Of Cook or De Quiros, nor of the empire-builders;
By missionary bishops and the tourist trade

They are not annexed; they claim no fixed position;
They take no pride in a favoured latitude;
The committee of atolls inspires in them no devotion
And the earthquake belt no special attitude.

A refuge only for the shipwrecked sailor;
He sits on the shore and sullenly masturbates,
Dreaming of rescue, the pubs in the ports of call or
The big-hipped harlots at the dockyard gates.

But the wandering islands drift on their own business,
Incurious whether the whales swim round or under,
Investing no fear in ultimate forgiveness.
If they clap together, it is only casual thunder

And yet they are hurt—for the social polyps never
Girdle their bare shores with a moral reef;
When the icebergs grind them they know both beauty and
    terror;
They are not exempt from ordinary grief;

And the sudden ravages of love surprise
Them like acts of God—its irresistible function
They have never treated with convenient lies
As a part of geography or an institution.

An instant of fury, a bursting mountain of spray,
They rush together, their promontories lock,
An instant the castaway hails the castaway,
But the sounds perish in that earthquake shock.

And then, in the crash of ruined cliffs, the smother
And swirl of foam, the wandering islands part.

But all that one mind ever knows of another,
Or breaks the long isolation of the heart,

Was in that instant. The shipwrecked sailor senses
His own despair in a retreating face.
Around him he hears in the huge monotonous voices
Of wave and wind: 'The Rescue will not take place.'

Conquistador

I sing of the decline of Henry Clay
Who loved a white girl of uncommon size.
Although a small man in a little way,
He had in him some seed of enterprise.

Each day he caught the seven-thirty train
To work, watered his garden after tea,
Took an umbrella if it looked like rain
And was remarkably like you or me.

He had his hair cut once a fortnight, tried
Not to forget the birthday of his wife,
And might have lived unnoticed till he died
Had not ambition entered Henry's life.

He met her in the lounge of an hotel
—A most unusual place for him to go—
But there he was and there she was as well,
Sitting alone. He ordered beers for two.

She was so large a girl that when they came
He gave the waiter twice the usual tip.
She smiled without surprise, told him her name,
And as the name trembled on Henry's lip,

His parched soul, swelling like a desert root,
Broke out its delicate dream upon the air;
The mountains shook with earthquake under foot;
An angel seized him suddenly by the hair;

The sky was shrill with peril as he passed;
A hurricane crushed his senses with its din;
The wildfire crackled up his reeling mast;
The trumpet of a maelstrom sucked him in;

The desert shrivelled and burnt off his feet;
His bones and buttons an enormous snake
Vomited up; still in the shimmering heat
The pygmies showed him their forbidden lake

And then transfixed him with their poison darts;
He married six black virgins in a bunch,
Who, when they had drawn out his manly parts,
Stewed him and ate him lovingly for lunch.

Adventure opened wide its grisly jaws;
Henry looked in and knew the Hero's doom.
The huge white girl drank on without a pause
And, just at closing time, she asked him home.

The tram they took was full of Roaring Boys
Announcing the world's ruin and Judgment Day;
The sky blared with its grand orchestral voice
The Götterdämmerung of Henry Clay.

But in her quiet room they were alone.
There, towering over Henry by a head,
She stood and took her clothes off one by one,
And then she stretched herself upon the bed.

Her bulk of beauty, her stupendous grace
Challenged the lion heart in his puny dust.
Proudly his Moment looked him in the face:
He rose to meet it as a hero must;

Climbed the white mountain of unravished snow,
Planted his tiny flag upon the peak.
The smooth drifts, scarcely breathing, lay below.
She did not take the trouble to smile or speak.

And afterwards, it may have been in play,
The enormous girl rolled over and squashed him flat;
And, as she could not send him home that way,
Used him thereafter as a bedside mat.

Speaking at large, I will say this of her:
She did not spare expense to make him nice.
Tanned on both sides and neatly edged with fur,
The job would have been cheap at any price.

And when, in winter, getting out of bed,
Her large soft feet pressed warmly on the skin,
The two glass eyes would sparkle in his head,
The jaws extend their papier-mâché grin.

Good people, for the soul of Henry Clay
Offer your prayers, and view his destiny!
He was the Hero of our Time. He may
With any luck, one day, be you or me.

Pyramis or The House of Ascent

This is their image: the desert and the wild,
A lone man digging, a nation piling stones
Under the lash in fear, in sweat, in haste;
Image of those demonic minds who build
To outlast time, spend life to house old bones—
This pyramid rising squarely in the waste!

I think of the great work, its secret lost;
The solid, blind, invincible masonry
Still challenges the heart. Neglect and greed
Have left it void and ruin; sun and frost
Free it away; yet, all foretold, I see
The builder answering: 'Let the work proceed!'

I think of how the work was hurried on:
Those terrible souls, the Pharaohs, those great Kings
Taking, like genius, their prerogative
Of blood, mind, treasure: 'Tomorrow I shall be gone;
If you lack slaves, make war! The measure of things
Is man, and I of men. By this you live.'

No act of time limits the procreant will
And to subdue men seems a little thing,
Seeing that in another world than this
The gods themselves unwilling await him still
And must be overcome; for thus the King
Takes, for all men, his apotheosis.

I think of other pyramids, not in stone,
The great, incredible monuments of art,
And of their builders, men who put aside

10

20

Consideration, dared, and stood alone,
Strengthening those powers that fence the failing heart:
Intemperate will and incorruptible pride.

The man alone digging his bones a hole;
The pyramid in the waste—whose images?
Blake's tower of vision defying the black air;
Milton twice blind groping about his soul
For exit, and Swift raving mad in his—
The builders of the pyramid everywhere!

The Death of the Bird

For every bird there is this last migration:
Once more the cooling year kindles her heart;
With a warm passage to the summer station
Love pricks the course in lights across the chart.

Year after year a speck on the map, divided
By a whole hemisphere, summons her to come;
Season after season, sure and safely guided,
Going away she is also coming home.

And being home, memory becomes a passion
With which she feeds her brood and straws her nest,
Aware of ghosts that haunt the heart's possession
And exiled love mourning within the breast.

The sands are green with a mirage of valleys;
The palm-tree casts a shadow not its own;
Down the long architrave of temple or palace
Blows a cool air from moorland scarps of stone.

And day by day the whisper of love grows stronger;
That delicate voice, more urgent with despair,
Custom and fear constraining her no longer,
Drives her at last on the waste leagues of air.

A vanishing speck in those inane dominions,
Single and frail, uncertain of her place,
Alone in the bright host of her companions,
Lost in the blue unfriendliness of space,

She feels it close now, the appointed season:
The invisible thread is broken as she flies;
Suddenly, without warning, without reason,
The guiding spark of instinct winks and dies.

30 Try as she will, the trackless world delivers
No way, the wilderness of light no sign,
The immense and complex map of hills and rivers
Mocks her small wisdom with its vast design.

And darkness rises from the eastern valleys,
And the winds buffet her with their hungry breath,
And the great earth, with neither grief nor malice,
Receives the tiny burden of her death.

Meditation on a Bone

A piece of bone, found at Trondhjem in 1901, with the following
runic inscription (about A.D. 1050) cut on it:
*I loved her as a maiden; I will not trouble Erlend's detestable wife; better
she should be a widow.*

Words scored upon a bone,
Scratched in despair or rage—
Nine hundred years have gone;
Now, in another age,
They burn with passion on
A scholar's tranquil page.

The scholar takes his pen
And turns the bone about,
And writes those words again.
10 Once more they seethe and shout,
And through a human brain
Undying hate rings out.

'I loved her when a maid;
I loathe and love the wife
That warms another's bed: .
Let him beware his life!'
The scholar's hand is stayed;
His pen becomes a knife

To grave in living bone
The fierce archaic cry.
He sits and reads his own
Dull sum of misery.
A thousand years have flown
Before that ink is dry.

And, in a foreign tongue,
A man, who is not he,
Reads and his heart is wrung
This ancient grief to see,
And thinks: When I am dung,
What bone shall speak for me?

The Double Looking Glass

See how she strips her lily for the sun:
The silk shrieks upward from her wading feet;
Down through the pool her wavering echoes run;
Candour with candour, shade and substance meet.

From where a wet meniscus rings the shin
The crisp air shivers up her glowing thighs,
Swells round a noble haunch and whispers in
The dimple of her belly. . . . Surely eyes

Lurk in the laurels, where each leafy nest
Darts its quick bird-glance through the shifting screen.
. . . Yawn of the oxter, lift of liquid breast
Splinter their white shafts through our envious green

Where thuds this rage of double double hearts.
. . . My foolish fear refracts a foolish dream.
Here all things have imagined counterparts:
A dragon-fly dim-darting in the stream

Follows and watches with enormous eyes
His blue narcissus glitter in the air.
The flesh reverberates its own surprise
And startles at the act which makes it bare.

Laced with quick air and vibrant to the light,
Now my whole animal breathes and knows its place

In the great web of being, and its right;
The mind learns ease again, the heart finds grace.

I am as all things living. Man alone
Cowers from his world in clothes and cannot guess
How earth and water, branch and beast and stone
Speak to the naked in their nakedness.

30
. . . A silver rising of her arms, that share
Their pure and slender crescent with the pool
Plunders the braided treasure of her hair.
Loosed from their coils uncrowning falls the full

Cascade of tresses whispering down her flanks,
And idly now she wades a step, and stays
To watch the ripples widen to the banks
And lapse in mossy coves and rushy bays.

Look with what bliss of motion now she turns
And seats herself upon a sunny ledge,
Leans back, and drowsing dazzles, basking burns.
40
Susannah! . . . what hiss, what rustle in the sedge;

What fierce susurrus shifts from bush to bush?
. . . Susannah! Susannah, Susannah! . . . Foolish heart,
It was your own pulse lisping in a hush
So deep, I hear the water-beetle dart

And trace from bank to bank his skein of light,
So still the sibilance of a breaking bud
Speaks to the sense; the hairy bee in flight
Booms a brute chord of danger in my blood.

What danger though? The garden wall is high
50
And bolted and secure the garden door;
The bee, bold ravisher, will pass me by
And does not seek my honey for his store;

The speckled hawk in heaven, wheeling slow
Searches the tufts of grass for other prey;
Safe in their sunny banks the lilies grow,
Secure from rough hands for another day.

Alert and brisk, even the hurrying ant
Courses these breathing ranges unafraid.

The fig-tree, leaning with its leaves aslant,
Touches me with broad hands of harmless shade.

And if the urgent pulses of the sun
Quicken my own with a voluptuous heat,
They warm me only as they warm the stone
Or the thin liquid paddling round my feet.

My garden holds me like its private dream,
A secret pleasure, guarded and apart.
Now as I lean above the pool I seem
The image of my image in its heart.

In that inverted world a scarlet fish
Drifts through the trees and swims into the sky,
So in the contemplative mind a wish
Drifts through its mirror of eternity.

A mirror for man's images of love
The nakedness of woman is a pool
In which her own desires mount and move,
Alien, solitary, purposeful

Yet in this close were every leaf an eye,
In those green limbs the sap would mount as slow.
One with their life beneath an open sky,
I melt into the trance of time, I flow

Into the languid current of the day
. . . The sunlight sliding on a breathing flank
Fades and returns again in tranquil play;
Her eyelids close; she sleeps upon the bank.

Now, now to wreak upon her Promised Land
The vengeance of the dry branch on the bud.
Who shall be first upon her? Who shall stand
To watch the dragon sink its fangs in blood?

Her ripeness taunts the ignominy of age;
Seethes in old loins with hate and lust alike.
Now in the plenitude of shame and rage
The rod of chastisement is reared to strike.

And now to take her drowsing; now to fall
With wild-fire on the cities of the plain;

Susannah! . . . Yet once more that hoarse faint call,
That rustle from the thicket comes again?

Ah, no! Some menace from the edge of sleep
Imposes its illusion on my ear.
Relax, return, Susannah; Let the deep
Warm tide of noonday bear you; do not fear,

But float once more on that delicious stream.
Suppose some lover watches from the grove;
Suppose, only suppose, those glints, the gleam
Of eyes; the eyes of a young man in love.

Shall I prolong this fancy, now the sense
Impels, the hour invites? Shall I not own
Such thoughts as women find to recompense
Their hidden lives when secret and alone?

Surprise the stranger in the heart, some strong
Young lion of the rocks who found his path
By night, and now he crouches all day long
Beside the pool to see me at my bath.

He would be there, a melancholy shade
Caught in the ambush of his reckless joy,
Afraid to stir for fear I call, afraid
In one unguarded moment to destroy

At once the lover and the thing he loves.
Who should he be? I cannot guess; but such
As desperate hope or lonelier passion moves
To tempt his fate so far, to dare so much;

Who having seen me only by the way,
Or having spoken with me once by chance,
Fills all his nights with longing, and the day
With schemes whose triumph is a casual glance.

Possessed by what he never can possess,
He forms his wild design and ventures all
Only to see me in my nakedness
And lurk and tremble by the garden wall.

He lives but in my dream. I need repel
No dream for I may end it when I please;

And I may dream myself in love as well
As dream my lover in the summer trees,

Suppose myself desired, suppose desire,
Summon that wild enchantment of the mind,
Kindle my fire at his imagined fire,
Pity his love and call him and be kind.

Now think he comes, and I shall lie as still
As limpid waters that reflect their sun,
And let him lie between my breasts and fill
My loins with thunder till the dream be done.

The kisses of my mouth are his; he lies
And feeds among the lilies; his brown knees
Divide the white embraces of my thighs.
Wake not my love nor stir him till he please,

For now his craft has passed the straits and now
Into my shoreless sea he drives alone.
Islands of spice await his happy prow
And fabulous deeps support and bear him on.

He rides the mounting surge, he feels the wide
Horizon draw him onward mile by mile;
The reeling sky, the dark rejoicing tide
Lead him at last to this mysterious isle.

In ancient woods that murmur with the sea,
He finds once more the garden and the pool.
And there a man who is and is not he
Basks on the sunny margin in the full

Noon of another and a timeless sky,
And dreams but never hopes to have his love;
And there the woman who is also I
Watches him from the hollow of the grove;

Till naked from the leaves she steals and bends
Above his sleep and wakes him with her breast
And now the vision begins, the voyage ends,
And the great phoenix blazes in his nest.

. . . Ah, God of Israel, even though alone,
We take her with a lover, in the flush
Of her desires. SUSANNAH! . . . I am undone!
What beards, what bald heads burst now from the bush!

140

150

160

Ode on the Death of
Pius the Twelfth

To every season its proper act of joy,
To every age its natural mode of grace,
Each vision its hour, each talent we employ
    Its destined time and place.

I was at Amherst when this great pope died;
The northern year was wearing towards the cold;
The ancient trees were in their autumn pride
    Of russet, flame and gold.

Amherst in Massachusetts in the Fall:
10 I ranged the college campus to admire
Maple and beech, poplar and ash in all
    Their panoply of fire.

Something that since a child I longed to see,
This miracle of the other hemisphere:
Whole forests in their annual ecstasy
    Waked by the dying year.

Not budding Spring, not Summer's green parade
Clothed in such glory these resplendent trees;
The lilies of the field were not arrayed
20   In riches such as these.

Nature evolves their colours as a call,
A lure which serves to fertilize the seed;
How strange then that the splendour of the Fall
    Should serve no natural need

And, having no end in nature, yet can yield
Such exquisite natural pleasure to the eye!
Who could have guessed in summer's green concealed
    The leaf's resolve to die?

Yet from the first spring shoots through all the year,
30 Masked in the chlorophyll's intenser green,
The feast of crimson was already there,
    These yellows blazed unseen.

Now in the bright October sun the clear
Translucent colours trembled overhead
And as I walked, a voice I chanced to hear
    Announced: The Pope is dead!

A human voice, yet there the place became
Bethel: each bough with pentecost was crowned;
The great trunks rapt in unconsuming flame
    Stood as on holy ground.

I thought of this old man whose life was past,
Who in himself and his great office stood
Against the secular tempest as a vast
    Oak spans the underwood;

Who in the age of Armageddon found
A voice that caused all men to hear it plain,
The blood of Abel crying from the ground
    To stay the hand of Cain;

Who found from that great task small time to spare:
—For him and for mankind the hour was late—
So much to snatch, to save, so much to bear
    That Mary's part must wait,

Until in his last years the change began:
A strange illumination of the heart,
Voices and visions such as mark the man
    Chosen and set apart.

His death, they said, was slow, grotesque and hard,
Yet in that gross decay, until the end
Untroubled in his joy, he saw the Word
    Made spirit and ascend.

Those glorious woods and that triumphant death
Prompted me there to join their mysteries:
This Brother Albert, this great oak of faith,
    Those fire-enchanted trees.

Seven years have passed, and still, at times, I ask
Whether in man, as in those plants, may be
A splendour, which his human virtues mask,
    Not given to us to see?

If to some lives at least there comes a stage
When, all the active man now left behind,
They enter on the treasure of old age,
    This autumn of the mind.

Then, while the heart stands still, beyond desire
The dying animal knows a strange serene:
Emerging in its ecstasy of fire
    The burning soul is seen.

Who sees it? Since old age appears to men
Senility, decrepitude, disease,
What Spirit walks among us, past our ken,
    As we among these trees,

Whose unknown nature, blessed with keener sense
Catches its breath in wonder at the sight
And feels its being flood with that immense
    Epiphany of light?

On an Engraving by Casserius

For Dr John Z. Bowers

Set on this bubble of dead stone and sand,
Lapped by its frail balloon of lifeless air,
Alone in the inanimate void, they stand,
These clots of thinking molecules who stare
Into the night of nescience and death,
And, whirled about with their terrestrial ball,
Ask of all being its motion and its frame:
This of all human images takes my breath;
Of all the joys in being a man at all,
10 This folds my spirit in its quickening flame.

Turning the leaves of this majestic book
My thoughts are with those great cosmographers,
Surgeon adventurers who undertook
To probe and chart time's other universe.
This one engraving holds me with its theme:
More than all maps made in that century
Which set true bearings for each cape and star,
De Quiros' vision or Newton's cosmic dream,
This reaches towards the central mystery
20 Of whence our being draws and what we are.

It came from that great school in Padua:
Casserio and Spiegel made this page.
Vesalius, who designed the *Fabrica*,

There strove, but burned his book at last in rage;
Fallopius by its discipline laid bare
The elements of this humanity,
Without which none knows that which treats the soul;
Fabricius talked with Galileo there:
Did those rare spirits in their colloquy
30   Divine in their two skills the single goal?

'One force that moves the atom and the star,'
Says Galileo; 'one basic law beneath
All change!' 'Would light from Achernar
Reveal how embryon forms within its sheath?'
Fabricius asks, and smiles. Talk such as this,
Ranging the bounds of our whole universe,
Could William Harvey once have heard? And once
Hearing, strike out that strange hypothesis,
Which in *De Motu Cordis* twice recurs,
40   Coupling the heart's impulsion with the sun's?

Did Thomas Browne at Padua, too, in youth
Hear of their talk of universal law
And form that notion of particular truth
Framed to correct a science they foresaw,
That darker science of which he used to speak
In later years and called the Crooked Way
Of Providence? Did *he* foresee perhaps
An age in which all sense of the unique,
And singular dissolves, like ours today,
50   In diagrams, statistics, tables, maps?

Not here! The graver's tool in this design
Aims still to give not general truth alone,
Blue-print of science or data's formal line:
Here in its singularity he has shown
The image of an individual soul;
Bodied in this one woman, he makes us see
The shadow of his anatomical laws.
An artist's vision animates the whole,
Shines through the scientist's detailed scrutiny
60   And links the person and the abstract cause.

Such were the charts of those who pressed beyond
Vesalius their master, year by year
Tracing each bone, each muscle, every frond
Of nerve until the whole design lay bare.
Thinking of this dissection, I descry

The tiers of faces, their teacher in his place,
The talk at the cadaver carried in:
'A woman—with child!'; I hear the master's dry
Voice as he lifts a scalpel from its case:
70   'With each new step in science, we begin.'

Who was she? Though they never knew her name,
Dragged from the river, found in some alley at dawn,
This corpse none cared, or dared perhaps, to claim;
The dead child in her belly still unborn,
Might have passed, momentary as a shooting star,
Quenched like the misery of her personal life,
Had not the foremost surgeon of Italy,
Giulio Casserio of Padua,
Bought her for science, questioned her with his knife,
80   And drawn her for his great *Anatomy*;

Where still in the abundance of her grace,
She stands among the monuments of time
And with a feminine delicacy displays
His elegant dissection: the sublime
Shaft of her body opens like a flower
Whose petals, folded back expose the womb,
Cord and placenta and the sleeping child,
Like instruments of music in a room
Left when her grieving Orpheus left his tower
90   Forever, for the desert and the wild.

Naked she waits against a tideless shore,
A sibylline stance, a noble human frame
Such as those old anatomists loved to draw.
She turns her head as though in trouble or shame,
Yet with a dancer's gesture holds the fruit
Plucked, though not tasted, of the Fatal Tree.
Something of the first Eve is in this pose
And something of the second in the mute
Offering of her child in death to be
100   Love's victim and her flesh its mystic rose.

No figure with wings of fire and back-swept hair
Swoops with his: Blessed among Women!; no sword
Of the spirit cleaves or quickens her; yet there
She too was overshadowed by the Word,
Was chosen, and by her humble gift of death
The lowly and the poor in heart give tongue,
Wisdom puts down the mighty from their seat;

The vile rejoice and rising, hear beneath
Scalpel and forceps, tortured into song,
Her body utter their magnificat.

Four hundred years since first that cry rang out:
Four hundred years, the patient, probing knife
Cut towards its answer—yet we stand in doubt:
Living, we cannot tell the source of life.
Old science, old certainties that lit our way
Shrink to poor guesses, dwindle to a myth.
Today's truths teach us how we were beguiled;
Tomorrow's how blind our vision of today.
The universals we thought to conjure with
Pass: there remain the mother and the child.

Loadstone, loadstar, alike to each new age,
There at the crux of time they stand and scan,
Past every scrutiny of prophet or sage,
Still unguessed prospects in this venture of Man.
To generations, which we leave behind,
They taught a difficult, selfless skill: to show
The mask beyond the mask beyond the mask;
To ours another vista, where the mind
No longer asks for answers, but to know:
What questions are there which we fail to ask?

Who knows, but to the age to come they speak
Words that our own is still unapt to hear:
'These are the limits of all you sought and seek;
More our yet unborn nature cannot bear.
Learn now that all man's intellectual quest
Was but the stirrings of a foetal sleep;
The birth you cannot haste and cannot stay
Nears its appointed time; turn now and rest
Till that new nature ripens, till the deep
Dawns with that unimaginable day.'

Moschus Moschiferus

A Song for St Cecilia's Day

In the high jungle where Assam meets Tibet
The small Kastura, most archaic of deer,
Were driven in herds to cram the hunters' net
And slaughtered for the musk-pods which they bear;

But in those thickets of rhododendron and birch
The tiny creatures now grow hard to find.
Fewer and fewer survive each year. The search
Employs new means, more exquisite and refined:

The hunters now set out by two or three;
Each carries a bow and one a slender flute.
Deep in the forest the archers choose a tree
And climb; the piper squats against the root.

And there they wait until all trace of man
And rumour of his passage dies away.
They melt into the leaves and, while they scan
The glade below, their comrade starts to play.

Through those vast listening woods a tremulous skein
Of melody wavers, delicate and shrill:
Now dancing and now pensive, now a rain
Of pure, bright drops of sound and now the still,

Sad wailing of lament; from tune to tune
It winds and modulates without a pause;
The hunters hold their breath; the trance of noon
Grows tense; with its full power the music draws

A shadow from a juniper's darker shade;
Bright-eyed, with quivering muzzle and pricked ear,
The little musk-deer slips into the glade
Led by an ecstasy that conquers fear.

A wild enchantment lures him, step by step,
Into its net of crystalline sound, until
The leaves stir overhead, the bowstrings snap
And poisoned shafts bite sharp into the kill.

10

20

30

Then, as the victim shudders, leaps and falls,
The music soars to a delicious peak,
And on and on its silvery piping calls
Fresh spoil for the rewards the hunters seek.

But when the woods are emptied and the dusk
Draws in, the men climb down and count their prey,
Cut out the little glands that hold the musk
And leave the carcasses to rot away.

A hundred thousand or so are killed each year;
Cause and effect are very simply linked:
Rich scents demand the musk, and so the deer,
Its source, must soon, they say, become extinct.

Divine Cecilia, there is no more to say!
Of all who praised the power of music, few
Knew of these things. In honour of your day
Accept this song I too have made for you.

Hay Fever

Time, with his scythe honed fine,
Takes a pace forward, swings from the hips; the flesh
Crumples and falls in wind-rows curving away.
Waiting my turn as he swings—(Not yet, not mine!)
I recall the sound of the scythe on an earlier day:
Late spring in my boyhood; learning to mow with the
        men;
Eight of us mowing together in echelon line,
Out of the lucerne patch and into the hay,
And I at the end on the left because I was fresh,
Because I was new to the game and young at the skill—
As though I were Time himself, I remember it still.

The mild Tasmanian summer; the men are here
To mow for my minister father and make his hay.
They have brought a scythe for me. I hold it with pride.
The lucerne is up to my knee, the grass to my waist.
I set the blade into the grass as they taught me the way;
The still dewy stalks nod, tremble and tilt aside,
Cornflowers, lucerne and poppies, sugar-grass,
        summer-grass, laced
With red-stemmed dock; I feel the thin steel crunch
Through hollow-stalk milk thistle, self-sown oats and rye;

I snag on a fat-hen clump; chick-weed falls in a bunch,
But sorrel scatters; dandelion casts up a golden eye,
To a smell of cows chewing their cuds, the sweet
      hay-breath:
The boy with the scythe never thinks it the smell of death.

The boy with the scythe takes a stride forward, swings
From the hips, keeping place and pace, keeping time
30   By the sound of the scythes, by the swish and ripple, the
      sigh
Of the dying grass like an animal breathing, a rhyme
Falling pat on the ear that matches the steel as it sings
True through the tottering stems. Sweat runs into my eye.
How long to a break? How long can I hold out yet?
I nerve my arms to go on; I am running with, flooding
      with, sweat.

How long ago was it?—Why, the scythe is as obsolete now
As arrows and bow. I have lived from one age to another;
40   And I have made hay while I could and the sun still shone.
Time drives a harvester now: he does not depend on the
      weather.
Well, I have rolled in his hay, in my day, and now it is
      gone;
But I still have a barn stacked high with that good dry
      mow,
Shrivelled and fragrant stems, the grass and the flowers
      together
And a thistle or two in the pile for the prick of remorse.
50   It is good for a man when he comes to the end of his course
In the barn of his brain to be able to romp like a boy in the
      heap . . .
To lie still in well-cured hay . . . to drift into sleep.

Tasmanian Magpies

Ethiopia! they used to say,
Fluting at dawn through pure, clear rills of sound,
The magpies of that earlier day,
Ethiopia! Ethiopia! from all around.
Dulcimer of no Abyssinian maid
Was ever so plangent or so doucely played.
Ethiópia, Ethiopiá!
Echoes went through me of Mount Abora.

Another country, another age! I still
Hear them at early morning in the trees;
The same pure grace-notes, the same exquisite trill,
The lilt, the liquid ease,
But not the enchantment of that warbled name;
The magpie dialect here is not the same;
The magic syllables have gone
That brought me full awake and roused the sun.

Lost Ethiopia. Is that loss in me?
Monaro magpies bursting into song
Soar through new cadences, fresh jubilee;
But in an unknown tongue
Rejoice. Can it perhaps be true
That I have lost those languages I knew
In boyhood, when each bird,
Stone, cloud and every tree that grew
Spoke and I had by heart all that I heard?

JUDITH WRIGHT

(b. 1915)

JUDITH WRIGHT was born on the family station property at Armidale, New South Wales. She had, as A.D. Hope has said, 'the great advantage, for a poet, of being a lonely child in a literate family and with plenty of time to read'. After finishing her schooling, she went to Sydney University where she read French and Italian as well as English literature, history, psychology and anthropology and philosophy but did not take a degree. In 1937 she travelled in Europe, and on returning to Australia did secretarial work. After the outbreak of war she returned to help run the family property for a time. She had been writing poetry at university, but now she began to explore her feelings about the New England landscape ('country that built my heart') and wrote some of the poems that were collected in her first book, *The Moving Image* (1946). By the time that book appeared she had married the philosopher, J.P. McKinney, and was living in Queensland. The forest on Mount Tamborine, where she lived until 1974, was a stimulus to her imagination as the landscapes of her childhood had been. Since her husband's death in 1966 she has become a very active public figure, a forthright crusader for the environment and for the rights of the Aborigines. In 1959 she published a family history, *Generations of Men*, and in 1982 she published *The Cry for the Dead*, a factual study which sets the story of her family in the larger context of the pastoral history of the area.

Her first two books of poetry created great excitement and firmly established her as a major presence on the Australian poetic scene. In particular, her second book— *Woman to Man* (1949)—was hailed for its success in expressing a woman's view of love-making and the process of gestation and birth. Though she has continued to follow a metaphysical path in her poetry, it is the early poems with their sensuous immediacy that have made the greatest impact; and the selection of poems for this anthology reflects this. The poems are in the order in which they appear in her *Collected Poems 1942–1970*. Judith Wright has been an influential critic of poetry, and has contributed to the renewed interest in Harpur, on whom she has written in the Australian Writers and their Work series, and in Shaw Neilson, whose work she has helped to edit. Her major critical work is *Preoccupations in Australian Poetry* (1965). She has also written books for children and short stories, and has edited several poetry anthologies.

Bora Ring

The song is gone; the dance
is secret with the dancers in the earth,
the ritual useless, and the tribal story
lost in an alien tale.

Only the grass stands up
to mark the dancing-ring: the apple-gums
posture and mime a past corroboree,
murmur a broken chant.

The hunter is gone: the spear
is splintered underground; the painted bodies
a dream the world breathed sleeping and forgot.
The nomad feet are still.

Only the rider's heart
halts at a sightless shadow, an unsaid word
that fastens in the blood the ancient curse,
the fear as old as Cain.

Bullocky

Beside his heavy-shouldered team,
thirsty with drought and chilled with rain,
he weathered all the striding years
till they ran widdershins in his brain:

Till the long solitary tracks
etched deeper with each lurching load
were populous before his eyes,
and fiends and angels used his road.

All the long straining journey grew
a mad apocalyptic dream,
and he old Moses, and the slaves
his suffering and stubborn team.

Then in his evening camp beneath
the half-light pillars of the trees
he filled the steepled cone of night
with shouted prayers and prophecies.

While past the campfire's crimson ring
the star-struck darkness cupped him round,

and centuries of cattlebells
rang with their sweet uneasy sound.

Grass is across the waggon-tracks,
and plough strikes bone beneath the grass,
and vineyards cover all the slopes,
where the dead teams were used to pass.

O vine, grow close upon that bone
and hold it with your rooted hand.
The prophet Moses feeds the grape,
and fruitful is the Promised Land.

Brother and Sisters

The road turned out to be a cul-de-sac;
stopped like a lost intention at the gate
and never crossed the mountains to the coast.
But they stayed on. Years grew like grass and leaves
across the half-erased and dubious track
until one day they knew the plans were lost,
the blue-print for the bridge was out of date,
and now their orchards never would be planted.
The saplings sprouted slyly; day by day
the bush moved one step nearer, wondering when.
The polished parlour grew distrait and haunted
where Millie, Lucy, John each night at ten
wound the gilt clock that leaked the year away.

The pianola—oh, listen to the mocking-bird—
wavers on Sundays and has lost a note.
The wrinkled ewes snatch pansies through the fence
and stare with shallow eyes into the garden
where Lucy shrivels waiting for a word,
and Millie's cameos loosen round her throat.
The bush comes near, the ranges grow immense.

Feeding the lambs deserted in early spring
Lucy looked up and saw the stockman's eye
telling her she was cracked and old.
                              The wall
groans in the night and settles more awry.
O how they lie awake. Their thoughts go fluttering
from room to room like moths: 'Millie, are you awake?'
'Oh John, I have been dreaming.' 'Lucy, do you cry?'
—meet tentative as moths. Antennae stroke a wing.
'There is nothing to be afraid of. Nothing at all.'

For New England

Your trees, the homesick and the swarthy native,
blow all one way to me, this southern weather
that smells of early snow:
                              And I remember
The house closed in with sycamore and chestnut
fighting the foreign wind.
Here I will stay, she said; be done with the black north,
the harsh horizon rimmed with drought.—
Planted the island there and drew it round her.
10   Therefore I find in me the double tree.

And therefore I, deserted on the wharves,
have watched the ships fan out their web of streamers
(thinking of how the lookout at the heads
leaned out towards the dubious rims of sea
to find a sail blown over like a message
you are not forgotten),
or followed through the taproot of the poplar ...
But look, oh look, the Gothic tree's on fire
with blown galahs, and fuming with wild wings.

20   The hard inquiring wind strikes to the bone
and whines division.
                              Many roads meet here
in me, the traveller and the ways I travel.
All the hills' gathered waters feed my seas
who am the swimmer and the mountain river;
and the long slopes' concurrence is my flesh
who am the gazer and the land I stare on;
and dogwood blooms within my winter blood,
and orchards fruit in me and need no season.
30   But sullenly the jealous bones recall
what other earth is shaped and hoarded in them.

Where's home, Ulysses? Cuckolded by lewd time
he never found again the girl he sailed from,
but at his fireside met the islands waiting
and died there, twice a stranger.
                              Wind, blow through me
till the nostalgic candles of laburnum
fuse with the dogwood in a single flame
to touch alight these sapless memories.
40   Then will my land turn sweetly from the plough
and all my pastures rise as green as spring.

Woman to Man

The eyeless labourer in the night,
the selfless, shapeless seed I hold,
builds for its resurrection day—
silent and swift and deep from sight
foresees the unimagined light.

This is no child with a child's face;
this has no name to name it by:
yet you and I have known it well.
This is our hunter and our chase,
the third who lay in our embrace.

This is the strength that your arm knows,
the arc of flesh that is my breast,
the precise crystals of our eyes.
This is the blood's wild tree that grows
the intricate and folded rose.

This is the maker and the made;
this is the question and reply;
the blind head butting at the dark,
the blaze of light along the blade.
Oh hold me, for I am afraid.

Woman to Child

You who were darkness warmed my flesh
where out of darkness rose the seed.
Then all a world I made in me;
all the world you hear and see
hung upon my dreaming blood.

There moved the multitudinous stars,
and coloured birds and fishes moved.
There swam the sliding continents.
All time lay rolled in me, and sense,
and love that knew not its beloved.

O node and focus of the world;
I hold you deep within that well
you shall escape and not escape—

that mirrors still your sleeping shape;
that nurtures still your crescent cell.

I wither and you break from me;
yet though you dance in living light
I am the earth, I am the root,
I am the stem that fed the fruit,
20   the link that joins you to the night.

The Bull

In the olive darkness of the sally-trees
silently moved the air from night to day.
The summer-grass was thick with honey-daisies
where he, a curled god, a red Jupiter,
heavy with power among his women lay.

But summer's bubble-sound of sweet creek-water
dwindles and is silent; the seeding grasses
grow harsh, and wind and frost in the black sallies
roughen the sleek-haired slopes. Seek him out, then,
10   the angry god betrayed, whose godhead passes,

and down the hillsides drive him from his mob.
What enemy steals his strength—what rival steals
his mastered cows? His thunders powerless,
the red storm of his body shrunk with fear,
runs the great bull, the dogs upon his heels.

The Old Prison

The rows of cells are unroofed,
a flute for the wind's mouth,
who comes with a breath of ice
from the blue caves of the south.

O dark and fierce day:
the wind like an angry bee
hunts for the black honey
in the pits of the hollow sea.

Waves of shadow wash
the empty shell bone-bare,
and like a bone it sings
a bitter song of air.

Who built and laboured here?
The wind and the sea say
—Their cold nest is broken
and they are blown away.

They did not breed nor love.
Each in his cell alone
cried as the wind now cries
through this flute of stone.

Train Journey

Glassed with cold sleep and dazzled by the moon,
out of the confused hammering dark of the train
I looked and saw under the moon's cold sheet
your delicate dry breasts, country that built my heart;

and the small trees on their uncoloured slope
like poetry moved, articulate and sharp
and purposeful under the great dry flight of air,
under the crosswise currents of wind and star.

Clench down your strength, box-tree and ironbark.
Break with your violent root the virgin rock.
Draw from the flying dark its breath of dew
till the unliving come to life in you.

Be over the blind rock a skin of sense,
under the barren height a slender dance ...

I woke and saw the dark small trees that burn
suddenly into flowers more lovely than the white moon.

Request to a Year

If the year is medtating a suitable gift,
I should like it to be the attitude
of my great-great-grandmother,
legendary devotee of the arts,

who, having had eight children
and little opportunity for painting pictures,
sat one day on a high rock
beside a river in Switzerland

and from a difficult distance viewed
her seond son, balanced on a small ice-floe,
drift down the current towards a waterfall
that struck rock-bottom eighty feet below,

while her second daughter, impeded,
no doubt, by the petticoats of the day,
stretched out a last-hope alpenstock
(which luckily later caught him on his way).

Nothing, it was evident, could be done;
and with the artist's isolating eye
my great-great-grandmother hastily sketched the scene.
The sketch survives to prove the story by.

Year, if you have no Mother's day present planned;
reach back and bring me the firmness of her hand.

The Harp and the King

Old king without a throne,
the hollow of despair
behind his obstinate unyielding stare,
knows only, God is gone:
and, fingers clenching on his chair,
feels night and the soul's terror coming on.

Bring me that harp, that singer. Let him sing.
Let something fill the space inside the mind,
that's a dry stream-bed for the flood of fear.

Song's only sound; but it's a lovely sound,
a fountain through the drought. Bring David here,
said the old frightened king.

Sing something. Comfort me.
Make me believe the meaning in the rhyme.
The world's a traitor to the self-betrayed;
but once I thought there was a truth in time,
while now my terror is eternity.
So do not take me outside time.
Make me believe in my mortality,
since that is all I have, the old king said.

I sing the praise of time, the harp replied:
the time of aching drought when the black plain
cannot believe in roots or leaves or rain.
Then lips crack open in the stone-hard peaks;
and rock begins to suffer and to pray
when all that lives has died
and withered in the wind and blown away;
and earth has no more strength to bleed.

I sing the praise of time and of the rain—
the word creation speaks.
Four elements are locked in time;
the sign that makes them fertile is the seed,
and this outlasts all death and springs again,
the running water of the harp-notes cried.

But the old king sighed obstinately,
How can that comfort me?
Night and the terror of the soul come on,
and out of me both water and seed have gone.
What other generations shall I see?
But make me trust my failure and my fall,
said the sad king, since these are now my all.

I sing the praise of time, the harp replied.
In time we fail, alone with hours and tears,
ruin our followers and traduce our cause,
and give our love its last and fatal hurt.
In time we fail and fall.
In time the company even of God withdraws
and we are left with our own murderous heart.

Yet it is time that holds,
somewhere although not now,
the peal of trumpets for us; time that bears,
made fertile even by those tears,
even by this darkness, even by this loss,
incredible redemptions—hours that grow,
as trees grow fruit, in a blind holiness,
the truths unknown, the loves unloved by us.

But the old king turned his head sullenly.
How can that comfort me,
who sees into the heart as deep as God can see?
Love's sown in us; perhaps it flowers; it dies.
I failed my God and I betrayed my love.
Make me believe in treason; that is all I have.

This is the praise of time, the harp cried out—
that we betray all truths that we possess.
Time strips the soul and leaves it comfortless
and sends it thirsty through a bone-white drought.
Time's subtler treacheries teach us to betray.
What else could drive us on our way?
Wounded we cross the desert's emptiness,
and must be false to what would make us whole.
For only change and distance shape for us
some new tremendous symbol for the soul.

The Forest

When first I knew this forest
its flowers were strange.
Their different forms and faces
changed with the seasons' change—

white violets smudged with purple,
the wild-ginger spray,
ground-orchids small and single
haunted my day;

the thick-fleshed Murray-lily,
flame-tree's bright blood,
and where the creek runs shallow,
the cunjevoi's green hood.

When first I knew this forest,
time was to spend,
and time's renewing harvest
could never reach an end.

Now that its vines and flowers
are named and known,
like long-fulfilled desires
those first strange joys are gone.

My search is further.
There's still to name and know
beyond the flowers I gather
that one that does not wither—
the truth from which they grow.

Remembering an Aunt

Her room was large enough—you would say, private
from the rest of the house, until you looked again
and saw it supervised by her mother's window.
She kept there, face to the wall, some of the pictures
she had once painted; in a cupboard she had carved
was closed some music she had wished to play.

Her hands were pricked and blackened. At the piano
she played the pieces her mother liked to hear—
Chopin and Chaminade, In a Persian Market.
Her smile was awkward. When they said to her,
'Why not take up your sketching again? So pretty—'
she was abrupt. For she remembered Rome,
Florence, the galleries she saw at thirty,
she who had won art prizes at local shows
and played to country women from her childhood.
Brushes, paints, Beethoven put aside
(for ignorant flattery's worse than ignorant blame),
she took her stance and held it till she died.

I praise her for her silence and her pride;
art lay in both. Yet in her, all the same,
sometimes there sprang a small unnoticed flame—
grief too unseen, resentment too denied.

DAVID CAMPBELL

(1917–1979)

DAVID CAMPBELL was born (in his own words) 'in a brass bed on a sheep station in New South Wales not far from Gundagai, the town most often celebrated in the early songs and ballads of shearers, bullockies and bushrangers'. His father, a doctor who practised in the district, was part-owner of the station on which Campbell grew up. His education began with governesses on the family station, but he was eventually sent to King's School, Parramatta, and then, at the age of eighteen, to Cambridge to study history. At school and university he was an outstanding sportsman, achieving the distinction of playing Rugby for England. At Cambridge he discovered that his real interest was literature, and wrote his first poems. However, it was not until 1942, by which time he was an R.A.A.F. pilot in action in New Guinea, that he began writing poetry seriously. About the same time that Judith Wright in New England was writing about her relationship to Australia David Campbell had begun writing such poems as 'Harry Pearce' (Pearce was the bullock-driver on the family station of his childhood). He was wounded while on active service and was awarded the DFC and Bar. After the war he settled on a pastoral property north of Canberra, moving further away as the capital spread. In this country, where he spent the rest of his life, he found much of the inspiration for his poetry: 'at times I had the sense of riding around my own world of the imagination, my own creation'. In his later years, along with A.D. Hope and Rosemary Dobson, he became a focal point for the young poets in Canberra. With Rosemary Dobson, he wrote *Moscow Trefoil* (1975), a collection of versions in English of poems by the two Russian poets, Osip Mandelstam and Anna Akhmatova. The poems in this anthology are to be found in his *Selected Poems* (1968), with the exception of 'Bell Birds', which is from *Deaths and Pretty Cousins* (1975). David Campbell wrote two volumes of short stories, and edited an anthology of modern Australian poetry.

Harry Pearce

I sat beside the red stock route
And chewed a blade of bitter grass
And saw in mirage on the plain
A bullock wagon pass.
Old Harry Pearce was with his team.
'The flies are bad,' I said to him.

The leaders felt his whip. It did
Me good to hear old Harry swear,
And in the heat of noon it seemed
His bullocks walked on air.
Suspended in the amber sky
They hauled the wool to Gundagai.

He walked in Time across the plain,
An old man walking in the air;
For years he wandered in my brain,
And now he lodges here.
And he may drive his cattle still
When Time with us has had his will.

Windy Gap

As I was going through Windy Gap
A hawk and a cloud hung over the map.

The land lay bare and the wind blew loud
And the hawk cried out from the heart of the cloud,

'Before I fold my wings in sleep
I'll pick the bones of your travelling sheep,

'For the leaves blow back and the wintry sun
Shows the tree's white skeleton.'

A magpie sat in the tree's high top
Singing a song on Windy Gap

That streamed far down to the plain below
Like a shaft of light from a high window.

From the bending tree he sang aloud,
And the sun shone out of the heart of the cloud

And it seemed to me as we travelled through
That my sheep were the notes that trumpet blew.

And so I sing this song of praise
For travelling sheep and blowing days.

Who Points the Swallow

Love who points the swallow home
And scarves the russet at his throat,
Dreaming in the needle's eye,
Guide us through the maze of glass
Where the forceful cannot pass,
With your silent clarity.

There where blood and sap are one,
Thrush's heart and daisy's root
Keep the measure of the dance,
Though within their cage of bone
Griefs and tigers stalk alone,
Locked in private arrogance.

Lay the shadow of our fear
With the brilliance of your light,
Naked we can meet the storm,
Travellers who journeyed far
To find you at our own front door,
O love who points the swallow home.

Night Sowing

O gentle, gentle land
Where the green ear shall grow,
Now you are edged with light:
The moon has crisped the fallow,
The furrows run with night.

This is the season's hour:
While couples are in bed,
I sow the paddocks late,
Scatter like sparks the seed
And see the dark ignite.

O gentle land, I sow
The heart's living grain.
Stars draw their harrows over,
Dews send their melting rain:
I meet you as a lover.

On the Birth of a Son

For Andrew

The day the boy was born, the wall fell down
That flanks our garden. There's an espaliered pear,
And then the wall I laboured with such care,
Such sweat and foresight, locking stone with stone,
To build. Well, just a wall, but it's my own,
I built it. Sitting in a garden chair
With flowers against the wall, it's good to stare
Inwards. But now some freak of wind has blown
And tumbled it across the lawn—a sign
Perhaps. Indeed, when first I saw the boy,
I thought, he's humble now, but wait a few
Years and we'll see!—out following a line
Not of our choice at all. And then with joy
I looked beyond the stones and saw the view.

Mothers and Daughters

The cruel girls we loved
Are over forty,
Their subtle daughters
Have stolen their beauty;

And with a blue stare
Of cool surprise,
They mock their anxious mothers
With their mothers' eyes.

Droving

Down the red stock route, my tall son
Droves with his girl the white-faced steers
From the high country, as we would years
Ago beneath a daylight moon.
But now these two must bring them down
Between the snow-gums and the briars
Hung with their thousand golden tears,
To camp beside the creek at noon.
And finding them so sure and young,
The flower-fat mob their only care,
The days I thought beyond recall
Are ringed about with magpie song;
And it seems in spite of death and war
Time's not so desperate after all.

The Australian Dream

The doorbell buzzed. It was past three o'clock.
The steeple-of-Saint-Andrew's weathercock
Cried silently to darkness, and my head
Was bronze with claret as I rolled from bed
To ricochet from furniture. Light! Light
Blinded the stairs, the hatstand sprang upright,
I fumbled with the lock, and on the porch
Stood the Royal Family with a wavering torch.

'We hope,' the Queen said, 'we do not intrude.
The pubs were full, most of our subjects rude.
We came before our time. It seems the Queen's
Command brings only, "Tell the dead marines!"
We've come to you.' I must admit I'd half
Expected just this visit. With a laugh
That put them at their ease, I bowed my head.
'Your Majesty is most welcome here,' I said.
'My home is yours. There is a little bed
Downstairs, a boiler-room, might suit the Duke.'
He thanked me gravely for it and he took
Himself off with a wave. 'Then the Queen Mother?
She'd best bed down with you. There is no other
But my wide bed. I'll curl up in a chair.'
The Queen looked thoughtful. She brushed out her hair
And folded up *The Garter* on a pouf.
'Distress was the first commoner, and as proof
That queens bow to the times,' she said, 'we three
Shall share the double bed. Please follow me.'

I waited for the ladies to undress—
A sense of fitness, even in distress,
Is always with me. They had tucked away
Their state robes in the lowboy; gold crowns lay
Upon the bedside tables; ropes of pearls
Lassoed the plastic lampshade; their soft curls
Were spread out on the pillows and they smiled.
'Hop in,' said the Queen Mother. In I piled
Between them to lie like a stick of wood.
I couldn't find a thing to say. My blood
Beat, but like rollers at the ebb of tide.
'I hope your Majesties sleep well,' I lied.
A hand touched mine and the Queen said, 'I am
Most grateful to you, Jock. Please call me Ma'am.'

Bell Birds

Bell-miners ring like axemen in the green timber:
Chink ching and a water tree
Sways on its dappled bole, one hundred feet
Of waterfall, and falls; and the long reach
Rocks in pockets of light in the shocked silence
Of water tinkling over stone. *Ching Chink!*

The axes redouble their labour, falling like rain;
Lopping the branches, chopping the bole
Into lengths for the waiting jinker. And the bells
Ring out *ching chink* from the harness of the horses
As the forests melt away. In snowing sawmills
You can hear the thawing of the water. *Ching!*

Chink chink! Ching ching! To the song of tiny hammers
Houses go up in the clearing. Men squint down beams;
The beams arch over like ribs, barring the stars
That chime at night in the lonely tree by the window;
And two bell-miners cock their heads in their cage,
Rusty green birds that sometimes sing *ching chink*.

JAMES MCAULEY

(1917–1976)

JAMES MCAULEY was born at Lakemba, then on the out-
skirts of Sydney, New South Wales. Educated at Fort
Street High School, in 1935 he began an Arts course at
Sydney University, completing a Master's degree in 1941.
It was while at the university that he came to admire the
poetry of Christopher Brennan, then out of print and little
known. On graduating, he taught in schools before being
called up for the Army, in which he was involved in
education and research, including planning for the postwar
civil administration in New Guinea—an assignment which
led to a lifelong fascination with that country. After the
war he lectured in the military training school, which
became the Australian School of Pacific Administration,
remaining there until he became Reader in English at the
University of Tasmania in 1961. By this time he had
become a very prominent and controversial figure in
political and literary circles. McAuley, who had been born
an Anglican, became a Roman Catholic in 1952, and
quickly became a leading conservative within that church.
He was active in the formation of the Democratic Labor
Party, following the Labour split of 1955, and in 1956 he
was the founding editor of *Quadrant*, a magazine modelled
on the English publication, *Encounter*. The episode of
greatest public interest involving James McAuley was the
'Ern Malley' hoax which he and his fellow-poet, Harold
Stewart, perpetrated on Max Harris, then editing the *avant
garde* magazine, *Angry Penguins*. McAuley and Stewart
invented a poet, 'Ern Malley', and in one afternoon
concocted a series of poems in his name, with the intention

of exposing what they regarded as the lack of real crafts-
manship in the subjective verse encouraged by the *Angry
Penguins* group. In a more positive if less spectacular way
McAuley upheld classical values in his own poetry and
criticism. Despite his extraordinarily busy and varied
public life, his poetic output was substantial and wide-
ranging. His most ambitious work was the long poem,
'Captain Quiros', to which one of the poems included
here—'The Inception of the Poem'—refers. The poems in
this anthology are printed in the order in which they
appear in his *Collected Poems* (1971). Of McAuley's critic-
ism, the most interesting is his anthology, *A Map of
Australian Verse* (1975), in which he gives his considered
view of the development of Australian poetry in the
twentieth century.

Autumn

From R.M. Rilke

Lord, it is time. The fruitful summer yields;
The shadows fall across the figured dial,
The winds are loosed upon the harvest fields.
See that these last fruits swell upon the vine;
Grant them as yet a southern day or two
Then press them to fulfilment, and pursue
The last of sweetness in the heavy wine.

Who now is homeless shall not build this year.
He shall be solitary and long alone;
10   Shall wake, and read, and write long letters home,
And on deserted pavements here and there
Shall wander restless, as the leaves are blown.

Envoi

There the blue-green gums are a fringe of remote disorder
And the brown sheep poke at my dreams along the hillsides;
And there in the soil, in the season, in the shifting airs,
Comes the faint sterility that disheartens and derides.

Where once was a sea is now a salty sunken desert,
A futile heart within a fair periphery;
The people are hard-eyed, kindly, with nothing inside them,
The men are independent but you could not call them free.

And I am fitted to that land as the soul is to the body,
10   I know its contractions, waste, and sprawling indolence;
They are in me and its triumphs are my own,
Hard-won in the thin and bitter years without pretence.

Beauty is order and good chance in the artesian heart
And does not wholly fail, though we impede;
Though the reluctant and uneasy land resent
The gush of waters, the lean plough, the fretful seed.

Terra Australis

Voyage within you, on the fabled ocean,
And you will find that Southern Continent,
Quiros' vision—his hidalgo heart
And mythical Australia, where reside
All things in their imagined counterpart.

It is your land of similes: the wattle
Scatters its pollen on the doubting heart;
The flowers are wide-awake; the air gives ease.
There you come home; the magpies call you Jack
And whistle like larrikins at you from the trees.

There too the angophora preaches on the hillsides
With the gestures of Moses; and the white cockatoo,
Perched on his limbs, screams with demoniac pain;
And who shall say on what errand the insolent emu
Walks between morning and night on the edge of the plain?

But northward in valleys of the fiery Goat
Where the sun like a centaur vertically shoots
His raging arrows with unerring aim,
Stand the ecstatic solitary pyres
Of unknown lovers, featureless with flame.

Memorial

To Some Residents of New Guinea

When the sleeping isles were shaken
And many there bewildered fled,
Forsaking when they felt forsaken,
These no less bewildered made
Like reckoning of their chance, and stayed.
Hunted often and misled
By rumour, fear and stratagem,
Some died in horror without aid
And the years grow over them.
I write it brief and unadorned
That some remembrance may be paid
Far longer than they can be mourned.

An Art of Poetry

To Vincent Buckley

Since all our keys are lost or broken,
Shall it be thought absurd
If for an art of words I turn
Discreetly to the Word?

Drawn inward by his love, we trace
Art to its secret springs:
What, are we masters in Israel
And do not know these things?

Lord Christ from out his treasury
Brings forth things new and old:
We have those treasures in earthen vessels,
In parables he told,

And in the single images
Of seed, and fish, and stone,
Or, shaped in deed and miracle,
To living poems grown.

Scorn then to darken and contract
The landscape of the heart
By individual, arbitrary
And self-expressive art.

Let your speech be ordered wholly
By an intellectual love;
Elucidate the carnal maze
With clear light from above.

Give every image space and air
To grow, or as bird to fly;
So shall one grain of mustard-seed
Quite overspread the sky.

Let your literal figures shine
With pure transparency:
Not in opaque but limpid wells
Lie truth and mystery.

And universal meanings spring
From what the proud pass by:
Only the simplest forms can hold
A vast complexity.

We know, where Christ has set his hand
Only the real remains:
I am impatient for that loss
40   By which the spirit gains.

A Leaf of Sage

This is a tale from the Decameron;
Truant to good advice the poet returns
To the lost art, which he is told to shun,
Of narrative; hoping this time to have won
Some part of the perfections he discerns.

Let me be Love's cantor, and have power
To breathe the solemn neums of temple song
In pure unsweetened verse, neither harsh nor sour,
And may this five-leaved stanza come to flower
10   With graces that to youth and art belong.

A woolmonger's apprentice used to carry
Yarn to a poor household that was paid
To spin a weekly task of thread. And very
Often he would find excuse to tarry
For reasons not connected with his trade.

Pasquino lingered while Simona span;
And as he watched, her spindle seemed to draw
The fibre of his feelings till they ran
Twisting to coloured threads, which Love began
20   To weave into the pattern he foresaw.

Those fierce uncertain ardours of first love,
Who can quite recall them? Later, it's true,
Love may be jubilant in its summer grove,
Golden as noonday, pungent as the clove,
But gone is that trembling light like morning dew.

Clumsy, vehement, tongue-tied and aflame,
Pasquino's wishes yet found means to advance.
Each blurred encounter through the mesh of shame
And shyness was rewarded with the same
30   Confused surrender in Simona's glance.

Walking to her house he would devise
Conversations full of love's intent,
Supplying in his fancy her replies;
And if he ventured on these colloquies
She would return almost the words he'd lent.

They touched; they kissed; and passed incontinently
To the next stage of love (is it not so?)
Deceit of elders. Longing to be free,
She of her parents, of his master he,
40   They plotted what to say and where to go.

And thus one Sunday, with another pair,
They found a garden; each couple sat remote;
The sky laughed; a curling baroque air
Ruffled the colours of the bright parterre;
A bird sat by with soft recording note.

Spring had resumed its liturgy of light.
The sun's gladness like a festal garment
Fell on Simona's body and flowed bright
About her. Suppliant in her presence, sight
50   And touch and other senses sought preferment.

She seemed the virgin of Love's calendar.
Her mood of stillness, flushing with desire,
Resembled as Pasquino worshipped her
The delicate alternation of a star
Whose cold blue radiance has a pulse of fire.

A sage plant in this garden of their bliss
Like a small tree of knowledge grew at hand.
Laughing she plucked a leaf and said, 'Rub this
Against your teeth and it will give your kiss
60   Its aromatic virtue.' Her command

Pleased him, and he quoted the old saw,
'Eat sage in May if you would live for aye.'
He crushed the grey-green leaf as if to draw

Immortal joy from it under Love's law;
And then the thumb of Darkness bruised the day.

For not long after, as if plague-stricken, he
Grinced and sweated; livid spots appeared
Upon his face and hands; quite suddenly
His body swelled; he ceased to hear or see;
70 And while Simona, fixed in horror, stared,

The strange distemper with rough spasms tore
His life out by the cringing roots, and left
A swollen corpse. Beside the unseen door
The hidden bird sang sweetly as before.
And then the girl shrieked, utterly bereft.

O high untraceable permissive Will!
I stare into the whirlpool of your eye
Where our intentions, whether good or ill,
Sink to destruction swift and terrible:
80 These are your counsels, Lord, which terrify.

The other couple ran up at the sound,
And saw the spotted flesh, deformed and grim;
Then strangers too began to gather round,
And since no cause could readily be found
Suspicion grew that she had poisoned him.

The appetite for random accusation
Woke in a dozen mouths, which flowed with blame
And the sweet slaver of anticipation:
Our virtue loves the sauce of indignation
90 With which to eat another's life and name.

Hurried weeping to the magistrate,
She is too speechless to deny the crime.
He, unconvinced by what the accusers state,
Comes to the spot and bids the girls relate
Minutely all that happened at the time.

Then somewhat mastering her shock and grief,
Fearful of her accusers' lowering rage,
She tells the story, though her words are brief.
The tale seems hardly worthy of belief,
100 For why should death come from a harmless sage?

And now in her confusion and despair,
To show exactly how Pasquino died
She rubs the suspect herb against her bare
White teeth, commends her soul to Mercy's care,
And pitifully shows she has not lied.

In silence they cut down the shrub; beneath,
They find a foul toad squatting at the root,
The Satan of that bower, whose noisome breath
Proclaims it the dark minister of death;
110   For toads were venomous then by long repute.

I fear this business of the toad may seem
Unsatisfactory to those inclined
To live within a scientific scheme;
Why spend one's art upon a tale whose theme
Turns on a fable? But—ah well, never mind.

And then the keeper of the garden came
And with piled timber burned both bush and toad,
Cleansing the garden with a timely flame.
So may the lovers, purified from blame,
120   Ascend from fire to win a clear abode.

Rest now, my youth, under this hieroglyph,
This figured seal of silence; do not start
Up once more in agony and grief.
Sing, hidden bird, sing mercy and relief
To wanderers in the darkness of the heart.

Merry-Go-Round

Bright-coloured, mirror-plated, strung with lights,
With swan-shaped cars and prancing wooden horses,
The silent waiting merry-go-round invites
A swarm of eager riders for its courses.

It moves: a painted minature cosmos, turning
With planetary music blaring loud.
The riders lean intent, lips parted, faces burning;
Brief smiles float out towards the watching crowd.

On their brass poles the horses rise and fall
10 In undulant flight; the children ride through dreams.
How faery-bright to them, how magical,
The crude and gaudy mechanism seems!

Almost I see the marvel that they see,
And hear like them the music of the spheres;
They smile out of the enchanted whirl to me.
The lights and colours suddenly dim with tears.

But now their turning world is slowing, slowing;
Horses and music stop: how brief the ride!
New-comers clamber on as these are going
20 Reluctantly to join the crowd outside.

The Inception of the Poem

Midnight once more; the untended fire sinks low;
The lamp stares down upon the book unread;
The papers on my desk have nothing to show:
I have not learned the things I wished to know,
The things I wished to say remain unsaid.

Again the dead pause, the need for a new start;
The vanishing of every name and form
That seemed the very contours of the heart;
And all the working mystery of art
10 A queenless hive deserted by the swarm.

Then suddenly, unbidden, the theme returns
That visited my youth; over the vast
Pacific with the white wake at their sterns,
The ships of Quiros on their great concerns
Ride in upon the present from the past.

Pietà

A year ago you came
Early into the light.
You lived a day and night,
Then died; no-one to blame.

Once only, with one hand,
Your mother in farewell
Touched you. I cannot tell,
I cannot understand

A thing so dark and deep,
So physical a loss:
one touch, and that was all

She had of you to keep.
Clean wounds, but terrible,
Are those made with the Cross.

Because

My father and my mother never quarrelled.
They were united in a kind of love
As daily as the *Sydney Morning Herald*,
Rather than like the eagle or the dove.

I never saw them casually touch,
Or show a moment's joy in one another.
Why should this matter to me now so much?
I think it bore more hardly on my mother,

Who had more generous feeling to express.
My father had dammed up his Irish blood
Against all drinking praying fecklessness,
And stiffened into stone and creaking wood.

His lips would make a switching sound, as though
Spontaneous impulse must be kept at bay.
That it was mainly weakness I see now,
But then my feelings curled back in dismay.

Small things can pit the memory like a cyst:
Having seen other fathers greet their sons,
I put my childish face up to be kissed
After an absence. The rebuff still stuns

My blood. The poor man's curt embarrassment
At such a delicate proffer of affection
Cut like a saw. But home the lesson went:
My tenderness thenceforth escaped detection.

My mother sang *Because*, and *Annie Laurie*,
White Wings, and other songs; her voice was sweet.
I never gave enough, and I am sorry;
But we were all closed in the same defeat.

People do what they can; they were good people,
They cared for us and loved us. Once they stood
Tall in my childhood as the school, the steeple.
How can I judge without ingratitude?

Judgment is simply trying to reject
A part of what we are because it hurts.
The living cannot call the dead collect:
They won't accept the charge, and it reverts.

It's my own judgment day that I draw near,
Descending in the past, without a clue,
Down to that central deadness: the despair
Older than any hope I ever knew.

ROSEMARY DOBSON

(b. 1920)

ROSEMARY DOBSON was born in Sydney, New South Wales, where she spent her earliest years. Her father—a son of Austin Dobson, the late nineteenth-century English poet and essayist—died when she was five years old. With the help of scholarships she and her sister Ruth—the first Australian woman career diplomat—were educated at Frensham, a girl's boarding school at Mittagong in New South Wales. Later she had two years at Sydney University as an unmatriculated student, enjoying what she calls an 'under-the-counter education'. At school she developed early the enthusiasm for poetry and for painting which remains central to her life. Her art classes at school, and later with the professional artist, Thea Proctor, influenced her as a poet: 'I still find myself thinking of the technique of poetry in terms of the technique of painting'. She had begun writing poetry in childhood, and by 1944 she had published her first book of poems. She worked in the editorial department of Angus and Robertson for a number of years, and married a publisher, Alec Bolton, with whom she now lives in Canberra. Long before she went abroad in 1966 with her husband—they lived in England for five years—she had found inspiration in non-Australian subjects, and especially medieval and Renaissance painting. Her interest in painting has also led to her writing a monograph on the Australian painter, Ray Crooke. Rosemary Dobson is a poet whose reputation has grown steadily. The poems by which she is represented here are from her *Selected Poems* (1973).

Country Press

Under the dusty print of hobnailed boot,
Strewn on the floor the papers still assert
In ornamental gothic, swash italics
And bands of printer's flowers (traditional)
Mixed in a riot of typographic fancy,
This is the *Western Star*, the Farmer's Guide,
The Voice of Progress for the Nyngle District.
Page-proofs of double-spread with running headlines
Paper the walls, and sets of cigarette-cards
Where pouter-bosomed showgirls still display
The charms that dazzled in the nineteen hundreds.
Through gaping slats
Latticed with sun the ivy tendrils fall
Twining the disused platen thrust away
Under a pall of dust in nineteen-twenty.
Draw up a chair, sit down. Just shift the galleys.
You say you have a notice? There's no one dies
But what we know about it. Births, deaths and
            marriages,
Council reports, wool prices, river-heights,
The itinerant poem and the classified ads—
They all come homewards to the *Western Star*.
Joe's our type-setter. Meet Joe Burrell. Joe's
A promising lad—and Joe, near forty-seven,
Peers from a tennis-shade and, smiling vaguely,
Completes the headline for the Baptist Social.
The dance, the smoke-oh, and the children's picnic
Down by the river-flats beneath the willows—
They all come homewards and Joe sets them all,
Between the morning and the mid-day schooner.
Oh, *Western Star* that bringest all to fold,
The yarding sales, the champion shorthorn bull,
And Williams' pain-relieving liniment,
When I shall die
Set me up close against my fellow-men,
Cheer that cold column headed 'Deaths' with flowers,
Or mix me up with Births and Marriages;
Surround the tragic statement of my death
With euchre-drives and good-times-had-by-all
That, with these warm concomitants of life
Jostled and cheered, in lower-case italics
I shall go homewards in the *Western Star*.

The Bystander

I am the one who looks the other way,
In any painting you may see me stand
Rapt at the sky, a bird, an angel's wing,
While others kneel, present the myrrh, receive
The benediction from the radiant hand.

I hold the horses while the knights dismount
And draw their swords to fight the battle out;
Or else in dim perspective you may see
My distant figure on the mountain road
When in the plains the hosts are put to rout.

I am the silly soul who looks too late,
The dullard dreaming, second from the right.
I hang upon the crowd, but do not mark
(Cap over eyes) the slaughtered Innocents,
Or Icarus, his downward-plunging flight.

Once in a Garden—back view only there—
How well the painter placed me, stroke on stroke,
Yet scarcely seen among the flowers and grass—
I heard a voice say, 'Eat,' and would have turned—
I often wonder who it was that spoke.

Child with a Cockatoo

Portrait of Anne, Daughter of the Earl
of Bedford,
by S. Verelst

'Paid by my lord, one portrait, Lady Anne,
Full length with bird and landscape, twenty pounds
And framed withal. I say received. Verelst.'

So signed the painter, bowed, and took his leave.
My Lady Anne smiled in the gallery
A small, grave child, dark-eyed, half turned to show
Her five bare toes beneath the garment's hem,
In stormy landscape with a swirl of drapes.
And, who knows why, perhaps my lady wept
To stand so long and watch the painter's brush
Flicker between the palette and the cloth

While from the sun-drenched orchard all the day
She heard her sisters calling each to each.
And someone gave, to drive the tears away,
That sulphur-crested bird with great white wings,
The wise, harsh bird—as old and wise as Time
Whose well-dark eyes the wonder kept and closed.
So many years to come and still, he knew,
Brooded that great, dark island continent
20   Terra Australis.

               To those fabled shores
Not William Dampier, pirating for gold,
Nor Captain Cook his westward course had set
Jumped from the longboat, waded through the surf,
And clapt his flag ashore at Botany Bay.
Terra Australis, unimagined land—
Only that sulphur-crested bird could tell
Of dark men moving silently through trees,
Of stones and silent dawns, of blackened earth
30   And the long golden blaze of afternoon.
That vagrant which an ear-ringed sailor caught
(Dropped from the sky, near dead, far out to sea)
And caged and kept, till, landing at the docks,
Walked whistling up the Strand and sold it then,
The curious bird, its cynic eyes half-closed,
To the Duke's steward, drunken at an inn.
And he lived on, the old adventurer,
And kept his counsel, was a sign unread,
A disregarded prologue to an age.
40   So one might find a meteor from the sun
Or sound one trumpet ere the play's begun.

The Birth

A wreath of flowers as cold as snow
Breaks out in bloom upon the night:
That tree is rooted in the dark,
It draws from dew its breath of life,
It feeds on frost, it hangs in air
And like a glittering branch of stars
Receives, gives forth, its breathing light.

Eight times it flowered in the dark,
Eight times my hand reached out to break
That icy wreath to bear away
Its pointed flowers beneath my heart.
Sharp are the pains and long the way
Down, down into the depths of night
Where one goes for another's sake.

Once more it flowers, once more I go
In dream at midnight to that tree,
I stretch my hand and break the branch
And hold it to my human heart.
Now, as the petals of a rose
Those flowers unfold and grow to me—
I speak as of a mystery.

The Two Countries

Sometimes, waking, I would find
Long stalks of grasses wet with dew
Brushing against my hands, my cheeks
From that far country crossed in dream,
And leaning at the window-sill
Cry out like one in legendry
For the lost landscape of delight,
Its thickets, streams, and nightingales.

And sometimes, waking, I would find
Snowflakes fallen on my head
Bared beneath a frosty sky
As all night long I hastened down
The avenues of northern pine
That shook their snow-shawls over me.
Upon what errand was I bound
In dream, in darkness, and delight?

Enchanted country, spell-bewitched,
That changed beneath the cockcrow sky,
How rarely, rarely tread I now
The habitations of delight!
Yet in my sleeping daughter's hand
Treasured in darkness I have found
A diamond, dewdrop, flake of snow—
Something from that enchanted ground.

Cock Crow

Wanting to be myself, alone,
Between the lit house and the town
I took the road, and at the bridge
Turned back and walked the way I'd come.

Three times I took that lonely stretch,
Three times the dark trees closed me round,
The night absolved me of my bonds;
Only my footsteps held the ground.

My mother and my daughter slept,
One life behind and one before,
And I that stood between denied
Their needs in shutting-to the door.

And walking up and down the road
Knew myself, separate and alone,
Cut off from human cries, from pain,
And love that grows about the bone.

Too brief illusion! Thrice for me
I heard the cock crow on the hill
And turned the handle of the door
Thinking I knew his meaning well.

In a Strange House

Living in other people's houses, learning
The time of getting up, the cupboard in the kitchen
Where the blue cups go, the corner
Of the garden for compost:
Not fiddling with the fire, becoming
Familiar with noises, the clock's tick, the ivy
In a sudden wind restless at nightfall,
Learning the folk-lore, the neighbours, the customs.
All this was accomplished—was easy, given a certain
Quick-witted eagerness, given the warmth of your
    welcome,
My friends, my companions. Now I write as a guest in,
Compressed in, a house that will change and is changing.
I am guest. I am host. And the walls will contract and
    grow thinner,

The windows cloud over, darkness
Settle in drifts on the threshold. Footfalls
Outside will grow louder, frost lie till midday.
When the fire dies down will the stranger
20   Turn from the door?
                My friends, my companions,
And you who are closest to my heart, take note of
The name, the address. Remember I shall be trying
To learn to live in this house. Shall be listening with
      longing
For the voices of unborn children calling in the garden.

GWEN HARWOOD

(b. 1920)

GWEN HARWOOD was born in Brisbane, Queensland, where she grew up 'surrounded by words, music and philosophical argument'. Trained as a musician, she was a church organist before her marriage in 1945, after which 'I came to Tasmania, had four children, met Vivian Smith, Alec Hope, James McAuley, Vincent Buckley'. Although she had written poetry from childhood, her first collection did not appear until 1963. Her husband, who taught linguistics at the University of Tasmania, introduced her to the work of the philosopher Wittgenstein, whose writings have been important in her thinking about language. She has collaborated with the composer Larry Sitsky, writing the libretto for his opera, *The Fall of the House of Usher*. Gwen Harwood has published verse under pseudonyms—Francis Geyer, Walter Lehmann, Miriam Stone and Timothy Kline. In the guise of the latter, she proffered the following autobiographical note for a collection of younger poets: 'Hobbies, boat-building, sailmaking, bush-walking, cake-baking, gliding and soaring, drinking and whoring, cursing and praying, flogging and beating, mutton-bird eating, waving the flag and wearing drag, converting agnostics, writing acrostics, catching and chucking, kissing and collecting pictures of the Royal Family'. The poems printed under her name here are from her *Selected Poems* (1975), with the exception of 'Mother Who Gave Me Life', which is from *The Lion's Bride* (1981).

The Old Wife's Tale

Summer, transpose your haunting themes
into a key that all can sing.
How soon will winter's gadfly air
dart through the empty streets to sting
those dancers from the crowded square,
to spear their hopes and spike their dreams.

When I was young I danced so long
the fireworks stars wheeled round and burst
and showered their fierce chromatic rain
about my feet so long rehearsed
in dancing that I felt no pain
but far outdanced the dancing throng

until, beside a glass, I turned
to fix my hair and smooth my lace.
Then terror had me by the throat—
a vacant, crazed old woman's face
stared from my own. One vibrant note
cracked folly's bowl. The music burned

one moment, then its prism tones
fused into silence. Dazed and halt
I called on Christ, kind nurse, to wean
my foolish lips from sweet to salt,
erase in mercy what had been,
and melt with ease my tortured bones.

Silence for answer. So I caught
a young man's hand. He smiled and said,
'God's old and foolish, we can steal
more than our share of heavenly bread.
Rest in my arms, and I'll reveal
in darkness the true mode of thought.'

I bit the core of pain, to find
this world's true sweetness on my lips,
the virtuoso senses priced
at nothing, in one vast eclipse.
A moving fingertip sufficed
to draw love's orbit through the mind.

Better than love, what name for this:
our vanished childhood sealed in flesh,
the restless energy of joy
40   whipping a world still morning-fresh
to hum new notes, a spinning toy.
All sorrow mended in a kiss.

My children grew. Like wine I poured
knowledge and skill, fought love's long war
with trivial cares. My spirit gave
a cry of hunger: 'Grant me more
than this bare sustenance, I crave
some combat worthy of my sword.'

Powerless to temper or withold
50   time's raining blows, I watched him break
my cherished moulds and shape his own,
give strangers back for children, take
my husband, and I stood alone,
a shepherd with an empty fold.

Now with divining age I seek
the hidden seminal springs of peace,
hold mercy's spiral to my ear,
or stand in silence and release
the falcon mind to hunt down fear.
60   I stare at clouds until they break

in paradigms of truth, and spell
my sentence at the sun's assize.
My bone-bare, stark endurance frames
terror for fools, but to the wise
my winter-landscape face proclaims
life's last, and death's first parable.

In the Park

She sits in the park. Her clothes are out of date.
Two children whine and bicker, tug her skirt.
A third draws aimless patterns in the dirt.
Someone she loved once passes by—too late

to feign indifference to that casual nod.
'How nice,' et cetera. 'Time holds great surprises.'
From his neat head unquestionably rises
a small balloon ... 'but for the grace of God ...'

They stand a while in flickering light, rehearsing
the children's names and birthdays. 'It's so sweet
to hear their chatter, watch them grow and thrive,'
she says to his departing smile. Then, nursing
the youngest child, sits staring at her feet.
To the wind she says, 'They have eaten me alive.'

Suburban Sonnet

She practises a fugue, though it can matter
to no one now if she plays well or not.
Beside her on the floor two children chatter,
then scream and fight. She hushes them. A pot
boils over. As she rushes to the stove
too late, a wave of nausea overpowers
subject and counter-subject. Zest and love
drain out with soapy water as she scours
the crusted milk. Her veins ache. Once she played
for Rubinstein, who yawned. The children caper
round a sprung mousetrap where a mouse lies dead.
When the soft corpse won't move they seem afraid.
She comforts them; and wraps it in a paper
featuring: *Tasty dishes from stale bread.*

New Music

To Larry Sitsky

Who can grasp for the first time
these notes hurled into empty space?
Suddenly a tormenting nerve
affronts the fellowship of cells.
Who can tell for the first time
if it is love or pain he feels,
violence or tenderness that calls
plain objects by outrageous names

and strikes new sound from the old names?
10 At the service of a human vision,
not symbols, but strange presences
defining a transparent void,
these notes beckon the mind to move
out of the smiling context of
what's known; and what can guide it is
neither wisdom nor power, but love.

Who but a fool would enter these
regions of being with no name?
Secure among their towering junk
20 the wise and powerful congregate
fitting old shapes to old ideas,
rocked by their classical harmonies
in living sleep. The beggars' stumps
bang on the stones. Nothing will change.

Unless, wakeful with questioning,
some mind beats on necessity,
and being unanswered learns to bear
emptiness like a wound that no
word but its own can mend; and finds
30 a new imperative to summon
a world out of unmeasured darkness
pierced by a brilliant nerve of sound.

Father and Child

I   Barn Owl

Daybreak: the household slept.
I rose, blessed by the sun.
A horny fiend, I crept
out with my father's gun.
Let him dream of a child
obedient, angel-mild—

old No-Sayer, robbed of power
by sleep. I knew my prize
who swooped home at this hour
10 with daylight-riddled eyes
to his place on a high beam
in our old stables, to dream

light's useless time away.
I stood, holding my breath,
in urine-scented hay,
master of life and death,
a wisp-haired judge whose law
would punish beak and claw.

My first shot struck. He swayed,
ruined, beating his only
wing, as I watched, afraid
by the fallen gun, a lonely
child who believed death clean
and final, not this obscene

bundle of stuff that dropped,
and dribbled through loose straw
tangling in bowels, and hopped
blindly closer. I saw
those eyes that did not see
mirror my cruelty

while the wrecked thing that could
not bear the light nor hide
hobbled in its own blood.
My father reached my side,
gave me the fallen gun.
'End what you have begun.'

I fired. The blank eyes shone
once into mine, and slept.
I leaned my head upon
my father's arm, and wept,
owl-blind in early sun
for what I had begun.

II Nightfall

Forty years, lived or dreamed:
what memories pack them home.
Now the season that seemed
incredible is come.
Father and child, we stand
in time's long-promised land.

Since there's no more to taste
ripeness is plainly all.
Father, we pick our last
fruits of the temporal.
Eighty years old, you take
this late walk for my sake.

Who can be what you were?
Link your dry hand in mine,
my stick-thin comforter.
Far distant suburbs shine
with great simplicities.
Birds crowd in flowering trees,

sunset exalts its known
symbols of transience.
Your passionate face is grown
to ancient innocence.
Let us walk for this hour
as if death had no power

or were no more than sleep.
Things truly named can never
vanish from earth. You keep
a child's delight for ever
in birds, flowers, shivery-grass—
I name them as we pass.

'*Be your tears wet?*' You speak
as if air touched a string
near breaking-point. Your cheek
brushes on mine. Old king,
your marvellous journey's done.
Your night and day are one

as you find with your white stick
the path on which you turn
home with the child once quick
to mischief, grown to learn
what sorrows, in the end,
no words, no tears can mend.

Mother Who Gave Me Life

Mother who gave me life
I think of women bearing
women. Forgive me the wisdom
I would not learn from you.

It is not for my children I walk
on earth in the light of the living.
It is for you, for the wild
daughters becoming women,

anguish of seasons burning
backward in time to those other
bodies, your mother, and hers
and beyond, speech growing stranger

on thresholds of ice, rock, fire,
bones changing, heads inclining
to monkey bosom, lemur breast,
guileless milk of the word.

I prayed you would live to see
Halley's Comet a second time.
The Sister said, When she died
she was folding a little towel.

You left the world so, having lived
nearly thirty thousand days:
a fabric of marvels folded
down to a little space.

At our last meeting I closed
the ward door of heavy glass
between us, and saw your face
crumple, fine threadbare linen

worn, still good to the last,
then, somehow, smooth to a smile
so I should not see your tears.
Anguish: remembered hours:

a lamp on embroidered linen,
my supper set out, your voice
calling me in as darkness
falls on my father's house.

FRANCIS WEBB

(1925–1973)

FRANCIS WEBB was born in Adelaide, South Australia, where his father had a music studio and piano-importing business. Following the death of his mother two years later, he and his three sisters were sent to Sydney to live with grandparents. Educated at Christian Brothers schools, he won an Exhibition to Sydney University in 1942, but chose instead to join the R.A.A.F., in which he became an air gunner. He began university studies when the war was over, but abandoned them after a few months. He was only seventeen when his first poems appeared in the *Bulletin*. His first book, *A Drum for Ben Boyd*, was published in 1948, the impressive sequence from which the volume takes its name having been published in the *Bulletin* two years earlier. In 1949, while in England he suffered a breakdown, and the rest of his life was punctuated with periods of mental illness. The poems by which he is represented here are from his *Collected Poems* (1969).

Morgan's Country

This is Morgan's country: now steady, Bill.
(Stunted and grey, hunted and murderous.)
Squeeze for the first pressure. Shoot to kill.

Five: a star dozing in its cold cavern.
Six: first shuffle of boards in the cold house.
And the sun lagging on seven.

The grey wolf at his breakfast. He cannot think
Why he must make haste, unless because their eyes
Are poison at every well where he might drink.

Unless because their gabbling voices force
The doors of his grandeur—first terror, then only hate.
Now terror again. Dust swarms under the doors.

Ashes drift on the dead-sea shadow of his plate.
Why should he heed them? What to do but kill
When his angel howls, when the sounds reverberate

In the last grey pipe of his brain? At the window sill
A blowfly strums on two strings of air:
Ambush and slaughter tingle against the lull.

But the Cave, his mother, is close beside his chair,
Her sunless face scribbled with cobwebs, bones
Rattling in her throat when she speaks. And there

The stone Look-out, his towering father, leans
Like a splinter from the seamed palm of the plain.
Their counsel of thunder arms him. A threat of rain.

Seven: and a blaze fiercer than the sun.
The wind struggles in the arms of the starved tree,
The temple breaks on a threadbare mat of glass.

Eight: even under the sun's trajectory
This country looks grey, hunted and murderous.

A Leper

(*From* Canticle)

The town has a high wall. Yes, it is a man speaking,
Only for himself—no other will hear him, believe in him.
Here, in the town, cantering month and month,
Spring to winter; outside? spring to winter.
Once, I begged and prayed with these months as they
    passed me:
Once. Seasons, I tell myself, have the nostril to curl
Adroitly, and the heavy blue eyelid of judgment.
But whether they go in costly and cunning garments
10   With a staff prolonged as evening among the olives
Bridging a stern daylight and a stern darkness,
With equerries facile, glib, devoted as the birds,
Or are pale and circumspect, long cold fingers:
There is always *this* question, *this* something, in its yellow
Rags which prefigure the almost living ulcer
Beneath them, whose words are the filthy vivid trickling
Never quite congealed by a halfpenny's smug bandage.
O a pennyworth of shade from you, tree, before your
    charity
20   Is leafless under nibbling frost!

O a purse-paring of sunlight, O even the silver facing
Of rain's tribute in autumn! Now have you not played
    your parts?
Look aside, look aside. Yet this non-human thought
Cannot furl its bewildering pennon, must utter itself.
I am the graceless utterance, the question, the thought.

God's mercy upon all, then: a church is assigned me,
Of Santa Maria Maddelena—so there are stones, eyes
To contain my grossness without the blink of ruin?
30   For Santa Maria there was mercy; for me only vengeance,
An effigy sour as my body, and a scampering priest
Whose discreet senses dare not linger upon me.
Nor can I credit the Love aloft in those hands.

Acorn from oak—what a touching symptom of need.
The town has a high wall. Where has it fallen, this husk,
Small convulsed mouth pleading some harbourage?
The wall, only the wall: I do not howl for spires,
For the Rocca: only the whence, the height, the sureness,
Neither within the town nor outside it!

See, this high wall, tall oak, is mine by right—
Stone quartered to brace a crumbling skin, to appease
The festering ravenous gully:—for an eye closed
And desire gaping, the wall!
It is almost a man speaking.

A Death at Winson Green

There is a green spell stolen from Birmingham;
Your peering omnibus overlooks the fence,
Or the grey, bobbing lifelines of a tram.
Here, through the small hours, sings our innocence.
Joists, apathetic pillars plot this ward,
Tired timbers wheeze and settle into dust,
We labour, labour: for the treacherous lord
Of time, the dazed historic sunlight, must
Be wheeled in a seizure towards one gaping bed,
Quake like foam on the lip, or lie still as the dead.

Visitors' Day: the graven perpetual smile,
String-bags agape, and pity's laundered glove.
The last of the heathens shuffles down the aisle,
Dark glass to a beauty which we hate and love.
Our empires rouse against this ancient fear,
Longsufferings, anecdotes, levelled at our doom;
Mine-tracks of old allegiance, prying here,
Perplex the sick man raving in his room.
Outside, a shunting engine hales from bed
The reminiscent feast-day, long since dead.

Noon reddens, trader birds deal cannily
With Winson Green, and the slouch-hatted sun
Gapes at windows netted in wire, and we
Like early kings with book and word cast down
Realities from our squared electric shore.
Two orderlies are whistling-in the spring;
Doors slam; and a man is dying at the core
Of triumph won. As a tattered, powerful wing
The screen bears out his face against the bed,
Silver, derelict, rapt, and almost dead.

Evening gropes out of colour; yet we work
To cleanse our shore from limpet histories;
Traffic and factory-whistle turn berserk;
Inviolate, faithful as a saint he lies.
Twilight itself breaks up, the venal ship,
Upon the silver integrity of his face.
No bread shall tempt that fine, tormented lip.
Let shadow switch to light—he holds his place.
Unmarked, unmoving, from the gaping bed
40 Towards birth he labours, honour, almost dead.

The wiry cricket moiling at his loom
Debates a themeless project with dour night,
The sick man raves beside me in his room;
I sleep as a child, rouse up as a child might.
I cannot pray; that fine lip prays for me
With every gasp at breath; his burden grows
Heavier as all earth lightens, and all sea.
Time crouches, watching, near his face of snows.
He is all life, thrown on the gaping bed,
50 Blind, silent, in a trance, and shortly, dead.

Five Days Old

(For Christopher John)

Christmas is in the air.
Your are given into my hands
Out of quietest, loneliest lands.
My trembling is all my prayer.
To blown straw was given
All the fullness of Heaven.

The tiny, not the immense,
Will teach our groping eyes.
So the absorbed skies
10 Bleed stars of innocence.
So cloud-voice in war and trouble
Is at last Christ in the stable.

Now wonderingly engrossed
In your fearless delicacies,
I am launched upon sacred seas,

Humbly and utterly lost
In the mystery of creation,
Bells, bells of ocean.

Too pure for my tongue to praise,
That sober, exquisite yawn
Or the gradual, generous dawn
At an eyelid, maker of days:
To shrive my thought for perfection
I must breathe old tempests of action

For the snowflake and face of love,
Windfall and word of truth,
Honour close to death.
O eternal truthfulness, Dove,
Tell me what I hold—
Myrrh? Frankincense? Gold?

If this is man, then the danger
And fear are as lights of the inn,
Faint and remote as sin
Out here by the manger.
In the sleeping, weeping weather
We shall all kneel down together.

20

30

VINCENT BUCKLEY

(b. 1925)

VINCENT BUCKLEY was born in the country town of Rom-
sey, Victoria, but has spent most of his life in Melbourne
where he has long been an influential presence in intellec-
tual circles. He was educated at St Patrick's College and the
University of Melbourne, where he joined the teaching
staff in 1951 and is now Professor of English. He spent two
years at Cambridge, where he wrote a critical study, *Poetry
and Morality* (1959); and he has more recently spent a similar
period living in Ireland—he is of Irish descent—writing an
autobiography, *Cutting Green Hay* (1983). As a prominent
member of the Catholic laity, he has taken a public stand
on various religious and political issues; but his greatest
influence has been as a poet, critic and teacher of literature.
His first book of criticism, *Essays in Poetry, Mainly Austra-
lian* (1957), was one of the first studies of Australian
writing to come out of a university. *Poetry and the Sacred*
(1968) is an important contribution to the mainstream of
English literary criticism. He emerged rather more slowly
as a poet than as a critic, but by his third book, *Arcady and
Other Places* (1966), he had found his own voice as a poet.
His poetry has continued to develop in interesting ways,
and his long (twenty-seven sections) poetic sequence,
'Golden Builders', has attracted much attention. Vincent
Buckley has shown a particular interest in writing poems
that form a sequence. In this anthology he is represented
by a complete sequence of seven poems, 'Stroke', in which
the personal feelings of a son are shaped into a religious
meditation; it is taken from *Arcady and Other Places*.

Stroke

I

In the faint blue light
We are both strangers; so I'm forced to note
His stare that comes moulded from deep bone,
The full mouth pinched in too far, one hand
Climbing an aluminium bar.
Put, as though for the first time,
In a cot from which only a hand escapes,
He grasps at opposites, knowing
This room's a caricature of childhood.
'I'm done for.'

'They're treating you all right?'
We talk from the corners of our mouths
Like old lags, while his body strains
To notice me, before he goes on watching
At the bed's foot
His flickering familiars,
Skehan, Wilson, Ellis, dead men, faces,
Bodies, paused in the aluminium light,
Submits his answer to his memories,
'Yes, I'm all right. But still it's terrible.'

Words like a fever bring
The pillar of cloud, pillar of fire
Travelling the desert of the mind and face.
The deep-set, momentarily cunning eyes
Keep trying for a way to come
Through the bed's bars to his first home.
And almost find it. Going out I hear
Voices calling requiem, where the cars
Search out the fog and gritty snow,
Hushing its breathing under steady wheels.
Night shakes the seasonable ground.

II

Decorous for the dying's sake
The living talk with eyes and hands
Of football, operations, work;
The pussyfooting nurses take
Their ritual peep; the rule demands

I stand there with a stiff face
Ready, at a word or gleam,
To conjure off the drops of sweat.
So small a licit breathing-space
Brings each inside the other's dream.

Across the bright unechoing floors
The trolleys and attendants rove;
On tiptoe shine, by scoured walls,
The nearly speechless visitors
Skirt the precipice of love.

III

Oaks, pines, the willows with their quiet
Terror; the quiet terror of my age;
The seven-year-old bookworm sitting out
At night, in the intense cold, the horse
Tethered, the stars almost moving,
The cows encroaching on the night grass.
The frost stung my lips; my knees burned;
Darkness alone was homely. The hawthorn tree
Glimmered as though frost had turned to language
And language into sharp massy blossoms.
Once, I even scraped my father's hand
And glimpsed the white underside of poplars
That, moving, almost touched the flashing stars.
Squat, steep-browed, the Methodist Church nestled
Halfway between the distant police station
And the near barn; a whole world
Gave neither words nor heat, but merely
A geometry of the awakening sight.
I had forgotten that night, or nights;
And if I think back, there's nothing mythical:
A cross-legged kid with a brooding nose
His hands were too chilled to wipe,
A book whose pages he could hardly turn,
A silent father he had hardly learned
To touch; cold he could bear,
Though chill-blooded; the dark heat of words.
A life neither calm nor animal.
Now, in the deeper quiet of my age,
I feel thirty years
Turning my blood inwards; neither trees nor stars,
But a hush and start of traffic; spasms of sound

Loosening tram rails, bluestone foundations,
Manuscripts, memories; too many tasks;
A body shrinking round its own
Corruption, though a long way from dying.
We suit our memories to our sufferings.

IV

Every clod reveals an ancestor.
They, the spirit hot in their bodies,
Burned to ash in their own thoughts; could not
Find enough water; rode in a straight line
Twenty miles across country
For hatred jumping every wire fence;
With uillean pipes taunted the air
Ferociously that taunted them;
Spoke with rancour, but with double meanings;
Proud of muscle, hated the bone beneath;
Married to gain forty acres
And a family of bond servants; died bound.
I, their grandson, do not love straight lines,
And talk with a measured voice—in double meanings—
Remembering always, when I think of death,
The grandfather, small, loveless, sinister,
    ('The most terrible man I ever seen,'
    Said Joe, who died thin as rice paper)
Horse-breaker, heart-breaker, whose foot scorches,
Fifty years after, the green earth of Kilmore.
It's his heat that lifts my father's frame
Crazily from the wheel-chair, fumbles knots,
Twists in the bed at night,
Considers every help a cruelty.

V

Indoors and out, weather and winds keep up
Time's passion: paddocks white for burning.
As usual, by his bed, I spend my time
Not in talk, but restless noticing:
If pain dulls, grief coarsens.
Each night we come and, voyeurs of decay,
Stare for minutes over the bed's foot,
Imagining, if we think at all,

The body turning ash, the near insane
Knowledge when, in the small hours,
Alone under the cold ceiling, above
The floor where the heating system keeps its pulse,
He grows accustomed to his own sweat
120 And sweats with helplessness, remembering
How, every day, at eight o'clock
The Polish nurse kisses him goodnight.
His arms are bent like twigs; his eyes
Are blown to the door after her; his tears
Are squeezed out not even for himself.
Where is the green that swells against the blade
Or sways in sap to the high boughs? To the root
He is dry wood, and in his sideways
Falling brings down lights. Our breath
130 Mingles,
Stirs the green air of the laurel tree.

VI

The roofs are lit with rain.
Winter. In that dark glow,
Now, as three months ago,
I pray that he'll die sane.

On tiles or concrete path
The old wheeling the old,
For whom, in this last world,
Hope is an aftermath.

140 And the damp trees extend
Branch and thorn. We live
As much as we believe.
All things covet an end.

Once, on the Kerrie road,
I drove with him through fire.
Now, in the burnt cold year,
He drains off piss and blood,

His wounded face tube-fed,
His arm strapped to a bed.

VII

150 At the merest handshake I feel his blood
Move with the ebb-tide chill. Who can revive
A body settled in its final mood?
To whom, on what tide, can we move, and live?

Later I wheel him out to see the trees:
Willows and oaks, the small plants he mistakes
For rose bushes; and there
In the front, looming, light green, cypresses.
His pulse no stronger than the pulse of air.

Dying, he grows more tender, learns to teach
160 Himself the mysteries I am left to trace.
As I bend to say 'Till next time', I search
For signs of resurrection in his face.

BRUCE BEAVER

(b. 1928)

BRUCE BEAVER was born at Manly, New South Wales, where he now lives. After completing his schooling at Sydney Boys High School, he worked at many jobs, ranging from manual labouring to proof-reading. He now lives by writing, having received—as he puts it in his part-verse part-prose autobiography, *As It Was* (1979)—'a willing life sentence in the quarry of words'. His first book of poetry was published in 1962, but it was only with his fourth volume—*Letters to Live Poets* (1969)—that he achieved prominence as a poet. This volume has been seen as marking the new direction which Australian poetry was to take in the 1970s, and Beaver's experiment in taking his own personal concerns and his identity as a poet as the subject of a series of 'letters' was important for younger poets of the period. His stature was publicly recognized by his being given the Patrick White Award in 1982. A selection of the 'Letters to Live Poets' sequence is printed here along with a previously uncollected poem from his *Selected Poems* (1979).

Letter I

God knows what was done to you.
I may never find out fully.
The truth reaches us slowly here,
is delayed in the mail continually
or censored in the tabloids. The war
now into its third year
remains undeclared.
The number of infants, among others, blistered
and skinned alive by napalm
has been exaggerated
by both sides we are told,
and the gas does not seriously harm;
does not kill but is merely
unbearably nauseating.
Apparently none of this
is happening to us.

I meant to write to you more than a year
ago. Then there was as much to hear,
as much to tell.
There was the black plastic monster
prefiguring hell
displayed on the roof
of the shark aquarium at the wharf.
At Surfer's Paradise were Meter Maids
glabrous in gold bikinis.
It was before your country's
president came among us like a formidable
virus. Even afterwards—
after I heard (unbelievingly)
you had been run down on an island
by a machine
apparently while renewing yourself;
that things were terminal again—
even then I might have written.

But enough of that. I could tell by the tone
of your verses there were times
when you had ranged around you,
looking for a lift from the gift horse,
your kingdom for a Pegasus.
But to be trampled by the machine
beyond protest . . .

I don't have to praise you; at least
I can say I had ears for your voice
but none of that really matters now.
Crushed though. Crushed on the littered sands.
Given the *coup de grace* of an empty beer can,
out of sight of the 'lordly and isolate satyrs'.
Could it have happened anywhere else
than in your country, keyed to obsolescence?

50   I make these words perform for you
knowing though you are dead, that you 'historically
belong to the enormous bliss of American death',
that your talkative poems remain
among the living things
of the sad, embattled beach-head.

Say that I am, as ever, the young-
old fictor of communications.
It's not that I wish to avoid
talking to myself or singing
60   the one-sided song.
It's simply that I've come to be
more conscious of the community
world-wide, of live, mortal poets.
Moving about the circumference
I pause each day
and speak to you and you.
I haven't many answers, few
enough; fewer questions left.
Even when I'm challenged 'Who
70   goes there?' I give ambiguous
replies as though the self linking
heart and mind had become a gap.

You see, we have that much in common
already. It's only when I stop
thinking of you living I remember
near by our home there's an aquarium
that people pay admission to,
watching sharks at feeding time:
the white, jagged rictus in the grey
80   sliding anonymity,
faint blur of red through green,
the continually spreading stain.

I have to live near this, if not quite with it.
I realize there's an equivalent
in every town and city in the world.
Writing to you keeps the local, intent
shark-watchers at bay
(who if they thought at all
would think me some kind of ghoul);
rings a bell for the gilded coin-slots
at the Gold Coast;
sends the president parliament's head on a platter;
writes Vietnam like a huge four-letter
word in blood and faeces on the walls
of government; reminds me when
the intricate machine stalls
there's a poet still living at this address.

LETTER XII

Three anti-depressants and one diuretic a day
seven and five times a week respectively
save me from the pit.
I pray while I'm taking them and in between doses
because, as Dylan Thomas says, *I have seen the gates*
of hell.

Once I drew back in distaste from the metho drinker
and his bleary lady friend—you've seen them
weaving a way through non-existent traffic.
He, swollen faced, with a backside kicked in
by what the tougher call life. She,
the terrible veteran doll of Pantagruel's nursery.
Let them pass into the peaceful holocaust.

In Rushcutters' park they congregated over bottles.
Walking, we avoided them as mined ground,
fearful of their implosions bloodying the day.
Later I fell so far into self-sickness

I envied them. My thoughts
haunted their submerged wreckage like a squid.
At their groaning subsidence I retreated
into a pall of ink.

             Whatever I tell you,
you have heard before.
                     I remembered Swift's
fascination with the insane. I whistled
Childe Roland to the Dark Tower Came
outside the grimy walls of Callan Park.

Inside—*il miglior fabbro*—the best of us all
chewing bloody knuckles, wept dry,
30   daft as a headless chicken circling in the dust.
Where are prayers said for him and the parkside
    horrors?

Some prayed for us, I know. I'm still here
partially, trying to live detachedly.
Is it only the exceptional ones, the broken
    battlers,
shred me into uselessness? Does it mean
I'd pick and choose in hell? Discriminative?
Like a dog in rut—no,
40   self-abasement's out. So is complacency.
I'm never likely to forget
the day I walked on hands and knees
like Blake's Nebuchadnezzar, scenting the pit.
So it's one day at a time spent checking
the menagerie of self; seeing
the two-headed man has half as much
of twice of everything; curbing the tiger;
sunning the snake; taking stock of
Monkey, Piggsy, Sandy's belt of skulls.

Letter XV

Who could be strong and refrain from murder?
Who in that age did not know that the worst was
    inevitable?
Each day brings news of atrocities
by mercenaries, patriots and the
professional automata of either side.
War spun out like an incredible
competition between two soap
and cereal kings, with consolation

prizes of self-satisfied
reactions for the observant.
Truly, the baby is dissolving in the bathwater.

You would have alluded to most of this
as a fable or mythologized it
or set it all down simply as prose notes
at the head of a personal lyric.
How may I, skulking thankfully
in this suburban backyard,
emotionally incapable of meeting
in debate opponents of my attitudes,
periodically psychotic—
retired from life, some would say—
how may I, tentatively sane,
comment sensibly upon
a wider spread insanity?

I would say no to patriotism's
inflated toad anywhere—
No to the nationalistic lie in the rotten teeth
of all democracies, communes,
imperialist church and police states,
witnessing impotently
fellow writers, poets and fictors, writhing
in a widespread poison of the word
(old vox populi, late edition,
gleaming upper and lower dentures,
charnel smile
and a breath like Vietnam)
abused by the mechanics of the state,
driven ranting mad by assassin facts
that kill by slow degrees
the imaginative mind and breed
the healthy body for the field of war.

I understand only the man
who is at war with war within himself.
The rest, it seems, are victims of
the fallacy of an external peace
in a life dependent on a ploy of tensions.
There is no just war among ourselves,
only the cannibalistic incursions
of the inveterately immature.

In another age, man, you and I
would have chronicled the bloody acts
of our mercenary gentlemen
and their automative cohorts
in fabulous song. Our consciousness
mutilated, our psyches singing
slaves, castratos of barbarians.
The women would have tapestried
the carnage and the circumstance

60 of politic thronings and dethronings,
all the dynasts' fustian
until their fingers bled and their bellies
cramped at the sour and proper task.

Look back and shudder. Move on.
End the tyranny of history,
that shambles of old blood and bones.
Learn at least how to live and die
without the fear of longevity's
objectiveless freedom,

70 without the hope
of an eternal adolescence.
The task is to survive the outer
lure of the bonfire's martyr, the inner
holocaust of consciousness.
To turn the entire being
into a veteran of the natural agon
whipping us into life between
a birth and a death.

Letter XIX

I welcome the anonymity of the middle years,
  years of the spreading
girth and conversational prolixity, when the whole
  being loosens
the stays of the thirties and lengthens out into
  paragraphs of perceptiveness
where once had bristled the pointed phrase. And the
  other aspect, the merely boring

10 raconteur, the redundant conversationalist; the not
  young

not old, twice-told tale teller; the paunched, bejowled
　　double-chinned
bumbler. These I welcome, also the watcher
　　unperceived on corners
from verandas of youth, voyeuristic, grateful beyond
　　the tang of sour
grapes to be no longer privy to the ingrowing
　　secret, the deathly
held breaths of years, the cold and burning self-trials.
　　The quaintly
acquainted with the antique masques of childhood,
　　the mummies and daddies,
the nurses and doctors, the pantomimic routines of
　　getting the hang of
living and dying young. No, childhood's well and truly
　　categorized
and pigeon-holed somewhere within that depot of
　　lapsed tenders, the unconscious. It's the witnessing
of the adolescent saga that sometimes chills me
　　to my still vulnerable
marrow, burns me down to the fire of being and sifts
　　me into a vacuum
of loveless nine-to-five nightmares on wretched
　　wages, the between grown
and ungrown, the lonely braggart loping like werewolf
　　past the
unattainable beauties on the peeling posters, past
　　the burning
girls that, plain as sisters, would, and onto the
　　illimitable
utmost, absolute and factual plateau of the self's
　　serfdom
to solitude, the sad king in the bone castle, the
　　bitter end
of beginnings and the beginning of fiddling
　　appetites and the myriad
arbitrations of early manhood (in my case,
　　alas, a prolongation
of mad simulated adolescence). Only now with
　　hypertensive
head and lazy bowels, with a heart as whole as a
　　tin of dog's meat
may I pause between poems of letters to you, my
　　alter egos, and pronounce
peace be occasionally with you all and, at no

matter what cost, with me here,
no longer (I pray) completely at odds with self
    and world, accommodating
room by room like a shabby genteel boarding
60   house, age.

The Entertainer

The sand modeller always began by heaping the sand
into large and small mounds. From these he shaped
by patting and moulding with palms of hands and
    wooden paddle
the forms of single beings or groups of people and
    symbols.
A most unsubtle artist. All his themes were as
    obvious
and known as intimately to his audience as
10   a Greek tragedy or comedy to Attic
onlookers, almost participants. Most of his hungry-
    eyed watchers
were children—I was a child then and venerated his
    homely
skill—I speak of a time when there were still familial
arts: the orchestra of parents, sons and daughters;
the singing, acting and recitations at home or on visits
to uncles, aunts and cousins. My own parents were
participants in amateur theatricals.
20   One day as a small child I'd 'made up' myself as
    a clown
with white, red and blue greasepaint from their kit.
I'd forgotten what I'd done and went on an errand to
the nearest grocer to be met with much hilarity
and questioning. I'd fled in shame, empty handed.
The sand modeller's colours were as straightforward as
    my parents'
make-up kit—pink and white water colours for
    flesh,
30   brown and black for hair, blue and brown for eyes,
white, red and something like purple for robes in
    folds.
He applied painstakingly layer on layer of swiftly
    absorbed
colour on the already dampened surface

of, perhaps, Britannia with shield sword and lion
or dog, maybe, if it came out that way. Or if
it was during the Christmas holidays, a holy family
(the earthly one) of Joseph, Mary, Jesus complete
with crib (dark brown) a calf and a sheep (dark
    brown and grey)
and once with three crowned kings (two pink and white,
    one black).
As he modelled, adults and children would quietly
    gather,
the parents giving their children pennies to toss on to
the handkerchief he'd spread at the base of his
    inventions.
Once, and once only, a gang of brutes had pelted his art
with penny pieces harsh and hard-edged as bullets,
slicing into and through the forms and serene faces
(I saw later something like them in the frescoes
of Giotto), scattering sand and bleeding colours
    over
his tableaux. Quietly he'd set to repairing the damage
then he'd spoken briefly with his sympathizers—
the only time I ever heard him say a word
(his thanks for the safely tossed coins was
    underwritten).
He seemed surprised at such an unnecessary
    display
of vandalism. His innocence in face of such
premeditated anti-art—was he not
an outright challenge to the youths (and
    had I not
imagined the effect of a stone in the face of Joseph,
Jesus even, Mary perhaps)—his innocence
was almost unbelievable. It seemed he belonged
to a time when no child did such things, at least openly.
While I had only a year before tossed into the maw
of a Punch and Judy tent a gramophone arm and
    headpiece
found in a bin, (Was not Punch a homicidal
maniac?) and had fled behind a nearby pine
to watch the puppet master emerge, rubbing his head
and accusing the seated children, who all pointed
    towards me
as I fled into another time, another season.
So up to the years of war the sand modeller
    returned.

With each season the tableaux simpler, less worked
        over,
the colours paler as though his eyes only retained
the memoried intensity of hues. The cloth
covered ever more sparsely with scattered copper
        coins.
The last groupings vaguely patriotic and
given over to stilted studies of the Royal
Family. Quite safe from harm. The vandals had enlisted
90 or absconded. The entire length of beach was suddenly
strung with rolls of barbed wire rusting overnight,
the sea-wall topped by another barbed wire fence with
        iron
stanchions. Though all knew the Japanese guns would
        aim
beyond us for another twenty miles then range
back to pulverize us as an afterthought.
For several years I took to modelling ships in sand
with a friend between the barbed beach and the wired
100   wall.
One of our friends was hospitalized with tetanus from
the wire. Then we had grown up suddenly and saw
the beach revert to the use of nominally pacific
bathers. Nobody noted the non-appearance of
the sand modeller. Nor did I before I began
to record the scenes of my childhood, then there came
        obliquely
the blank looks and wholly calm, coloured faces
of this and that grouping of his repertoire,
110 no larger than life yet agelessly impermanent
as the paradox itself, the brief and everlasting
human story written on the lapsing sands.

PETER PORTER

(b. 1929)

PETER PORTER was born in Brisbane, Queensland, and educated at grammar school there and in Toowoomba. He started his working life as a reporter in Brisbane, and then went into the clothing trade. In 1951 he moved to England where he settled and married; at first he had a variety of occupations, including copywriting, but in recent years he has made a living as a freelance writer 'of the highbrow kind', contributing to several of the more prestigious London journals and the B.B.C. He has been Poetry Editor of the London *Observer* for over ten years, and has become very well known in metropolitan literary circles for his work on behalf of the British Council and the Arts Council of Britain as well as in his own right as poet. Since 1961 he has published eight volumes of poetry, **including much-admired translations of the Latin satirist** Martial. He has kept his Australian passport, but has not regarded himself as an expatriate. When James McAuley consulted him about his inclusion in *A Map of Australian Verse* (1975), Porter 'gave it as his opinion that it would not be appropriate to represent him'. Nevertheless, interest in his poetry has grown steadily in Australia since his first volume was published in 1961—all his books have been published in England, where he is accepted as an English poet. The appearance of his *Collected Poems* in 1983 was an important literary event in both countries. Of the poems by which he is represented here, 'Phar Lap in the Melbourne Museum' is from *Once Bitten Twice Bitten* (1961); 'Sydney Cove 1788', 'How to Get a Girl Friend' and 'The Great Poet Comes Here in Winter' are from *Poems Ancient and Modern* (1964); 'An Australian Garden' from *Living in a Calm Country* (1975); and 'An Exequy' from *The Cost of Seriousness* (1978).

Phar Lap in the Melbourne Museum

A masterpiece of the taxidermist's art,
Australia's top patrician stares
Gravely ahead at crowded emptiness.
As if alive, the lustre of dead hairs,
Lozenged liquid eyes, black nostrils
Gently flared, otter-satin coat declares
That death cannot visit in this thin perfection.

The democratic hero full of guile,
Noble, handsome, gentle Houyhnhnm
10　　(In both Paddock and St Leger difference is
Lost in the welter of money)—to see him win
Men sold farms, rode miles in floods,
Stole money, locked up wives, somehow got in:
First away, he led the field and easily won.

It was his simple excellence to be best.
Tough men owned him, their minds beset
By stakes, bookies' doubles, crooked jocks.
He soon became a byword, public asset,
A horse with a nation's soul upon his back—
20　　Australia's Ark of the Covenant, set
Before the people, perfect, loved like God.

And like God to be betrayed by friends.
Sent to America, he died of poisoned food.
In Australia children cried to hear the news
(This Prince of Orange knew no bad or good).
It was, as people knew, a plot of life:
To live in strength, to excel and die too soon,
So they drained his body and they stuffed his skin.

Twenty years later on Sunday afternoons
30　　You still can't see him for the rubbing crowds.
He shares with Bradman and Ned Kelly some
Of the dirty jokes you still can't say out loud.
It is Australian innocence to love
The naturally excessive and be proud
Of a thoroughbred bay gelding who ran fast.

Sydney Cove, 1788

The Governor loves to go mapping—round and round
The inlets of the Harbour in his pinnace.
He fingers a tree-fern, sniffs the ground

And hymns it with a unison of feet—
We march to church and executions. No-one,
Even Banks, could match the flora of our fleet.

Grog from Madeira reminds us most of home,
More than the pork and British weevils do.
On a diet of flour, your hair comes out in your comb.

10   A seaman who tried to lie with a native girl
Ran off when he smelt her fatty hide.
Some say these oysters are the sort for pearls.

Green shoots of the Governor's wheat have browned.
A box of bibles was washed up today,
The chaplain gave them to two methodists. Ross found

A convict selling a baby for a jug of rum.
Those black hills which wrestle with
The rain are called Blue Mountains. Come

Genocide or Jesus we can't work this land.
20   The sun has framed it for our moralists
To dry the bones of forgers in the sand.

We wake in the oven of its cloudless sky,
Already the blood-encircled sun is up.
Mad sharks swim in the convenient sea.

The Governor says we musn't land a man
Or woman with gonorrhoea. Sound felons only
May leave their bodies in a hangman's land.

Where all is novel, the only rule's explore.
Amelia Levy and Elizabeth Fowles spent the night
30   With Corporal Plowman and Corporal Winxstead for

A shirt apiece. These are our home concerns.
The cantor curlew sings the surf asleep.
The moon inducts the lovers in the ferns.

How to Get a Girl Friend

I

Be concealed among the lower bushes
Under a mixture of shadows
Cast by the teasing sun,
Have the parts of a God straining to move,
Know the ways nymphs take through the woods,
Be even more knowing,
Have read the scholiasts and their heirs
The New Scholars,
Be finally knowing,
Have trained your nose away from familiar scents
To this difficult virgin undertaking.
Here she comes at the proper pubescence,
Step out and say: I am your fate.
Then the rest is parting of hairs.
Tuning her cries to the old scale,
Washing the country face in its own tears
And if found out a minor constellation
Or perhaps two old parents on a pension till death.

II

Be tubercular in a city
Where there have been two pogroms
Since the last census: be baptised
By old and doting parents, have been patted
On the head by the senile Emperor
On his morning walk across the park,
Have just spent too much on a minor example
Of rococo the same evening your avant-garde
Story is being read to the Literary Society,
Be snug in the knowledge
Of the great Diaries timed to explode
In at least three capitals when your lungs
Give out: then, at last, approach
That thin girl with the Missal
In the open-air café where the Hungarian Band plays,
Show her the entries for June 5th and August 9th
And while the lovely tubercule tunnels
Get beyond the Mimi stage, arrive at
The calm of many quarrels till
Surrounded by friends your unnecessary affair
Achieves its apotheosis and the Gods
Hang Heaven black with emblems for you.

When your girl dies they'll turn your summerhouse
Into a tram shelter where men write
I want it tonight and Nylon knickers give off sparks
And birds find nothing new whoever shelters there.

III

Be man enough to end those pointless weekends,
Bitching in her tiny kitchen, talking Zen,
Sneaking down the dark steps mined with bottles —
Take a new room across town, don't open her letters.

Put oriental wisdom and cryptic sense
Under your foot — dress well, get drunk once a week,
Build up debts: somebody has to take
Responsibility of all these girls.

Be exposed to mirrors and start to burn.
Then to work. That girl you're looking at
Who seemed to be with that appalling type
Is looking back: bring your leg across.

She's talking about the different tastes
Of oysters: she can't mean it. Now
Puff up those small feathers, they may dazzle.
You can grow wings flying to the sun.

IV

Be coaxed from parsing love's fine language,
Be the right man in the right place for once.
Suck the straw she passes you,
Lick the grass stain off her skinny knees—
The air of afternoon is hairy,
The ground thick in dismembered bees.
Soon enough, thundering in the distance,
She turns her Breughel landscape round
To trap the late sugar of the sun.
Say to her, Darling, kiss my hot ears,
Touch my eyes with your tongue,
Cure me of the plainness in my mind.
You are the great Atlas of my childhood,
All your names are furry caterpillars
Crawling to me across the tall Carpathians.
You have come so far to see me
I will sleep when you have gone. The outer

Suburbs are selling lime drinks though
The sun is now low down, the clang
Of iron gates carries like glockenspiels
Across the valley, the old quarry
Is filled with light, tadpole fishers
Are ready to hear their mothers' shouts.
It can never have been so beautiful
Or worth so many lies: I am at home here
In my nest of doubts. Open your eyes love,
The sun adorns us with its happenings.

The Great Poet Comes Here in Winter

Frau Antonia is a cabbage:
If I were a grub I'd eat a hole in her.
Here they deliver the milk up a private path
Slippery as spit—her goddess' hands
Turn it to milk puddings. Blow, little wind,
Steer in off this cardboard sea,
You are acclimatised like these vines
Warring on an inch of topsoil
You are agent of the Golden Republic,
So still blow for me—our flowers look one way,
If I were a good poet I would walk on the sea.

The sea is actually made of eyes.
Whether of drowned fishermen or of peasants
Accustomed to the hard bargains of the saints
I cannot say. Whether there will be
Any mail from Paris or even broccoli
For dinner is in doubt. My hat blew off the planet,
I knelt by the infinite sand of the stars
And prayed for all men. Being German, I have a lot of soul.
Nevertheless, why am I crying in this garden?
I refuse to die till fashion comes back to spats.

From this turret the Adriatic
Burns down the galley lanes to starved Ragusa,
How strange it can wash up condoms.
The world is coming unstitched at the seams.
All yesterday the weather was a taste
In my mouth, I saw the notes of Beethoven
Lying on the ground, from the horn

Of a gramophone I heard Crivelli's cucumbers
Crying out for paint. In the eyes of a stray bitch
30 Ribbed with hunger, heavy with young,
I saw the peneplain of all imagined
Misery, horizontal and wider than the world.
I gave her my unwrapped sugar. We said Mass
Together, she licking my fingers and me
Knowing how she would die, not glad to have lived.
She took her need away, I thought her selfish
But stronger than God and more beautiful company.

An Australian Garden

For Sally Lehmann

Here we enact the opening of the world
And everything that lives shall have a name
To show its heart; there shall be Migrants,
Old Believers, Sure Retainers; the cold rose
Exclaim perfection to the gangling weeds,
The path lead nowhere—this is like entering
One's self, to find the map of death
Laid out untidily, a satyr's grin
Signalling 'You are here': tomorrow
10 They are replanting the old court,
Puss may be banished from the sun-warmed stone.

See how our once-lived lives stay on to haunt us,
The flayed beautiful limbs of childhood
In the bole and branches of a great angophora—
Here we can climb and sit on memory
And hear the words which death was making ready
From the start. Such talking as the trees attempt
Is a lesson in perfectability. It stuns
The currawongs along the breaks of blue—
20 Their lookout cries have guarded Paradise
Since the expulsion of the heart, when man,
Bereft of joy, turned his red hand to gardens.

Spoiled Refugees nestle near Great Natives;
A chorus of winds stirs the pagoda'd stamens:
In this hierarchy of miniatures
Someone is always leaving for the mountains,
Civil servant ants are sure the universe

Stops at the hard hibiscus; the sun is drying
A beleaguered snail and the hydra-headed
Sunflowers wave like lights. If God were to plant
Out all His hopes, He'd have to make two more
Unknown Lovers, ready to find themselves
In innocence, under the weight of His green ban.

In the afternoon we change—an afterthought,
Those deeper greens which join the stalking shadows—
The lighter wattles look like men of taste
With a few well-tied leaves to brummel-up
Their poise. Berries dance in a southerly wind
And the garden tide has turned. Dark on dark.
Janus leaves are opening to the moon
Which makes its own grave roses. Old Man
Camellias root down to keep the sun intact,
The act is canopied with stars. A green sea
Rages through the landscape all the night.

We will not die at once. Nondescript pinks
Survive the death of light and over-refined
Japanese petals bear the weight of dawn's first
Insect. An eye makes damask on the dew.
Time for strangers to accustom themselves
To habitat. What should it be but love?
The transformations have been all to help
Unmagical creatures find their proper skins,
The virgin and the leonine. The past's a warning
That the force of joy is quite unswervable—
'Out of this wood do not desire to go.'

In the sun, which is the garden's moon, the barefoot
Girl espies her monster, all his lovely specialty
Like hairs about his heart. The dream is always
Midday and the two inheritors are made
Proprietors. They have multiplied the sky.
Where is the water, where the terraces, the Tritons
And the cataracts of moss? This is Australia
And the villas are laid out inside their eyes:
It would be easy to unimagine everything,
Only the pressure made by love and death
Holds up the bodies which this Eden grows.

An Exequy

In wet May, in the months of change,
In a country you wouldn't visit, strange
Dreams pursue me in my sleep,
Black creatures of the upper deep—
Though you are five months dead, I see
You in guilt's iconography,
Dear Wife, lost beast, beleaguered child,
The stranded monster with the mild
Appearance, whom small waves tease,
(Andromeda upon her knees
In orthodox deliverance)
And you alone of pure substance,
The unformed form of life, the earth
Which Piero's brushes brought to birth
For all to greet as myth, a thing
Out of the box of imagining.

This introduction serves to sing
Your mortal death as Bishop King
Once hymned in tetrametric rhyme
His young wife, lost before her time;
Though he lived on for many years
His poem each day fed new tears
To that unreaching spot, her grave,
His lines a baroque architrave
The Sunday poor with bottled flowers
Would by-pass in their mourning hours,
Esteeming ragged natural life
('Most dearly loved, most gentle wife'),
Yet, looking back when at the gate
And seeing grief in formal state
Upon a sculpted angel group,
Were glad that men of god could stoop
To give the dead a public stance
And freeze them in their mortal dance.

The words and faces proper to
My misery are private—you
Would never share your heart with those
Whose only talent's to suppose,
Nor from your final childish bed
Raise a remote confessing head—
The channels of our lives are blocked,
The hand is stopped upon the clock,

No-one can say why hearts will break
And marriages are all opaque:
A map of loss, some posted cards,
The living house reduced to shards,
The abstract hell of memory,
The pointlessness of poetry—
These are the instances which tell
50 Of something which I know full well,
I owe a death to you—one day
The time will come for me to pay
When your slim shape from photographs
Stands at my door and gently asks
If I have any work to do
Or will I come to bed with you.
O *scala enigmatica*,
I'll climb up to that attic where
The curtain of your life was drawn
60 Some time between despair and dawn—
I'll never know with what halt steps
You mounted to this plain eclipse
But each stair now will station me
A black responsibility
And point me to that shut-down room,
'This be your due appointed tomb.'
I think of us in Italy:
Gin-and-chianti-fuelled, we
Move in a trance through Paradise,
70 Feeding at last our starving eyes,
Two people of the English blindness
Doing each masterpiece the kindness
Of discovering it—from Baldovinetti
To Venice's most obscure jetty.
A true unfortunate traveller, I
Depend upon your nurse's eye
To pick the altars where no Grinner
Puts us off our tourists' dinner
And in hotels to bandy words
80 With Genevan girls and talking birds,
To wear your feet out following me
To night's end and true amity,
And call my rational fear of flying
A paradigm of Holy Dying—
And, oh my love, I wish you were
Once more with me, at night somewhere
In narrow streets applauding wines,
The moon above the Apennines

As large as logic and the stars,
Most middle-aged of avatars,
As bright as when they shone for truth
Upon untried and avid youth.

The rooms and days we wandered through
Shrink in my mind to one—there you
Lie quite absorbed by peace—the calm
Which life could not provide is balm
In death. Unseen by me, you look
Past bed and stairs and half-read book
Eternally upon your home,
The end of pain, the left alone.

I have no friend, or intercessor,
No psychopomp or true confessor
But only you who know my heart
In every cramped and devious part—
Then take my hand and lead me out,
The sky is overcast by doubt,
The time has come, I listen for
Your words of comfort at the door,
O guide me through the shoals of fear—
'Fürchte dich nicht, ich bin bei dir.'

BRUCE DAWE

(b. 1930)

BRUCE DAWE was born at Geelong, Victoria, but now lives
in Queensland, where he has been teaching literature at a
college of advanced education since graduating from the
University of Queensland in 1969. The youngest of a
working class family, he chose to leave school at the age of
sixteen, and worked at a variety of jobs, mostly labouring.
In 1954 he was converted to Roman Catholicism and
began an Arts course as a full-time student at the Universi-
ty of Melbourne: in the same year he began writing the
poems by which he has become known. He did not
continue with his studies full-time beyond the first year,
and worked as a postman and gardener until, in 1959, he
joined the R.A.A.F., in which he served for nine years. His
first book, *No Fixed Address* (1962), was an immediate
success, and he has remained consistently popular, appeal-
ing to a larger audience than any other contemporary
Australian poet. He has written of attempting in his poetry
'to capture something of the evanescence of contemporary
idiom, which is far richer and more allusive than the
stereotyped stone-the-crows popular concept of Australian
speech would have people believe'. The poems by which
he is represented here are in chronological order from the
revised edition of his collected poems, *Sometimes Gladness*
(1983).

The Not-so-good Earth

For a while there we had 25-inch Chinese peasant families
famishing in comfort on the 25-inch screen
and even Uncle Billy whose eyesight's going fast
by hunching up real close to the convex glass
could just about make them out—the riot scene
in the capital city for example
he saw that better than anything, using the contrast knob
to bring them up dark—all those screaming faces
and bodies going under the horses' hooves—he did a
10   terrific job
on that bit, not so successful though
on the quieter parts where they're just starving away
digging for roots in the not-so-good earth
cooking up a mess of old clay
and coming out with all those Confucian analects
to everybody's considerable satisfaction
(if I remember rightly Grandmother dies
with naturally a suspenseful break in the action
for a full symphony orchestra plug for Craven A
20   neat as a whistle probably damn glad
to be quit of the whole gang with their marvellous
      patience.)
We never did find out how it finished up . . . Dad
at this stage tripped over the main lead in the dark
hauling the whole set down smack on its inscrutable face,
wiping out in a blue flash and curlicue of smoke
600 million Chinese without a trace . . .

Life-Cycle

For Big Jim Phelan

When children are born in Victoria
they are wrapped in the club-colours, laid in beribboned
      cots,
having already begun a lifetime's barracking.

Carn, they cry, Carn . . . feebly at first
while parents playfully tussle with them
for possession of a rusk: Ah, he's a little Tiger! (And they
      are . . .)

Hoisted shoulder-high at their first League game
10 they are like innocent monsters who have been years
          swimming
    towards the daylight's roaring empyrean

    Until, now, hearts shrapnelled with rapture,
    they break surface and are forever lost,
    their minds rippling out like streamers

    In the pure flood of sound, they are scarfed with light, a
          voice
    like the voice of God booms from the stands
    Ooohh you bludger and the covenant is sealed.

20 Hot pies and potato-crisps they will eat,
    they will forswear the Demons, cling to the Saints
    and behold their team going up the ladder into Heaven,

    And the tides of life will be the tides of the home-team's
          fortunes
    —the reckless proposal after the one-point win,
    the wedding and honeymoon after the grand-final . . .

    They will not grow old as those from more northern States
          grow old,
    for them it will always be three-quarter-time
30 with the scores level and the wind advantage in the final
          term,

    That passion persisting, like a race-memory, through the
          welter of seasons,
    enabling old-timers by boundary-fences to dream of
          resurgent lions
    and centaur-figures from the past to replenish continually
          the present,

    So that mythology may be perpetually renewed
    and Chicken Smallhorn return like the maize-god
40 in a thousand shapes, the dancers changing

    But the dance forever the same—the elderly still
    loyally crying Carn . . . Carn . . . (if feebly) unto the very
          end,
    having seen in the six-foot recruit from Eaglehawk their
          hope of salvation.

Drifters

One day soon he'll tell her it's time to start packing,
and the kids will yell 'Truly?' and get wildly excited for no reason,
and the brown kelpie pup will start dashing about, tripping
                               everyone up,
and she'll go out to the vegetable-patch and pick all the green
                               tomatoes from the vines,
and notice how the oldest girl is close to tears because she was
                               happy here,
and how the youngest girl is beaming because she wasn't.
10 And the first thing she'll put on the trailer will be the bottling-set
                               she never unpacked from Grovedale,
and when the loaded ute bumps down the drive past the blackberry-
                               canes with their last shrivelled fruit,
she won't even ask why they're leaving this time, or where
                               they're heading for
—she'll only remember how, when they came here,
she held out her hands bright with berries,
the first of the season, and said:
'Make a wish, Tom, make a wish.'

Search and Destroy

A Bi-Centenary Poem

Fear no more the heat o' the sun
—its rays are filtered, every one.

The fumes from car-exhausts and fires
from dumps and furnaces aspires

to poison heaven where the bird
sings on a diminished third

or totters from the well-sprayed tree
replete with years and DDT.

Now nature grinds her basic gears,
10   the big-end knocks, the junk-yard nears ...

Now fish float belly-up downstream caught
by chemicals too vague to be fought,

the forests sigh and fall, the hills
blink baldly as the new wind chills,

the grasslands waver and are gone,
the concrete Nothing blunders on,

black gold fountains to the sky,
the sands are mined, the sea-coasts die,

the land runs ruin to our pride!
20   Lord, give us, for our patricide,

two hundred more years like the last
and what shall then withstand the blast?

Homecoming

All day, day after day, they're bringing them home,
they're picking them up, those they can find, and bringing
them home,
they're bringing them in, piled on the hulls of Grants, in
trucks, in convoys,
they're zipping them up in green plastic bags,
they're tagging them now in Saigon, in the mortuary
coolness
they're giving them names, they're rolling them out of
10   the deep-freeze lockers—on the tarmac at Tan Son Nhut
the noble jets are whining like hounds,
they are bringing them home
—curly-heads, kinky-hairs, crew-cuts, balding non-coms
—they're high, now, high and higher, over the land, the
steaming *chow mein*
their shadows are tracing the blue curve of the Pacific
with sorrowful quick fingers, heading south, heading east,
home, home, home—and the coasts swing upward, the old
ridiculous curvatures
20   of earth, the knuckled hills, the mangrove-swamps, the
desert emptiness . . .
in their sterile housing they tilt towards these like skiers
—taxiing in, on the long runways, the howl of their
homecoming rises
surrounding them like their last moments (the mash, the
splendour)

then fading at length as they move
on to small towns where dogs in the frozen sunset
raise muzzles in mute salute,
30   and on to cities in whose wide web of suburbs
telegrams tremble like leaves from a wintering tree
and the spider grief swings in his bitter geometry
—they're bringing them home, now, too late, too early.

Exiles

More than ourselves we made these people strangers.
Israel is awash with Babylonians,
and where in Israel may the twelve tribes speak?

More than ourselves were outcast when we came
from the land between the rivers are these people,
driven derelict across the continent,

More sore, more sorry, loaded with more chains
than ever bound our forbears as they trudged
ashore in Botany, Moreton, or Port Phillip.

10   We took their hunting-grounds to graze our cattle,
we took their streams, we took, at will, their women,
we drove them from their temples in the land.

Whereas the engines of our endless spoilage
mould the horizons to our foreign dream,
and they, from their last sanctuaries, are turned out,

Who that observes them slowly moving now
along the fringes of our restlessness
could see them as they were before we came,

Or see them, on the banks of the broad rivers,
20   watching the convicts row in chiming rhythm,
still innocent of the song the sweet links sang?

LES A. MURRAY

(b. 1938)

LES A. MURRAY was born at Nabiac and grew up on the family dairy farm at Bunyah on the North Coast of New South Wales. According to his own account he learned to read from *Cassell's Encyclopedia*. After attending various country schools he went to Sydney in 1957 and began studying Arts at Sydney University. In 1962 he married and settled in Canberra, where he worked as a translator—translating scholarly material in a dozen West European languages—at the Australian National University. Since then, he has become a full-time writer, and now lives in the country. The poems in this anthology are from *The Vernacular Republic: Poems 1961–1981* (1982), in which Murray has collected 'all of the verse, apart from the novel sequence, *The Boys Who Stole the Funeral*, which the author wishes to preserve from his first twenty years' work'. On the basis of this volume Murray has been judged as a foremost Australian poet. He shares with Bruce Dawe a fascination with the vernacular ('I set out at one time to make Australian language into a literary language'); but his wide poetic interests embrace Aboriginal forms and themes as well as the literature of his own Gaelic ancestors. A man of definite views, he has written—at times provocatively—on a range of literary and general topics: the collections, *The Peasant Mandarin: Prose Pieces* (1978) and *Persistence in Folly* (1984), contain a number of essays dealing with topics relevant to his poetry.

The Burning Truck

It began at dawn with fighter planes:
they came in off the sea and didn't rise,
they leaped the sandbar one and one and one
coming so fast the crockery they shook down
off my kitchen shelves was spinning in the air
when they were gone.

They came in off the sea and drew a wave
of lagging cannon-shells across our roofs.
Windows spat glass, a truck took sudden fire,
out leaped the driver, but the truck ran on,
growing enormous, shambling by our street-doors,
coming and coming....

By every right in town, by every average
we knew of in the world, it had to stop,
fetch up against a building, fall to rubble
from pure force of burning, for its whole
body and substance were consumed with heat
but it would not stop.

And all of us who knew our place and prayers
clutched our verandah-rails and window-sills,
begging that truck between our teeth to halt,
keep going, vanish, strike ... but set us free.
And then we saw the wild boys of the street
go running after it.

And as they followed, cheering, on it crept,
windshield melting now, canopy-frame a cage
torn by gorillas of flame, and it kept on
over the tramlines, past the church, on past
the last lit windows, and then out of the world
with its disciples.

Noonday Axeman

Axe-fall, echo and silence. Noonday silence.
Two miles from here, it is the twentieth century:
cars on the bitumen, powerlines vaulting the farms.
Here, with my axe, I am chopping into the stillness.

Axe-fall, echo and silence. I pause, roll tobacco,
twist a cigarette, lick it. All is still.
I lean on my axe. A cloud of fragrant leaves
hangs over me moveless, pierced everywhere by sky.

Here, I remember all of a hundred years:
candleflame, still night, frost and cattle bells,
the draywheels' silence final in our ears,
and the first red cattle spreading through the hills

and my great-great-grandfather here with his first sons,
who would grow old, still speaking with his Scots accent,
having never seen those highlands that they sang of.
A hundred years. I stand and smoke in the silence.

A hundred years of clearing, splitting, sawing,
a hundred years of timbermen, ringbarkers, fencers
and women in kitchens, stoking loud iron stoves
year in, year out, and singing old songs to their children

have made this silence human and familiar
no farther than where the farms rise into foothills,
and, in that time, how many have sought their graves
or fled to the cities, maddened by this stillness?

Things are so wordless. These two opposing scarves
I have cut in my red-gum squeeze out jewels of sap
and stare. And soon, with a few more axe-strokes,
the tree will grow troubled, tremble, shift its crown

and, leaning slowly, gather speed and colossally
crash down and lie between the standing trunks.
And then, I know, of the knowledge that led my forebears
to drink and black rage and wordlessness, there will be
    silence.

After the tree falls, there will reign the same silence
as stuns and spurs us, enraptures and defeats us,

as seems to some a challenge, and seems to others
to be waiting here for something beyond imagining.

Axe-fall, echo and silence. Unhuman silence.
A stone cracks in the heat. Through the still twigs,
40   radiance
stings at my eyes. I rub a damp brow with a handkerchief
and chop on into the stillness. Axe-fall and echo.

The great mast murmurs now. The scarves in its trunk
crackle and squeak now, crack and increase as the hushing
weight of high branches heels outward, and commences
tearing and falling, and the collapse is tremendous.

Twigs fly, leaves puff and subside. The severed trunk
slips off its stump and drops along its shadow.
And then there is no more. The stillness is there
50   as ever. And I fall to lopping branches.

Axe-fall, echo and silence. It will be centuries
before many men are truly at home in this country,
and yet, there have always been some, in each generation,
there have always been some who could live in the
presence of silence.

And some, I have known them, men with gentle broad
        hands,
who would die if removed from these unpeopled places,
some again I have seen, bemused and shy in the cities,
60   you have built against silence, dumbly trudging through
        noise

past the railway stations, looking up through the traffic
at the smoky halls, dreaming of journeys, of stepping
down from the train at some upland stop to recover
the crush of dry grass underfoot, the silence of trees.

Axe-fall, echo and silence. Dreaming silence.
Though I myself run to the cities, I will forever
be coming back here to walk, knee-deep in ferns,
up and away from this metropolitan century,

to remember my ancestors, axemen, dairymen,
       ·   horse-breakers,
now coffined in silence, down with their beards and
       dreams,
who, unwilling or rapt, despairing or very patient,
made what amounts to a human breach in the silence,

made of their lives the rough foundation of legends—
men must have legends, else they will die of strangeness—
then died in their turn, each, after his own fashion,
resigned or agonized, from silence into great silence.

Axe-fall, echo and axe-fall. Noonday silence.
Though I go to the cities, turning my back on these hills,
for the talk and dazzle of cities, for the sake of belonging
for months and years at a time to the twentieth century,

the city will never quite hold me. I will be always
coming back here on the up-train, peering, leaning
out of the window to see, on far-off ridges
the sky between the trees, and over the racket
of the rails to hear the echo and the silence.

I shoulder my axe and set off home through the stillness.

Evening Alone at Bunyah

I

My father, widowed, fifty-six years old,
sits washing his feet.
The innocent sly charm
is back in his eye of late years, and tonight
he's going dancing.

I wouldn't go tonight, he says to me
by way of apology. *You sure you won't come?*
What for? I ask. *You know I only dance
on bits of paper.* He nods and says, *Well, if*
. *any ghosts come calling, don't let 'em eat my cake.*

I bring him a towel and study his feet afresh:
they make my own feel coarse. They are so small,
so delicate he can scarcely bear to walk
barefoot to his room to find his dancing shoes
and yet all day he works in hobnailed boots
out in the forest, clearing New South Wales.

No ghosts will come, Dad. I know you dote on cake.
I know how some women who bake it dote on you.
It gets them nowhere.
You are married still.

II

Home again from the cities of the world.
Cool night, and the valley relaxes after heat,
the earth contracts, the planks of the old house creak,
making one more adjustment, joist to nail,
nail to roof, roof to the touch of dew.

Smoke stains, rafters, whitewash rubbed off planks . . .
yet this is one house that Jerry built to last:
when windstorms came, and other houses lost
roofs and verandahs, this gave just enough
and went unscathed, for all the little rain
that sifted through cracks, the lamps puffed out by wind
sucked over the wallplate, and the occasional bat
silly with fear at having misplaced the dark.

When I was a child, my father was ashamed
of this shabby house. It signified for him
hard work and unjust poverty. There would come
a day when he'd tear it down and build afresh.
The day never came. But that's another poem.

No shame I felt in those days was my own.
It can be enough to read books and camp in a house.
Enough, at fourteen, to watch your father sit
at the breakfast table nursing his twelve-gauge
shotgun, awaiting the doubtful reappearance
of a snake's head at a crack in the cement
of the skillion fireplace floor.

The blood's been sluiced
away, and the long wrecked body of the snake
dug out and gone to ash these thirteen years,
but the crack's still there,
and the scores the buckshot ripped beside the stove.

There is a glow in the kitchen window now
that was not there in the old days. They have set
three streetlights up along the Gloucester road
for cows to stray by, and night birds to shun,
for the road itself's not paved, and there's no town
in the valley yet at all.
It is hoped there will be.

Today, out walking, I considered stones.
It used to be said that I must know each one
on the road by its first name, I was such a dawdler,
such a head-down starer.
I picked up
a chunk of milk-seamed quartz, thumbed off the clay,
let the dry light pervade it and collect,
eliciting shifting gleams, revealing how
the specific strength of a stone fits utterly
into its form and yet reflects the grain
and tendency of the mother-lode, the mass
of a vanished rock-sill tipping one small stone
slightly askew as it weighs upon your palm,
and then I threw it back towards the sun
to thump down on a knoll
where it may move a foot in a thousand years.

Today, having come back, summer was all mirror
tormenting me. I fled down cattle tracks
chest-deep in the earth, and pushed in under twigs
to sit by cool water seeping over rims
of blackened basalt, the tall light reaching me.

Since those moth-grimed streetlamps came,
my dark is threatened.

IV

I stand, and turn, and wander through the house,
avoiding those floorboards that I know would creak,
to the other verandah. Here is where I slept,
and here is where, one staring day, I felt
a presence at my back, and whirled in fright
to face my father's suit, hung out to air.

This country is my mind. I lift my face
and count my hills, and linger over one:
Deer's, steep, bare-topped, where eagles nest below
the summit in scrub oaks, and where I take
my city friends to tempt them with my past.

Across the creek and the paddocks of the moon
four perfect firs stand dark beside a field
lost long ago, which holds a map of rooms.
This was the plot from which we transplants sprang.
The trees grew straight. We burgeoned and spread far.
I think of doors and rooms beneath the ground,
deep rabbit rooms, thin candlelight of days ...
and, turning quickly, walk back through the house.

V

Night, and I watch the moonrise through the door.
Sitting alone's a habit of mind with me ...
for which I'll pay in full. That has begun.
But meanwhile I will sit and watch the moon.

My father will be there now, at a hall
in the dark of the country, shining at the waltz,
spry and stately, twirling at formal speeds
on a roaring waxed-plank floor.
The petrol lamps
sizzle and glare now the clapping has died down.
They announce some modern dance. He steps outside
to where cigarettes glow sparsely in the dark,
joins some old friends and yarns about his son.

Beneath this moon, an ancient radiance comes
back from far hillsides where the tall pale trunks
of ringbarked trees haphazardly define
the edge of dark country I could not afford
to walk in at night alone
lest I should hear
the barking of dogs from a clearing where no house
has ever stood, and, walking down a road
in the wilderness, meet a man who waited there
beside a creek to tell me what I sought.

Father, come home soon.
Come home alive.

An Absolutely Ordinary Rainbow

The word goes round Repins,
the murmur goes round Lorenzinis,
at Tattersalls, men look up from sheets of numbers,
the Stock Exchange scribblers forget the chalk in their
    hands
and men with bread in their pockets leave the Greek Club:
There's a fellow crying in Martin Place. They can't stop
    him.
The traffic in George Street is banked up for half a mile
and drained of motion. The crowds are edgy with talk
and more crowds come hurrying. Many run in the back
    streets
which minutes ago were busy main streets, pointing:
There's a fellow weeping down there. No one can stop
    him.

The man we surround, the man no one approaches
simply weeps, and does not cover it, weeps
not like a child, not like the wind, like a man
and does not declaim it, nor beat his breast, or even
sob very loudly—yet the dignity of his weeping

holds us back from his space, the hollow he makes about
    him
in the midday light, in his pentagram of sorrow,
and uniforms back in the crowd who tried to seize him
stare out at him, and feel, with amazement, their minds
longing for tears as children for a rainbow.

Some will say, in the years to come, a halo
or force stood around him. There is no such thing.
Some will say they were shocked and would have stopped
    him
but they will not have been there. The fiercest manhood,
the toughest reserve, the slickest wit amongst us

trembles with silence, and burns with unexpected
judgements of peace. Some in the concourse scream
who thought themselves happy. Only the smallest
    children
and such as look out of Paradise come near him
and sit at his feet, with dogs and dusty pigeons.

Ridiculous, says a man near me, and stops
his mouth with his hands, as if it uttered vomit—
and I see a woman, shining, stretch her hand
and shake as she receives the gift of weeping;
as many as follow her also receive it

and many weep for sheer acceptance, and more
refuse to weep for fear of all acceptance,
but the weeping man, like the earth, requires nothing,
the man who weeps ignores us, and cries out
of his writhen face and ordinary body

not words, but grief, not messages, but sorrow
hard as the earth, sheer, present as the sea—
and when he stops, he simply walks between us
mopping his face with the dignity of one
man who has wept, and now has finished weeping.

Evading believers, he hurries off down Pitt Street.

The Ballad of Jimmy Governor

H.M. Prison, Darlinghurst,
18th January 1901

You can send for my breakfast now, Governor.
The colt from Black Velvet's awake
and the ladies all down from the country
are gathered outside for my sake.

Soon be all finished, the running.
No tracks of mine lead out of here.
Today, I take that big step
on the bottom rung of the air
and be in Heaven for dinner.
Might be the first jimbera there.

The Old People don't go to Heaven,
good thing. My mother might meet
that stockman feller my father
and him cut her dead in the street.
Mother, today I'll be dancing
your way and his way on numb feet.

But a man's not a rag to wipe snot on,
I got that much into their heads,
them hard white sunbonnet ladies
that turned up their short lips and said
my wife had a slut's eye for colour.
I got that into their head

and the cow-cockies' kids plant up chimneys
they got horse soldiers out with the Law
after Joe and lame Jack and tan Jimmy—
but who learnt us how to make war
on women, old men, babies?
It ain't all one way any more.

The papers, they call us bushrangers:
That would be our style, I daresay,
bushrangers on foot with our axes.
It sweetens the truth, anyway.
They don't like us killing their women.
Their women kill us every day.

And the squatters are peeing their moleskins,
that's more than a calf in the wheat,
it's Jimmy the fencer, running
along the top rail in the night,
it's the Breelong mob crossing the ranges
with rabbitskins soft on their feet.

But now Jack in his Empire brickyard
has already give back his shoes
and entered the cleanliness kingdom,
the Commonwealth drums through the walls
and I'm weary of news.

I'm sorry, old Jack, I discharged you,
you might have enjoyed running free
of plonk and wet cornbags and colour
with us pair of outlaws. But see,
you can't trust even half a whitefeller.
You died of White Lady through me.

They tried me once running, once standing:
one time ought to do for the drop.
It's more trial than you got, I hear, Joe,
your tommyhawk's chipped her last chop.
I hope you don't mind I got lazy
when the leaks in my back made me stop.

If any gin stands in my print
I'll give her womb sorrow and dread,
if a buck finds our shape in the tussocks
I'll whiten the hair in his head,
but a man's not a rag to wipe boots on
and I got that wrote up, bright red,

where even fine ladies can read it
who never look at the ground
for a man that ain't fit to breed from
may make a terrible bound
before the knacker's knife gets him.
Good night to you, father. Sleep sound.

Fetch in my breakfast, Governor,
I have my journey to make
and the ladies all down from the country
are howling outside for my sake.

The Buladelah-Taree Holiday
Song Cycle

I

The people are eating dinner in that country north of
    Legge's Lake;
behind flywire and venetians, in the dimmed cool, town
    people eat Lunch.
Plying knives and forks with a peek-in sound, with a
    tuck-in sound
they are thinking about relatives and inventory, they are
    talking about customers and visitors.
In the country of memorial iron, on the creek-facing hills
    there,
they are thinking about bean plants, and rings of tank
    water, of growing a pumpkin by Christmas;
rolling a cigarette, they say thoughtfully Yes, and their
    companion nods, considering.
Fresh sheets have been spread and tucked tight, childhood
    rooms have been seen to,
for this is the season when children return with their
    children
to the place of Bingham's Ghost, of the Old Timber
    Wharf, of the Big Flood That Time,

the country of the rationalized farms, of the day-and-
    night farms, and of the Pitt Street farms,
of the Shire Engineer and many other rumours, of the
    tractor crankcase furred with chaff,
the places of sitting down near ferns, the snake-fear
    places, the cattle-crossing-long-ago places.

II

It is the season of the Long Narrow City; it has crossed
    the Myall, it has entered the North Coast,
that big stunning snake; it is looped through the hills,
    burning all night there.
Hitching and flying on the downgrades, processionally
    balancing on the climbs,
it echoes in O'Sullivan's Gap, in the tight coats of the
    flooded-gum trees;
the tops of palms exclaim at it unmoved, there near
    Wootton.
Glowing all night behind the hills, with a north-shifting
    glare, burning behind the hills;
through Coolongolook, through Wang Wauk, across the
    Wallamba,
the booming tarred pipe of the holiday slows and spurts
    again; Nabiac chokes in glassy wind,
the forests on Kiwarric dwindle in cheap light; Tuncurry
    and Forster swell like cooking oil.
The waiting is buffed, in timber villages off the highway,
    the waiting is buffeted:
the fumes of fun hanging above ferns; crime flashes in
    strange windscreens, in the time of the Holiday.
Parasites weave quickly through the long gut that
    paddocks shine into;
powerful makes surging and pouncing: the police,
    collecting Revenue.
The heavy gut winds over the Manning, filling
    northward, digesting the towns, feeding the towns;
they all become the narrow city, they join it;
girls walking close to murder discard, with excitement,
    their names.
Crossing Australia of the sports, the narrow city,
    bringing home the children.

III

₆₀ It is good to come out after driving and walk on bare
          grass;
walking out, looking all around, relearning that country.
Looking out for snakes, and looking out for rabbits as
          well;
going into the shade of myrtles to try their cupped
          climate, swinging by one hand around them,
in that country of the Holiday . . .
stepping behind trees to the dam, as if you had a gun,
to that place of the Wood Duck,
₇₀ to that place of the Wood Duck's Nest,
proving you can still do it; looking at the duck who hasn't
          seen you,
the mother duck who'd run Catch Me (broken wing) I'm
          Fatter (broken wing), having hissed to her children.

IV

The birds saw us wandering along.
Rosellas swept up crying out *we think we think;* they
          settled farther along;
knapping seeds off the grass, under dead trees where their
          eggs were, walking around on their fingers,
₈₀ flying on into the grass.
The heron lifted up his head and elbows; the magpie
          stepped aside a bit,
angling his chopsticks into pasture, turning things over in
          his head.
At the place of the Plough Handles, of the Apple Trees
          Bending Over, and of the Cattlecamp,
there the vealers are feeding; they are loosely at work,
          facing everywhere.
They are always out there, and the forest is always on the
₉₀   hills;
around the sun are turning the wedgetail eagle and her
          mate, that dour brushhook-faced family:
they settled on Deer's Hill away back when the sky was
          opened,
in the bull-oak trees way up there, the place of fur tufted
          in the grass, the place of bone-turds.

V

The Fathers and the Great-Grandfathers, they are out in
    the paddocks all the time, they live out there,
at the place of the Rail Fence, of the Furrows Under
    Grass, at the place of the Slab Chimney.
We tell them that clearing is complete, an outdated
    attitude, all over;
we preach without a sacrifice, and are ignored; flowering
    bushes grow dull to our eyes.
We begin to go up on the ridge, talking together, looking
    at the kino-coloured ants,
at the yard-wide sore of their nest, that kibbled peak, and
    the workers heaving vast stalks up there,
the brisk compact workers; jointed soldiers pour out
    then, tense with acid; several probe the mouth of a
    lost gin bottle:
Innuendo, we exclaim, *literal minds!* and go on up the
    ridge, announced by finches;
passing the place of the Dingo Trap, and that farm hand it
    caught, and the place of the Cowbails,
we come to the road and watch heifers,
little unjoined devons, their teats hidden in fur, and the
    cousin with his loose-slung stockwhip driving them.
We talk with him about rivers and the lakes; his polished
    horse is stepping nervously,
printing neat omegas in the gravel, flexing its skin to
    shake off flies;
his big sidestepping horse that has kept its stones; it
    recedes gradually, bearing him;
we murmur *stone-horse* and *devilry* to the grinners under
    grass.

VI

Barbecue smoke is rising at Legge's Camp; it is steaming
    into the midday air,
all around the lake shore, at the Broadwater, it is going
    up among the paperbark trees,
a heat-shimmer of sauces, rising from tripods and flat
    steel, at that place of the Cone-shells,
at that place of the Seagrass, and the tiny segmented
    things swarming in it, and of the Pelican.
Dogs are running around disjointedly; water escapes
    from their mouths,
confused emotions from their eyes; humans snarl at them
    Gwanout and Hereboy, not varying their tone

much;

140 the impoverished dog people, suddenly sitting down to
        nuzzle themselves; toddlers side with them:
toddlers, running away purposefully at random, among
        cars, into big drownie-water (come back,
        Cheryl-Ann!).
They rise up as charioteers, leaning back on the tow-bar;
        all their attributes bulge at once;
swapping swash shoulder-wings for the white-sheeted
        shoes that bear them,
they are skidding over the flat glitter, stiff with grace, for
150 once not travelling to arrive.
From the high dunes over there, the rough blue distance,
        at length they come back behind the boats,
and behind the boats' noise, cartwheeling, or sitting
        down, into the lake's warm chair;
they wade ashore and eat with the families, putting off
        that up-rightness, that assertion,
eating with the families who love equipment, and the
        freedom from equipment,
with the fathers who love driving, and lighting a fire
160 between stones.

VII

Shapes of children were moving in the standing corn, in
        the child-labour districts;
coloured flashes of children, between the green and
        parching stalks, appearing and disappearing.
Some places, they are working, racking off each cob like
        a lever, tossing it on the heaps;
other places, they are children of child-age, there playing
        jungle:
in the tiger-striped shade, they are firing hoehandle
170 machine guns, taking cover behind fat pumpkins;
in other cases, it is Sunday and they are lovers.
They rise and walk together in the sibilance, finding
        single rows irksome, hating speech now,
or, full of speech, they swap files and follow defiles,
        disappearing and appearing;
near the rain-grey barns, and the children building
        cattleyards beside them;
the standing corn, gnawed by pouched and rodent mice;
        generations are moving among it.
180 the parrot-hacked, medicine-tasseled corn, ascending all
        the creek flats, the wire-fenced alluvials.
    going up in patches through the hills, towards the Steep
        Country.

VIII

Forests and State Forests, all down off the steeper
    country; mosquitoes are always living in there:
they float about like dust motes and sink down, at the
    places of the Stinging Tree,
and of the Staghorn Fern; the males feed on plant-stem
    fluid, absorbing that watery ichor;
190   the females meter the air, feeling for the warm-blooded
    smell, needing blood for their eggs.
They find the dingo in his sleeping-place, they find his
    underbelly and his anus;
they find the possum's face, they drift up the ponderous
    pleats of the fig tree, way up into its rigging,
the high camp of the fruit bats; they feed on the
    membranes and ears of bats; tired wings cuff air at
    them;
their eggs burning inside them, they alight on the
200   muzzles of cattle,
the half-wild bush cattle, there at the place of the Sleeper
    Dump, at the place of the Tallowwoods.
The males move about among growth tips; ingesting
    solutions, they crouch intently;
the females sing, needing blood to breed their young;
    their singing is in the scrub country;
their tune comes to the name-bearing humans, who
    dance to it and irritably grin at it.

IX

The warriors are cutting timber with brash chainsaws;
210   they are trimming hardwood pit-props and loading
    them;
Is that an order? they hoot at the peremptory lorry driver,
    who laughs; he is also a warrior.
They are driving long-nosed tractors, slashing pasture in
    the dinnertime sun;
they are fitting tappets and valves, the warriors, or giving
    finish to a surfboard.
Addressed on the beach by a pale man, they watch waves
    break and are reserved, refusing pleasantry;
220   they joke only with fellow warriors, chaffing about
    try-ons and the police, not slighting women.
Making Timber a word of power, Con-rod a word of
    power, Sense a word of power, the Regs. a word of
    power,
they know belt-fed from spring-fed; they speak of being
    stiff, and being *history;*

LES A. MURRAY   213

the warriors who have killed, and the warriors who
        eschewed killing,
the solemn, the drily spoken, the life peerage of
        endurance; drinking water from a tap,
they watch boys who think hard work a test, and boys
        who think it is not a test.

X

Now the ibis are flying in, hovering down on the
        wetlands,
on those swampy paddocks around Darawank, curving
        down in ragged dozens,
on the riverside flats along the Wang Wauk, on the
        Boolambayte pasture flats,
and away towards the sea, on the sand moors, at the place
        of the Jabiru Crane.
leaning out of their wings, they step down; they take out
        their implement at once,
out of its straw wrapping, and start work; they dab
        grasshopper and ground-cricket
with nonexistence . . . spiking the ground and puncturing
        it . . . they swallow down the outcry of a frog;
they discover titbits kept for them under cowmanure lids,
        small slow things.
Pronging the earth, they make little socket noises, their
        thoughtfulness jolting down-and-up suddenly;
there at Bunyah, along Firefly Creek, and up through
        Germany,
the ibis are all at work again, thin-necked ageing men
        towards evening; they are solemnly all back
at Minimbah, and on the Manning, in the rye-and clover
        irrigation fields;
city storemen and accounts clerks point them out to their
        wives,
remembering things about themselves, and about the
        ibis.

XI

Abandoned fruit trees, moss-tufted, spotted with dim
        lichen paints; the fruit trees of the Grandmothers,
they stand along the creekbanks, in the old home
        paddocks, where the houses were;
they are reached through bramble-grown front gates,
        they creak at dawn behind burnt skillions,

at Belbora, at Bucca Wauka, away in at Burrell Creek,
    at Telararee of the gold-sluices.
The trees are split and rotten-elbowed; they bear the
270   old-fashioned summer fruits,
    the annual bygones: china pear, quince, persimmon;
    the fruit has the taste of former lives, of sawdust and
      parlour song, the tang of Manners;
children bite it, recklessly,
    at what will become for them the place of the Slab Wall,
      and of the Coal Oil Lamp,
    the place of moss-grit and swallows' nests, the place of
      the Crockery.

XII

Now the sun is an applegreen blindness through the
280   swells, a white blast on the sea-face, flaking and
      shoaling;
    now it is burning off the mist; it is emptying the density
      of trees, it is spreading upriver,
hovering above the casuarina needles, there at Old Bar
      and Manning Point;
flooding the island farms, it abolishes the milkers'
      munching breath
as they walk towards the cowyards; it stings a bucket
      here, a teacup there.
290 Morning steps into the world by ever more southerly
      gates; shadows weaken their north skew
on Middle Brother, on Cape Hawke, on the dune scrub
      toward Seal Rocks;
    steadily the heat is coming on, the butter-water time, the
      clothes-sticking time;
grass covers itself with straw; abandoned things are
      thronged with spirits;
everywhere wood is still with strain; birds hiding down
      the creek galleries, and in the cockspur canes;
300 the cicada is hanging up her sheets; she takes wing off her
      music-sheets.
Cars pass with a rational zoom, panning quickly towards
      Wingham,
through the thronged and glittering, the shale-topped
      ridges, and the cattlecamps,
towards Wingham for the cricket, the ball knocked hard
      in front of smoked-glass ranges, and for the
      drinking.
In the time of heat, the time of flies around the mouth, the

310 time of the west verandah;
looking at that umbrage along the ranges, on the New
England side;
clouds begin assembling vaguely, a hot soiled heaviness
on the sky, away there towards Gloucester;
a swelling up of clouds, growing there above Mount
George, and above Tipperary;
far away and hot with light; sometimes a storm takes root
there, and fills the heavens rapidly;
darkening, boiling up and swaying on its stalks, pulling
320 this way and that, blowing round by Krambach;
coming white on Bulby, it drenches down on the
paddocks, and on the wire fences;
the paddocks are full of ghosts, and people in cornbag
hoods approaching;
lights are lit in the house; the storm veers mightily on its
stem, above the roof; the hills uphold it;
the stony hills guide its dissolution; gullies opening and
crumbling down, wrenching tussocks and rolling
them;
330 the storm carries a greenish-grey bag; perhaps it will find
hail and send it down, starring cars, flattening
tomatoes,
in the time of the Washaways, of the dead trunks braiding
water, and of the Hailstone Yarns.

XIII

The stars of the holiday step out all over the sky.
People look up at them, out of their caravan doors and
their campsites;
people look up from the farms, before going back; they
gaze at their year's worth of stars.
340 The Cross hangs head-downward, out there over
Markwell;
it turns upon the Still Place, the pivot of the Seasons, with
one shoulder rising:
'Now I'm beginning to rise, with my Pointers and my
Load . . .'
hanging eastwards, it shines on the sawmills and the
lakes, on the glasses of the Old People.
Looking at the Cross, the galaxy is over our left shoulder,
slung up highest in the east;
350 there the Dog is following the Hunter; the Dog Star
pulsing there above Forster; it shines down on the
Bikies,

and on the boat-hire sheds, there at the place of the
  Oyster; the place of the Shark's Eggs and her Hide;
the Pleiades are pinned up high on the darkness, away
  back above the Manning;
they are shining on the Two Blackbutt Trees, on the
  rotted river wharves, and on the towns;
standing there, above the water and the lucerne flats, at
360 the place of the Families;
their light sprinkles down on Taree of the Lebanese
  shops, it mingles with the streetlights and their glare.
People recover the starlight, hitching north,
travelling north beyond the seasons, into that country of
  the Communes, and of the Banana:
the Flying Horse, the Rescued Girl, and the Bull, burning
  steadily above that country.
Now the New Moon is low down in the west, that
  remote direction of the Cattlemen,
370 and of the Saleyards, the place of steep clouds, and of the
  Rodeo;
the New Moon who has poured out her rain, the moon of
  the Planting-times.
People go outside and look at the stars, and at the
  melonrind moon,
the Scorpion going down into the mountains, over there
  towards Waukivory, sinking into the tree-line,
in the time of the Rockmelons, and of the Holiday . . .
the Cross is rising on his elbow, above the glow of the
380 horizon;
carrying a small star in his pocket, he reclines there
  brilliantly,
above the Alum Mountain, and the lakes threaded on the
  Myall River, and above the Holiday.

PART TWO
Selected Poems

Notes on the Poets

The notes that follow are intended to do no more than place the authors in the most rudimentary way for the benefit of readers unacquainted with their work, by recording their life-dates, the regions with which they are associated, their occupations, and the titles of their publications from which the poems come.

ADAM LINDSAY GORDON (1833–1870). Born in the Azores, educated in England, Gordon was sent by his parents in 1853 to South Australia where he acquired a reputation as a horseman. Following various reverses, he committed suicide the day after the publication of the volume on which his fame chiefly rests, *Bush Ballads and Galloping Rhymes*, from which 'The Sick Stockrider' comes.

ADA CAMBRIDGE (1844–1926). A prolific novelist as well as a poet, Norfolk-born Ada Cambridge arrived in Victoria in 1870 as the wife of an Anglican clergyman. Her first book of poems, *The Manor House and Other Poems*, appeared in 1875 and her last, *The Hand in the Dark*, in which 'Vows' appeared, in 1913.

MARY GILMORE (1865–1962). After a bush childhood in New South Wales, a school-teaching career and involvement in the Labour movement, in 1896 Gilmore joined William Lane's New Australia venture in Paraguay. On her return to Australia she began to write, and quickly became a prominent and prolific journalist. She published seven volumes of verse and two of prose anecdotes and recollections. 'Old Botany Bay' and 'Nationality' first appeared in, respectively, *The Passionate Heart* (1918) and *Fourteen Men* (1954).

BARCROFT BOAKE (1866–1892). Boake hanged himself at the age of twenty-six. Like Gordon, that earlier suicide whom Boake admired, he found his poetic inspiration in the bush, though his view of it is a much darker one. 'Where the Dead Men Lie' is the title poem of his only book of poetry, published five years after his death.

BERNARD O'DOWD (1866–1953). With both a Law and an Arts degree from the University of Melbourne, O'Dowd had a long career as a public servant in Victoria. He produced five major volumes of poetry, and is today best known for 'Australia', which appeared in his first book, *Dawnward?* (1903).

'JOHN O'BRIEN' [Patrick Joseph Hartigan] (1878–1952). An ordained Catholic priest, Hartigan wrote articles about the pioneer clergy in Australia and, under the O'Brien pseudonym, two popular volumes of ballad poetry, *Around the Boree Log and Other*

Verses (1911) and the posthumously published *The Parish of St. Mel's* (1954). 'Said Hanrahan' comes from the earlier volume.

DOROTHEA MACKELLAR (1885–1968). Mackellar's best-known poem, 'My Country', appeared first in the London *Spectator* as 'Core of My Heart' in 1908, then in revised form in her first book, *The Closed Door* (1911). Born in Sydney, she was educated privately and at the University of Sydney. She wrote three further volumes of poetry and three novels.

LESBIA HARFORD (1891–1927). Despite congenital ill-health, Harford gained a Law degree at the University of Melbourne, was active in radical and union politics, worked in a clothing factory, and completed her articles in a solicitor's office just before her death. The first collection of her verse was not published until 1941. The three poems in this anthology are from a second, and more extensive, collection, *The Poems of Lesbia Harford*, edited by Drusilla Modjeska and Marjorie Pizer, which appeared in 1985.

R.D. FITZGERALD (1902–1987). Born in Sydney, FitzGerald had a long career as a surveyor. His first collection of verse, *The Greater Apollo: Seven Metaphysical Songs*, appeared in 1927 when he was under the influence of Norman Lindsay, and his most recent volume of verse appeared in 1977. 'The Wind at Your Door' comes from *Southmost Twelve* (1962) and 'Song in Autumn' from *This Night's Orbit* (1953).

RONALD MCCUAIG (b. 1908). Born in Newcastle, McCuaig practised his profession of journalism in Sydney. He has produced several volumes of poetry, much of it topical and satirical, but none since 1961. 'Love Me and Never Leave Me' and 'The Passionate Clerk' are from *Quod Ronald McCuaig* (1946).

IAN MUDIE (1911–1976). A South Australian, Mudie was a prolific freelance writer, closely identified with the Jindyworobak movement in Australian poetry; he produced nine volumes of verse as well as editing others. His most popular poem, 'They'll Tell You About Me', first appeared in *The Blue Crane* (1959).

WILLIAM HART-SMITH (b. 1911). Like Mudie, the English-born Hart-Smith was associated with the Jindyworobak movement in the 1940s. His poetry reflects his experience of living in New Zealand as well as in Australia. 'Space' was included in his first volume of poetry, which was privately printed in 1941 or 1942, and appears in his *Selected Poems 1936–1984*, edited by Brian Dibble in 1985.

ROLAND ROBINSON (b. 1912). Born in Ireland, Robinson had a wide range of jobs after schooling in Australia, and was an early member of the Jindyworobaks. His poetry has often reflected sympathetically on the Aboriginal inhabitants of this country. 'Altjeringa' comes from *Deep Well*, published in 1962.

JOHN BLIGHT (b. 1913). Blight has spent most of his life on the Queensland coast, and many of his poems explore his fascination with the sea. He has published eight volumes of verse. 'A Sailor's Grave' and 'Death of a Whale' are from *A Beachcomber's Diary* (1963).

DOUGLAS STEWART (1913–1985). A New Zealander who settled in Australia in 1939 and became literary editor of the *Bulletin*, Stewart was one of the most versatile Australian literary figures, noted as a playwright and an editor as well as a poet. His earlier poetry reflects his New Zealand experience. 'Terra Australis' comes from *Sun Orchids* (1952) and 'B Flat' from *Collected Poems* (1967).

KENNETH MACKENZIE (1913–1955). After an unsettled education in Western Australia, Mackenzie became a journalist in Sydney, where he was influenced by Norman Lindsay. He published novels as Seaforth Mackenzie but his four volumes of poetry (two of them posthumous) appeared under his real name. 'An Old Inmate' and 'The Children Go' are from *Selected Poems* (1961).

JOHN MANIFOLD (1915–1985). Born in Melbourne into one of the oldest grazing families in Victoria, Manifold went to Cambridge University in the late 1930s and remained abroad until 1949, having served in the British Army during the Second World War. 'The Tomb of Lt. John Learmonth, A.I.F.', an elegy in memory of a school friend, first appeared in the *New Republic* in 1945, and was included in his *Selected Verse* (1946).

DOROTHY AUCHTERLONIE (b. 1915). Born in England, Auchterlonie has been a lecturer in English at several Australian universities, has contributed substantially (as Dorothy Green) to Australian literary criticism, and has published two volumes of poetry, the second of which is *The Dolphin* (1967), from which 'The Tree' comes.

HAROLD STEWART (b. 1916). With James McAuley, Stewart created the mythical poet 'Ern Malley' in the 1944 *Angry Penguins* hoax. He now lives in Japan, and two of his published volumes of poetry are translations of Japanese haiku. 'Orpheus and the Wild Beasts' comes from his second collection, *Orpheus and Other Poems* (1956).

ANNE ELDER (1918–1976). Elder came from New Zealand to Australia at the age of three and, after a career as a ballet dancer, published her first book of poetry, *For the Record*, in 1972. 'Farmer

Goes Berserk' is from *Crazy Woman and Other Poems*, which was published posthumously in 1976.

OODGEROO NOONUCCAL [Kath Walker] (b. 1920). A part-Aborigine from Stradbroke Island off the Queensland coast near Brisbane, Noonuccal has campaigned strenuously for Aboriginal rights. 'We are Going' is from the first of her two poetry collections, *We are Going* (1964) and *The Dawn is at Hand* (1966). In 1988 she publicly rejected the European name by which she had been known as a writer.

MAX HARRIS (b. 1921). A South Australian who co-edited the literary and artistic journal, *Angry Penguins*, and established the Mary Martin bookshop chain, Harris has been a regular commentator on Australian culture, as well as the author of several volumes of poetry. 'The Tantanoola Tiger' comes from *A Window at Night* (1967).

DIMITRIS TSALOUMAS (b. 1921). A Greek poet who settled in Australia in 1952, Tsaloumas has published in both Greece and Australia. 'Autumn Supper' comes from his first collection of poems written in English, *Falcon Drinking* (1988).

DOROTHY HEWETT (b. 1923). Born in Western Australia where she grew up, but now living in Sydney, Hewett is well known as both a playwright and a poet. Her most-performed play is *The Chapel Perilous* (1972); and her five volumes of poetry include *Rapunzel in Suburbia* (1975), in which 'Anniversary' appears.

R.A. SIMPSON (b. 1929). A Melbourne poet, Simpson has been poetry editor of the *Bulletin* and of the *Age*, and a lecturer in Art at Chisholm Institute of Technology. He has produced nine volumes of poetry. 'Captain Oates, 1912' comes from *This Real Pompeii* (1964), and 'Ethel' from *After the Assassination* (1968).

DAVID LAKE (b. 1929). A Cambridge graduate, Lake was born in India and taught in South East Asian tertiary institutions from 1959 to 1967. A regular contributor of verse to periodicals, he has published one collection, *Hornpipes and Funerals* (1973), and several novels. 'To Horace' is taken from *Recent Queensland Poetry*, edited by Greg McCart in 1975.

PHILIP MARTIN (b. 1931). Melbourne born and educated, Martin teaches English at Monash University. He has published several volumes of verse since *Voice Unaccompanied* appeared in 1970. 'Reading the Lines' and 'Christmas Ghosts' come from *A Flag for the Wind* (1982).

VIVIAN SMITH (b. 1933). Born in Hobart but now living in Sydney, Smith has taught in the universities of Hobart and of

Melbourne. He is the author of a number of critical studies as well as of four collections of verse. 'Deathbed Sketch' is from *An Island South* (1967), and 'Twenty Years of Sydney' is from *Tide Country* (1982).

JENNIFER STRAUSS (b. 1933). A graduate of the University of Melbourne, Victorian-born Strauss now teaches literature at Monash University. Her first collection, *Children and Other Strangers*, appeared in 1975, and her second, *Winter Driving*, from which 'Migrant Woman on a Melbourne Tram' comes, in 1981.

FAY ZWICKY (b. 1934). Born in Melbourne, Zwicky was a concert pianist but is now an academic at the University of Western Australia. She is a critic and short story writer, as well as the author of two collections of poetry. 'Kaddish' comes from *Kaddish and Other Poems* (1982).

CHRIS WALLACE-CRABBE (b. 1934). Born and educated in Melbourne and a professor at the University of Melbourne, Wallace-Crabbe is the author of a number of critical studies, is the editor of three poetry anthologies, and has published nine volumes of poetry. 'Melbourne' comes from *In Light and Darkness* (1963).

DAVID MALOUF (b. 1934). Born in Brisbane of Lebanese and English parents, Malouf now lives partly in Australia and partly in Italy. He has written several novels, beginning with *Johnno* (1975), and has published six volumes of verse. 'Suburban' comes from *Neighbours in a Thicket* (1974).

ANTIGONE KEFALA (b. 1935). Born in Romania of Greek parents, Kefala lived in New Zealand where she completed her education before coming to Australia. She has published two short novels as well as three volumes of poetry. 'Freedom Fighter' comes from *Mrs Noah and the Minoan Queen* (1983).

RANDOLPH STOW (b. 1935). Stow, who now lives in England, was born and educated in Western Australia. A well-known novelist, he has also published a popular children's novel, *Midnite* (1967), and several volumes of poetry. 'The Utopia of Lord Mayor Howard' is from *Outsider* (1962) and 'The Singing Bones' is from *A Counterfeit Silence* (1969).

JUDITH RODRIGUEZ (b. 1936). A graduate of Queensland and Cambridge universities, Rodriguez taught English at La Trobe University for many years, but now lives in Sydney. She has published five collections of verse; 'Eskimo Occasion' comes from *Water Life* (1976).

MUDROOROO NAROGIN [Colin Johnson] (b. 1939). Narogin, who was born in Western Australia, spent eight years in India as a Buddhist, and is now a lecturer at the University of Queensland. The first of the three novels that he has so far published, *Wild Cat Falling* (1965), was also the first to be published by an Aborigine. His poem 'Under an Aboriginal Tree' is from his first collection of poetry, *The Song Cycle of Jacky and Selected Poems* (1987).

GEOFFREY LEHMANN (b. 1940). Sydney-born Lehmann now lectures in Law at the University of New South Wales. An editor and anthologist (co-editor with Robert Gray of *The Younger Australian Poets*, 1983), he is the author of several collections of verse. 'Five Days Late' comes from his *Selected Poems* (1976).

ANDREW TAYLOR (b. 1940). Born in Victoria, Taylor has lectured in English at the universities of Melbourne and of Adelaide. He has published seven collections of poetry. 'Developing a Wife' comes from *The Cool Change* (1971).

GEOFF PAGE (b. 1940). Page, born in New South Wales and educated in Canberra, has published five volumes of poetry and edited an anthology of recent poetry about the First World War. 'Smalltown Memorials' is from *Smalltown Memorials* (1975).

KATE LLEWELLYN (b. 1940). Born in South Australia, Llewellyn is associated with feminist writing in Australia; she co-edited (with Susan Hampton) *The Penguin Book of Australian Women Poets* (1986). 'Eve' comes from *Luxury* (1985), the second of the two volumes of poetry she has so far published.

ROGER MCDONALD (b. 1941). A teacher, a producer with the ABC, and a professional editor, Sydney-born McDonald was responsible for the *Paperback Poets* series of the early 1970s. He has published several novels as well as poetry. '1915' first appeared in *Airship* (1975).

ROBERT GRAY (b. 1945). Gray, born in New South Wales, has worked at various jobs, including poetry reviewing. He has published four volumes of poetry and co-edited (with Geoffrey Lehmann) an anthology, *The Younger Australian Poets* (1983). 'In the early hours . . .' comes from *The Skylight* (1983).

MARK O'CONNOR (b. 1945). Melbourne born and educated, since 1970 O'Connor has identified himself with the Great Barrier Reef and the tropical rainforest of northern Queensland. He has published three collections of poetry, including *The Fiesta of Men* (1983) from which 'Letter from the Barrier Reef' comes.

RHYLL MCMASTER (b. 1947). Brisbane-born McMaster now lives near Canberra. She has published short stories as well as poetry. 'The Journey' comes from her collection, *The Brineshrimp* (1972).

GARY CATALANO (b. 1947). Born in Queensland, educated in Sydney, now resident in Melbourne, Catalano has published works on Australian art as well as two volumes of poetry. 'Australia' first appeared in the *Age Monthly Review* and was chosen by Les A. Murray for inclusion in *The New Oxford Book of Australian Verse* (1986).

PETER KOCAN (b. 1947). Newcastle-born Kocan discovered his talent for writing while in a psychiatric hospital following his conviction for the attempted murder in Sydney of Labor leader, Arthur Calwell, in 1966. He has published two novels and two collections of verse. 'Barbecue' appeared in *Southerly* No. 2 of 1987, and has not yet been collected.

MICHAEL DRANSFIELD (1948–1973). Born in Sydney, Dransfield abandoned his university studies there, and led an unsettled life in various parts of eastern Australia. His early death following a motor-cycle accident and his involvement in the drug subculture have led to his becoming a cult-hero. An extraordinarily prolific poet, he published three volumes of verse during his lifetime, and three further have been posthumously published. 'Like this for Years' come from *Streets of the Long Voyage* (1970).

ALAN WEARNE (b. 1948). A Melbourne poet, Wearne has published a prize-winning verse novel, *The Nightmarkets* (1986), as well as two collections of poetry. 'St Bartholomew Remembers Jesus Christ as an Athlete' comes from *Public Relations* (1972).

KEVIN HART (b. 1954). Born in London, educated at the Australian National University, Hart now lectures at Deakin University. He has published three collections of verse; 'A Dream of France' and 'The Old' come from his first, *The Departure* (1978).

Adam Lindsay Gordon
The Sick Stockrider

Hold hard, Ned! Lift me down once more, and lay me in
    the shade:
Old man, you've had your work cut out to guide
Both horses, and to hold me in the saddle when I sway'd,
All through the hot, slow, sleepy, silent ride.

The dawn at 'Moorabinda' was a mist rack dull and
    dense,
The sunrise was a sullen, sluggish lamp;
I was dozing in the gateway at Arbuthnot's bound'ry
10   fence,
I was dreaming on the Limestone cattle camp.

We crossed the creek at Carricksford, and sharply
    through the haze,
And suddenly, the sun shot flaming forth;
To the southward lay 'Katawa', with the sandpeaks all
    ablaze,
And the flush'd fields of Glen Lomond lay to north.

Now westward winds the bridle path that leads to
    Lindisfarm,
20   And yonder looms the double-headed Bluff;
From the far side of the first hill, when the skies are clear
    and calm,
You can see Sylvester's woolshed fair enough.

Five miles we used to call it from our homestead to the
    place
Where the big tree spans the roadway like an arch;
'Twas here we ran the dingo down that gave us such a
    chase
Eight years ago—or was it nine?—last March.

30   'Twas merry in the glowing morn, among the gleaming
    grass,
To wander as we've wandered many a mile,
And blow the cool tobacco cloud, and watch the white
    wreaths pass,
Sitting loosely in the saddle all the while.

'Twas merry 'mid the blackwoods, when we spied the
    station roofs,

To wheel the wild scrub cattle at the yard,
With a running fire of stockwhips and a fiery run of
40   hoofs;
Oh! the hardest day was never then too hard!

Aye! we had a glorious gallop after 'Starlight' and his
           gang,
When they bolted from Sylvester's on the flat;
How the sun-dried reed-beds crackled, how the
           flint-strewn ranges rang
To the strokes of 'Mountaineer' and 'Acrobat'!

Hard behind them in the timber, harder still across the
           heath,
50   Close beside them through the tea-tree scrub we dashed;
And the golden-tinted fern leaves, how they rustled
           underneath!
And the honeysuckle osiers, how they crash'd!

We led the hunt throughout, Ned, on the chestnut and
           the grey,
And the troopers were three hundred yards behind,
While we emptied our six-shooters on the bushrangers at
           bay,
In the creek with stunted box-tree for a blind!

60   There you grappled with the leader, man to man and
           horse to horse,
And you roll'd together when the chestnut rear'd;
He blazed away and missed you in that shallow
           watercourse—
A narrow shave—his powder singed your beard!

In these hours when life is ebbing, how those days when
           life was young
Come back to us; how clearly I recall
Even the yarns Jack Hall invented, and the songs Jem
70   Roper sung;
And where are now Jem Roper and Jack Hall?

Aye! nearly all our comrades of the old colonial school,
Our ancient boon companions, Ned, are gone;
Hard livers for the most part, somewhat reckless as a
           rule,
It seems that you and I are left alone.

There was Hughes, who got in trouble through that
    business with the cards,
It matters little what became of him;
But a steer ripp'd up MacPherson in the Cooraminta
    yards,
And Sullivan was drown'd at Sink-or-swim.

And Mostyn—poor Frank Mostyn—died at last a fearful
    wreck,
In 'the horrors', at the Upper Wandinong;
And Carisbrooke, the rider, at the Horsefall broke his
    neck—
Faith! the wonder was, he saved his neck so long!

Ah! those days and nights we squandered at the Logans'
    in the glen—
The Logans, man and wife, have long been dead.
Elsie's tallest girl seems taller than your little Elsie then;
And Ethel is a woman grown and wed.

I've had my share of pastime, and I've done my share of
    toil,
And life is short—the longest life a span;
I care not now to tarry for the corn or for the oil,
Or for the wine that maketh glad the heart of man.

For good undone and gifts misspent and resolutions vain,
'Tis somewhat late to trouble. This I know—
I should live the same life over, if I had to live again;
And the chances are I go where most men go.

The deep blue skies wax dusky, and the tall green trees
    grow dim,
The sward beneath me seems to heave and fall;
And sickly, smoky shadows through the sleepy sunlight
    swim,
And on the very sun's face weave their pall.

Let me slumber in the hollow where the wattle blossoms
    wave,
With never stone or rail to fence my bed;
Should the sturdy station children pull the bush flowers
    on my grave,
I may chance to hear them romping overhead.

I don't suppose I shall, though, for I feel like sleeping
    sound.
That sleep they say is doubtful. True; but yet
At least it makes no difference to the dead man
    underground
120   What the living men remember or forget.

Enigmas that perplex us in the world's unequal strife,
The future may ignore or may reveal.
Yet some, as weak as water, Ned! to make the best of life,
Have been, to face the worst, as true as steel.

Ada Cambridge
Vows

Nay, ask me not. I would not dare pretend
    To constant passion and a life-long trust.
    They will desert thee, if indeed they must.
How can we guess what Destiny will send—
Smiles of fair fortune, or black storms to rend
    What even now is shaken by a gust?
    The fire will burn, or it will die in dust.
We cannot tell until the final end.

And never vow was forged that could confine
10   Aught but the body of the thing whereon
Its pledge was stamped. The inner soul divine,
    That thinks of going, is already gone.
When faith and love need bolts upon the door,
Faith is not faith, and love abides no more.

Mary Gilmore
Old Botany Bay

    'I'm old
    Botany Bay;
    Stiff in the joints,
    Little to say.

    I am he
    Who paved the way,

That you might walk
At your ease to-day;

I was the conscript
Sent to hell
To make in the desert
The living well;

I bore the heat,
I blazed the track—
Furrowed and bloody
Upon my back.

I split the rock;
I felled the tree:
The nation was—
Because of me!'

Old Botany Bay
Taking the sun
From day to day ...
Shame on the mouth
That would deny
The knotted hands
That set us high!

Nationality

I have grown past hate and bitterness,
I see the world as one:
Yet, though I can no longer hate,
My son is still my son.

All men at God's round table sit
And all men must be fed;
But this loaf in my hand,
This loaf is my son's bread.

Barcroft Boake
Where the Dead Men Lie

Out on the wastes of the Never Never—
   That's where the dead men lie!
There where the heat-waves dance for ever—
   That's where the dead men lie!
That's where the Earth's loved sons are keeping
Endless tryst: not the west wind sweeping
Feverish pinions can wake their sleeping—
   Out where the dead men lie!

Where brown Summer and Death have mated—
   That's where the dead men lie!
Loving with fiery lust unsated—
   That's where the dead men lie!
Out where the grinning skulls bleach whitely
Under the saltbush sparkling brightly;
Out where the wild dogs chorus nightly—
   That's where the dead men lie!

Deep in the yellow, flowing river—
   That's where the dead men lie!
Under the banks where the shadows quiver—
   That's where the dead men lie!
Where the platypus twists and doubles,
Leaving a train of tiny bubbles;
Rid at last of their earthly troubles—
   That's where the dead men lie!

East and backward pale faces turning—
   That's how the dead men lie!
Gaunt arms stretched with a voiceless yearning—
   That's how the dead men lie!
Oft in the fragrant hush of nooning
Hearing again their mother's crooning,
Wrapt for aye in a dreamful swooning—
   That's how the dead men lie!

Only the hand of Night can free them—
   That's when the dead men fly!
Only the frightened cattle see them—
   See the dead men go by!
Cloven hoofs beating out one measure,
Bidding the stockmen know no leisure—

That's when the dead men take their pleasure!
  That's when the dead men fly!

Ask, too, the never-sleeping drover:
  He sees the dead pass by;
Hearing them call to their friends—the plover,
  Hearing the dead men cry;
Seeing their faces stealing, stealing,
Hearing their laughter, pealing, pealing,
Watching their grey forms wheeling, wheeling
  Round where the cattle lie!

Strangled by thirst and fierce privation—
  That's how the dead men die!
Out on Moneygrub's farthest station—
  That's how the dead men die!
Hard-faced greybeards, youngsters callow;
Some mounds cared for, some left fallow;
Some deep down, yet others shallow;
  Some having but the sky.

Moneygrub, as he sips his claret,
  Looks with complacent eye
Down at his watch-chain, eighteen carat—
  There, in his club, hard by:
Recks not that every link is stamped with
Names of the men whose limbs are cramped with
Too long lying in grave-mould, cramped with
  Death where the dead men lie.

Bernard O'Dowd
Australia

Last sea-thing dredged by sailor Time from Space,
Are you a drift Sargasso, where the West
In halcyon calm rebuilds her fatal nest?
Or Delos of a coming Sun-God's race?
Are you for Light, and trimmed, with oil in place,
Or but a Will o' Wisp on marshy quest?
A new demesne for Mammon to infest?
Or lurks millennial Eden 'neath your face?

The cenotaphs of species dead elsewhere
That in your limits leap and swim and fly,

Or trail uncanny harp-strings from your trees,
Mix omens with the auguries that dare
To plant the Cross upon your forehead sky,
A virgin helpmate Ocean at your knees.

'John O'Brien'
Said Hanrahan

'We'll all be rooned,' said Hanrahan,
 In accents most forlorn,
Outside the church, ere Mass began,
 One frosty Sunday morn.

The congregation stood about,
 Coat-collars to the ears,
And talked of stock, and crops, and drought,
 As it had done for years.

'It's lookin' crook,' said Daniel Croke;
 'Bedad, it's cruke, me lad,
For never since the banks went broke
 Has seasons been so bad.'

'It's dry, all right,' said young O'Neil,
 With which astute remark
He squatted down upon his heel
 And chewed a piece of bark.

And so around the chorus ran
 'It's keepin' dry, no doubt.'
'We'll all be rooned,' said Hanrahan
 'Before the year is out.

'The crops are done; ye'll have your work
 To save one bag of grain;
From here way out to Back-o'-Bourke
 They're singin' out for rain.

'They're singin' out for rain,' he said,
 'And all the tanks are dry.'
The congregation scratched its head,
 And gazed around the sky.

'There won't be grass, in any case,
 Enough to feed an ass;

10

20

30

There's not a blade on Casey's place
    As I came down to Mass.'

'If rain don't come this month,' said Dan,
    And cleared his throat to speak—
'We'll all be rooned,' said Hanrahan,
    'If rain don't come this week.'

A heavy silence seemed to steal
    On all at this remark;
And each man squatted on his heel,
    And chewed a piece of bark.

'We want a inch of rain, we do,'
    O'Neil observed at last;
But Croke "maintained" we wanted two
    To put the danger past.

'If we don't get three inches, man,
    Or four to break this drought,
We'll all be rooned,' said Hanrahan,
    'Before the year is out.'

In God's good time down came the rain;
    And all the afternoon
On iron roof and window-pane
    It drummed a homely tune.

And through the night it pattered still,
    And lightsome, gladsome elves
On dripping spout and window-still
    Kept talking to themselves.

It pelted, pelted all day long,
    A-singing at its work,
Till every heart took up the song
    Way out to Back-o'-Bourke.

And every creek a banker ran,
    And dams filled overtop;
'We'll all be rooned,' said Hanrahan,
    'If this rain doesn't stop.'

And stop it did, in God's good time;
    And spring came in to fold

A mantle o'er the hills sublime
    Of green and pink and gold.

And days went by on dancing feet,
    With harvest-hopes immense,
And laughing eyes beheld the wheat
    Nid-nodding o'er the fence.

And, oh, the smiles on every face,
    As happy lad and lass
Through grass knee-deep on Casey's place
    Went riding down to Mass.

While round the church in clothes genteel
    Discoursed the men of mark,
And each man squatted on his heel,
    And chewed his piece of bark.

'There'll be bush-fires for sure, me man,
    There will, without a doubt;
We'll all be rooned,' said Hanrahan,
    'Before the year is out.'

Dorothea Mackellar
My Country

The love of field and coppice,
    Of green and shaded lanes,
Of ordered woods and gardens
    Is running in your veins;
Strong love of grey-blue distance,
    Brown streams and soft, dim skies—
I know but cannot share it,
    My love is otherwise.

I love a sunburnt country,
    A land of sweeping plains,
Of ragged mountain ranges,
    Of droughts and flooding rains.
I love her far horizons,
    I love her jewel-sea,
Her beauty and her terror—
    The wide brown land for me!

The stark white ring-barked forests,
    All tragic to the moon,
The sapphire-misted mountains,
20   The hot gold hush of noon.
Green tangle of the brushes,
    Where lithe lianas coil,
And orchids deck the tree-tops
    And ferns the warm dark soil.

Core of my heart, my country!
    Her pitiless blue sky,
When sick at heart, around us,
    We see the cattle die—
But then the grey clouds gather,
30   And we can bless again
The drumming of an army,
    The steady, soaking rain.

Core of my heart, my country!
    Land of the Rainbow Gold,
For flood and fire and famine,
    She pays us back threefold;
Over the thirsty paddocks,
    Watch, after many days,
The filmy veil of greenness
40   That thickens as we gaze.

An opal-hearted country,
    A wilful, lavish land—
All you who have not loved her,
    You will not understand—
Though earth holds many splendours,
    Wherever I may die,
I know to what brown country
    My homing thoughts will fly.

Lesbia Harford
Fatherless

I've had no man
To guard and shelter me,
Guide and instruct me
From mine infancy.

No lord of earth
To show me day by day
What things a girl should do
And what she should say.

I have gone free
Of manly excellence
And hold their wisdom
More than half pretence.

For since no male
Has ruled me or has fed,
I think my own thoughts
In my woman's head.

Periodicity

My friend declares
Being woman and virgin she
Takes small account of periodicity.

And she is right.
Her days are calmly spent
For her sex-function is irrelevant.

But I whose life
Is monthly broke in twain
Must seek some sort of meaning in my pain.

Women, I say,
Are beautiful in change
Remote, immortal, like the moon they range.

Or call my pain
A skirmish in the whole
Tremendous conflict between body and soul.

Meaning must lie,
Some beauty surely dwell
In the fierce depths and uttermost pits of hell.

Yet still I seek,
Month after month in vain,
Meaning and beauty in recurrent pain.

'Once I thought my love . . .'

Once I thought my love was worth the name
If tears came.

When the wound is mortal, now I know,
Few tears flow.

R.D. FitzGerald
The Wind at Your Door

(To Mary Gilmore)

My ancestor was called on to go out—
a medical man, and one such must by law
wait in attendance on the pampered knout
and lend his countenance to what he saw,
lest the pet, patting with too bared a claw,
be judged a clumsy pussy. Bitter and hard,
see, as I see him, in that jailhouse yard.

Or see my thought of him: though time may keep
elsewhere tradition or a portrait still,
I would not feel under his cloak of sleep
if beard there or smooth chin, just to fulfil
some canon of precision. Good or ill
his blood's my own; and scratching in his grave
could find me more than I might wish to have.

Let him then be much of the middle style
of height and colouring; let his hair be dark
and his eyes green; and for that slit, the smile
that seemed inhuman, have it cruel and stark,
but grant it could be too the ironic mark
of all caught in the system—who the most,
the doctor or the flesh twined round that post?

There was a high wind blowing on that day;
for one who would not watch, but looked aside,
said that when twice he turned it blew his way
splashes of blood and strips of human hide
shaken out from the lashes that were plied
by one right-handed, one left-handed tough,
sweating at this paid task, and skilled enough.

That wind blows to your door down all these years.
Have you not known it when some breath you drew
tasted of blood? Your comfort is in arrears
of just thanks to a savagery tamed in you
only as subtler fears may serve in lieu
of thong and noose—old savagery which has built
your world and laws out of the lives it spilt.

For what was jailyard widens and takes in
my country. Fifty paces of stamped earth
stretch; and grey walls retreat and grow so thin
that towns show through and clearings—new raw birth
which burst from handcuffs—and free hands go forth
to win tomorrow's harvest from a vast
ploughland—the fifty paces of that past.

But see it through a window barred across,
from cells this side, facing the outer gate
which shuts on freedom, opens on its loss
in a flat wall. Look left now through the grate
at buildings like more walls, roofed with grey slate
or hollowed in the thickness of laid stone
each side the court where the crowd stands this noon.

One there with the officials, thick of build,
not stout, say burly (so this obstinate man
ghosts in the eyes) is he whom enemies killed
(as I was taught) because the monopolist clan
found him a grit in their smooth-turning plan,
too loyally active on behalf of Bligh.
So he got lost; and history passed him by.

But now he buttons his long coat against
the biting gusts, or as a gesture of mind,
habitual; as if to keep him fenced
from stabs of slander sticking him from behind,
sped by the schemers never far to find
in faction, where approval from one source
damns in another clubroom as of course.

This man had Hunter's confidence, King's praise;
and settlers on the starving Hawkesbury banks
recalled through twilight drifting across their days
the doctor's fee of little more than thanks
so often; and how sent by their squeezed ranks

he put their case in London. I find I lack
the hateful paint to daub him wholly black.

Perhaps my life replies to his too much
through veiling generations dropped between.
My weakness here, resentments there, may touch
old motives and explain them, till I lean
to the forgiveness I must hope may clean
my own shortcomings; since no man can live
in his own sight if it will not forgive.

Certainly I must own him whether or not
it be my will. I was made understand
this much when once, marking a freehold lot,
my papers suddenly told me it was land
granted to Martin Mason. I felt his hand
heavily on my shoulder, and knew what coil
binds life to life through bodies, and soul to soil.

There, over to one corner, a bony group
of prisoners waits; and each shall be in turn
tied by his own arms in a human loop
about the post, with his back bared to learn
the price of seeking freedom. So they earn
three hundred rippling stripes apiece, as set
by the law's mathematics against the debt.

These are the Irish batch of Castle Hill,
rebels and mutineers, my countrymen
twice over: first, because of those to till
my birthplace first, hack roads, raise roofs; and then
because their older land time and again
enrolls me through my forbears; and I claim
as origin that threshold whence we came.

One sufferer had my surname, and thereto
'Maurice', which added up to history once;
an ignorant dolt, no doubt, for all that crew
was tenantry. The breed of clod and dunce
makes patriots and true men: could I announce
that Maurice as my kin I say aloud
I'd take his irons as heraldry, and be proud.

Maurice is at the post. Its music lulls,
one hundred lashes done. If backbone shows
then play the tune on buttocks! But feel his pulse;

that's what a doctor's for; and if it goes
110 lamely, then dose it with these purging blows—
which have not made him moan; though, writhing there,
'Let my neck be,' he says, 'and flog me fair.'

One hundred lashes more, then rest the flail.
What says the doctor now? 'This dog won't yelp;
he'll tire you out before you'll see him fail;
here's strength to spare; go on!' Ay, pound to pulp;
yet when you've done he'll walk without your help,
and knock down guards who'd carry him being bid,
and sing no song of where the pikes are hid.

120 It would be well if I could find, removed
through generations back—who knows how far?—
more than a surname's thickness as a proved
bridge with that man's foundations. I need some star
of courage from his firmament, a bar
against surrenders: faith. All trials are less
than rain-blacked wind tells of that old distress.

Yet I can live with Mason. What is told
and what my heart knows of his heart, can sort
much truth from falsehood, much there that I hold
130 good clearly or good clouded by report;
and for things bad, ill grows where ills resort:
they were bad times. None know what in his place
they might have done. I've my own faults to face.

Song in Autumn

Though we have put
white breath to its brief caper
in the early air,
and have known elsewhere
stiff fingers, frost underfoot,
sun thin as paper;

cold then was a lens
focussing sight, and showed that riggers' gear,
the spider's cables,
10 anchored between the immense
steel trusses of built grass. The hills were so near
you could pick up pebbles.

It is different at evening: damp rises
not crisp or definite like frost
but seeping into the blood and brain—
the end of enterprises.
And while, out of many things lost,
courage may remain,

this much is certain
20 from others' experience
and was indeed foretold:
noon's over; the days shorten.
Let there be no pretence;
none here likes the cold.

Ronald McCuaig
Love Me and Never Leave Me

Love me, and never leave me,
Love, nor ever deceive me,
And I shall always bless you
If I may undress you:
  This I heard a lover say
  To his sweetheart where they lay.

He, though he did undress her,
Did not always bless her;
She, though she would not leave him,
10 Often did deceive him;
  Yet they loved, and when they died
  They were buried side by side.

The Passionate Clerk to His Love

Live with me; be my wife;
We'll end flirtations;
You'll find it a slow life,
But with compensations.

And we'll get a flat
Of two witty
Rooms, a bath and kitchenette,
High over the city,

Where, in the evening
When dinner's over,
We'll wash up everything
And I'll be your lover,

And tie knot after knot
Of flesh aching,
Then cut the lot,
And without waking

You'll sleep till sunrise,
And we'll rise early,
And through each other's eyes
We'll see things clearly,

And never be dismayed
To find them shoddy,
And never be afraid
Of anybody;

And on Sunday afternoon
About three or four
I'll play the gramophone
While you pour

Afternoon tea
Into my soul,
And bending to me
With the sugar-bowl

You'll be a priestess
Swaying the sheathing
Of a flower-stained dress
With even breathing,

And in this atmosphere
Charmed from your breast
Half we shall hear
And feel the rest

As we talk scandal and
A kind of wit
We alone understand,
Or maybe just sit

Quiet while the clock chimes
Patient tomorrows,
And smile sometimes
At old sorrows.

Ian Mudie
They'll Tell You About Me

Me, I'm the man that dug the Murray for Sturt to sail
    down,
I am the one that rode beside the man from Snowy River,
and I'm Ned Kelly's surviving brother (or did I marry his
    sister?
I forget which), and it was my thumbnail that wrote that
    Clancy
had gone a–droving, and when wood was scarce I set the
    grass on fire
10   and ran with it three miles to boil my billy, only to find
I'd left the tea and sugar back with my tucker-bag,
and it was me, and only me, that shot through with the
    padre's daughter,
shot through with her on the original Bondi tram.
But it's a lie that I died hanging from a parrot's nest
with my arm in the hollow limb when my horse moved
    from under me;
I never die, I'm like the Leichhardt survivor I discovered
fifty years after the party had disappeared; I never die,
20   I'm Lasseter and Leichhardt both; I joined the wires of the
    O.T.
so that Todd could send the first message from Adelaide to
    Darwin;
I settled everywhere long before the explorers arrived;
my tracks criss-cross the Simpson Desert like city streets,
and I've hung my hat on Poeppel's Peg a thousand times.
It was me who boiled my billy under the coolabah,
told the bloke in the flash car to open his own flamin' gates,
put the goldfields pipe-line through where the experts said
30   nobody could,
wanted to know 'Who's robbing this coach, you or Ned
    Kelly?',
had the dog sit on my tucker-box outside of Gundagai,
yarned with Tom Collins while we fished for a cod
    someone'd caught years before,
and gave Henry Lawson the plots to make his stories from.

Me, I've found a hundred wrecked galleons on the
      Queensland coast,
dripping with doubloons, moidores and golden Inca
40   swords,
and dug a dozen piles of guilders from a Westralian beach;
I was the one that invented the hollow wood-heap,
and I built the Transcontinental, despite heat, dust, death,
      thirst, and flies.
I led the ragged thirteen; I fought at Eureka and Gallipoli
      and Lae;
and I was a day too early (or was it too late?) to discover
      Coolgardie,
lost my original Broken Hill share in a hand of euchre,
50 had the old man kangaroo pinch my coat and wallet,
threw fifty heads in a row in the big game at Kal,
took a paddle-steamer seventy miles out of the Darling on
      a heavy dew,
then tamed a Gippsland bunyip and sooled him on
to capture the Tantanoola Tiger and Fisher's Ghost
and become Billy Hughes's secretary for a couple of
      weeks.
Me, I outshore Jacky Howe, gave Buckley his chance,
and have had more lonely drinks than Jimmy Woods;
60 I jumped across Govett's Leap and wore an overcoat in
      Marble Bar,
seem to remember riding the white bull through the streets
      of Wagga,
sailed a cutter down the Kindur to the Inland Sea,
and never travelled until I went to Moonta.
Me, I was the first man ever to climb to the top of Ayers
      Rock,
pinched one of the Devil's Marbles for the kids to play
      with,
70 drained the mud from the Yarra, sold the Coathanger for a
      gold brick,
and asked for beer off the ice at Innamincka.
Me, yesterday I was rumour,
today I am legend,
tomorrow, history.
If you'd like to know more of me
inquire at the pub at Tennant Creek
or at any drover's camp
or shearing-shed,
80 or shout any bloke in any bar a drink,
or yarn to any bloke asleep on any beach;
they'll tell you about me,

they'll tell you more than I know myself.
After all, they were the ones that created me,
even though I'm bigger than any of them now
—in fact, I'm all of them rolled into one.

For anyone to kill me he'd have to kill
every single Australian,
every single one of them,
90   every single one.

William Hart-Smith
Space

Columbus looks towards the New World,
the sea is flat and nothing breaks the rim
of the world's disc;
he takes the sphere with him.

Day into night the same, the only change
the living variation at the core
of this man's universe;
and silent on the silver ship he broods.

Red gouts of weed, and skimming fish, to crack
10   the stupefying emptiness of sea;
night, and the unimpassioned gaze of stars . . .

And God be praised for the compass, oaths
bawled in the fo'c'sle,
broken heads and wine,
song and guitars,

the tramp of boots,
the wash and whip of brine.

Roland Robinson
Altjeringa

Nude, smooth, and giant-huge,
the torsos of the gums
hold up the vast dark cave
as the great moon comes.

Shock-headed black-boy stands,
with rigid, thrusting spear,
defiant and grotesque
against that glistening sphere.

In clenched, contorted birth
10   black banksias agonise;
out of the ferns and earth,
half-formed, beast-boulders rise;

because The Bush goes back,
back to a time unknown:
chaos that had not word,
nor image carved on stone.

John Blight
A Sailor's Grave

Shall I be buried at sea, or shall my bones wait
till the continents float apart, and at the gate
of my grave I hear the waves grinding
the granite back to sand, and feel the blinding,
stinging salt in the voids where my eyes were once?
I, wearing that white cap, my skull, a dunce,
should read the portents of each feasting tide;
should watch the ravenous currents devour the sand;
and I shall learn high up on a mountainside
10   is no safe place for a grave. What part of land
that has not been the sea bed? Then out to sea
bury me with all sailors, and I shall have
feel of that permanence that befits a grave
with, ever, the wind and wave to moan over me.

Death of a Whale

When the mouse died, there was a sort of pity:
the tiny, delicate creature made for grief.
Yesterday, instead, the dead whale on the reef
drew an excited multitude to the jetty.
How must a whale die to wring a tear?
Lugubrious death of a whale: the big
feast for the gulls and sharks; the tug
of the tide simulating life still there,

until the air, polluted, swings this way
10   like a door ajar from a slaughterhouse.
Pooh! pooh! spare us, give us the death of a mouse
by its tiny hole; not this in our lovely bay.
—Sorry we are, too, when a child dies;
but at the immolation of a race who cries?

Douglas Stewart
Terra Australis

I

Captain Quiros and Mr William Lane,
Sailing some highway shunned by trading traffic
Where in the world's skull like a moonlit brain
Flashing and crinkling rolls the vast Pacific,

Approached each other zigzag, in confusion,
Lane from the west, the Spaniard from the east,
Their flickering canvas breaking the horizon
That shuts the dead off in a wall of mist.

'Three hundred years since I set out from Lima
10   And off Espiritu Santo lay down and wept
Because no faith in men, no truth in islands
And still unfound the shining continent slept;

'And swore upon the Cross to come again
Though fever, thirst and mutiny stalked the seas
And poison spiders spun their webs in Spain,
And did return, and sailed three centuries,

'Staring to see the golden headlands wade
And saw no sun, no land, but this wide circle
Where moonlight clots the waves with coils of weed
20   And hangs like silver moss on sail and tackle,

'Until I thought to trudge till time was done
With all except my purpose run to waste;
And now upon this ocean of the moon,
A shape, a shade, a ship, and from the west!'

II

'What ship?' 'The *Royal Tar!*' 'And whither bent?'
'I seek the new Australia.' 'I, too, stranger;
Terra Australis, the great continent
That I have sought three centuries and longer;

30   'And westward still it lies, God knows how far,
Like a great golden cloud, unknown, untouched,
Where men shall walk at last like spirits of fire
No more by oppression chained, by sin besmirched.'

'Westward there lies a desert where the crow
Feeds upon poor men's hearts and picks their eyes;
Eastward we flee from all that wrath and woe
And Paraguay shall yet be Paradise.'

'Eastward,' said Quiros, as *San Pedro* rolled,
High-pooped and round in the belly like a barrel,
'Men tear each other's entrails out for gold;
40   And even here I find that men will quarrel.'

'If you are Captain Quiros you are dead.'
'The report has reached me; so is William Lane.'
The dark ships rocked together in the weed
And Quiros stroked the beard upon his chin:

'We two have run this ocean through a sieve
And though our death is scarce to be believed
Seagulls and flying-fish were all it gave
And it may be we both have been deceived.'

III

'Alas, alas, I do remember now;
50   In Paradise I built a house of mud
And there were fools who could not milk a cow
And idle men who would not though they could.

'There were two hundred brothers sailed this ocean
To build a New Australia in the east
And trifles of money caused the first commotion
And one small cask of liquor caused the last.

'Some had strange insects bite them, some had lust,
For wifeless men will turn to native women,
Yet who could think a world would fall in dust
And old age dream of smoke and blood and cannon

'Because three men got drunk?' 'With Indian blood
And Spanish hate that jungle reeked to Heaven;
And yet I too came once, or thought I did,
To Terra Australis, my dear western haven,

'And broke my gallows up in scorn of violence,
Gave land and honours, each man had his wish,
Flew saints upon the rigging, played the clarions:
Yet many there were poisoned by a fish

'And more by doubt; and so deserted Torres
And sailed, my seamen's prisoner, back to Spain.'
There was a certain likeness in the stories
And Captain Quiros stared at William Lane.

IV

Then 'Hoist the mainsail!' both the voyagers cried,
Recoiling each from each as from the devil;
'How do we know that we are truly dead
Or that the tales we tell may not be fable?

'Surely I only dreamed that one small bottle
Could blow up New Australia like a bomb?
A mutinous pilot I forebore to throttle
From Terra Australis send me demented home?

'The devil throws me up this Captain Quiros,
This William Lane, a phantom not yet born,
This Captain Quiros dead three hundred years,
To tempt me to disaster for his scorn—

'As if a blast of bony breath could wither
The trees and fountains shining in my mind,
Some traveller's tale, puffed out in moonlit weather,
Divert me from the land that I must find!

'Somewhere on earth that land of love and faith
In Labour's hands—the Virgin's—must exist,
And cannot lie behind, for there is death,
So where but in the west—but in the east?'

At that the sea of light began to dance
And plunged in sparkling brine each giddy brain;
The wind from Heaven blew both ways at once
And west went Captain Quiros, east went Lane.

B Flat

Sing softly, Muse, the Reverend Henry White
Who floats through time as lightly as a feather
Yet left one solitary gleam of light
Because he was the Selborne naturalist's brother

And told him once how on warm summer eves
When moonlight filled all Fyfield to the brim
And yearning owls were hooting to their loves
On church and barn and oak-tree's leafy limb

He took a common half-a-crown pitch-pipe
Such as the masters used for harpsichords
And through the village trod with silent step
Measuring the notes of those melodious birds

And found that each one sang, or rather hooted,
Precisely in the measure of B flat.
And that is all that history has noted;
We know no more of Henry White than that.

So, softly, Muse, in harmony and conformity
Pipe up for him and all such gentle souls
Thus in the world's enormousness, enormity,
So interested in music and in owls;

For though we cannot claim his crumb of knowledge
Was worth much more than virtually nil
Nor hail him for vast enterprise or courage,
Yet in my mind I see him walking still

With eager ear beneath his clerical hat
Through Fyfield village sleeping dark and blind,
Oh surely as he piped his soft B flat
The most harmless, the most innocent of mankind.

Kenneth MacKenzie
The Children Go

The children go.
They go for a year, with delight:
the boy with his cap just so—just right
on his hair that is mine (or is it?), and his brow
that is no one's in this family.
The girl—well, she
has a brow that is mine, I think,
Though the boy has my eyes ... So—
the children go.

10   They are gone now, and now
the whole house settles to sleep
with sigh that changes to a snore,
as though it had nothing to keep any more—
not even the toy worlds smashed and scattered on the floor;
its brisk blood suddenly stilled,
its dear life suddenly cheap, so cheap
that the spiders hidden away
come out and weave up day
to the deadly beauty of a net,

20   quickly—lest they forget
how often and why they have killed
what they have killed.

They are here, and so, too, are we—
parents of the two children, saying
Thank God they always go like that—happily
away from us to their school home
                    but saying
Who are we?
Knowing that in our death was their beginning;
and knowing, with a knowledge that must be borne,
30   that, from the moment they were got and born,
the children go.

They go out like flowers, from the seed to the sun,
having at first not much purpose
until some thing they have done,
some good deed or bad deed,
shows them the way: *before you walk you must run,*
and must fall down. But they pay no heed.

Let us
pretend to love one another
over a strangely silent meal at last
40   after so long: I am the father, you the mother
—or so we say; but the meal is a fast,
and the house is asleep already, the spiders' work half-done
and the children gone.

An Old Inmate

Joe Green Joe Green O how are you doing today?
I'm well, he said, and the bones of his head looked noble.
That night they wheeled Joe Green on a whisper away
but his voice rang on in the ward: I'm a terrible trouble
to all you girls. I make you work for your pay.
If I 'ad my way I'd see that they paid you double.

Joe Green Joe Green for eighty-two years and more
you walked the earth of your grandad's farm down-river
where oranges bigger than suns grow back from the shore
10   in the dark straight groves. Your love for life was a fever
that polished your eye and glowed in your cheek the more
the more you aged and pulsed in your voice for ever.

Joe Green looked down on his worked-out hands with scorn
and tears of age and sickness and pride and wonder
lay on his yellow cheek where the grooves were worn
shallow and straight: but the scorn of his look was tender
like a lover's who hears reproaches meet to be borne
and his voice no more than echoed its outdoor thunder:

Gi' me the good old days and the old-time folk.
20   You don't find that sort now you clever young fellers.
Wireless motorbikes all this American talk
and the pitchers and atom-bombs. O' course it follers
soon you'll forget 'ow to read or think or walk—
and there won't be one o' you sleeps at night on your pillers!

Joe Green Joe Green let us hear what your grandad said
when you were a lad and the oranges not yet planted
on the deep soil where the dark wild children played
the land that Governor King himself had granted
fifteen decades ago that the Green men made
30   a mile-square Eden where nothing that lived there wanted.

Joe Green lay back and smiled at the western sun:
'Fear God and the women, boy,' was his only lesson,
'and love 'em—but on the 'ole just leave 'em alone,
the women specially.' Maybe I didn't listen
all of the time. A man ain't made of stone . . .
But I done my share of praying and fearing and kissing.

No. I 'ad no dad nor mum of me own—
not to remember—but still I'd a good upbringing.
The gran'ma raised thirty-two of us all alone
40   child and grandchild. . . . Somewhere a bell goes ringing.
Steps and the shielded lanterns come and are gone.
The old voice rocks with laughter and tears and singing.

Gi' me the good old days. . . . Joe Green Joe Green
how are you doing tonight? Is it cold work dying?
Not 'alf so cold as some of the frosts I've seen
out Sackville way . . . The voice holds fast defying
sleep and silence, the whisper and the trifold screen
and the futile difficult sounds of his old girl's crying.

John Manifold
The Tomb of Lt. John Learmonth, A.I.F.

'At the end on Crete he took to the hills, and said he'd fight
it out with only a revolver. He was a great soldier.' . . .
            —*One of his men in a letter.*

This is not sorrow, this is work: I build
A cairn of words over a silent man,
My friend John Learmonth whom the Germans killed.

There was no word of hero in his plan;
Verse should have been his love and peace his trade,
But history turned him to a partisan.

Far from the battle as his bones are laid
Crete will remember him. Remember well,
Mountains of Crete, the Second Field Brigade!

10   Say Crete, and there is little more to tell
Of muddle tall as treachery, despair
And black defeat resounding like a bell;

But bring the magnifying focus near
And in contempt of muddle and defeat
The old heroic virtues still appear.

Australian blood where hot and icy meet
(James Hogg and Lermontov were of his kin)
Lie still and fertilise the fields of Crete.

*   *   *

Schoolboy, I watched his ballading begin:
Billy and bullocky and billabong,
Our properties of childhood, all were in.

I heard the air though not the undersong,
The fierceness and resolve; but all the same
They're the tradition, and tradition's strong.

Swagman and bushranger die hard, die game,
Die fighting, like that wild colonial boy—
Jack Dowling, says the ballad, was his name.

He also spun his pistol like a toy,
Turned to the hills like wolf or kangaroo,
And faced destruction with a bitter joy.

His freedom gave him nothing else to do
But set his back against his family tree
And fight the better for the fact he knew

He was as good as dead. Because the sea
Was closed and the air dark and the land lost,
'They'll never capture me alive', said he.

*   *   *

That's courage chemically pure, uncrossed
With sacrifice or duty or career,
Which counts and pays in ready coin the cost

Of holding course, Armies are not its sphere
Where all's contrived to achieve its counterfeit;
It swears with discipline, it's volunteer.

I could as hardly make a moral fit
Around it as around a lightning flash.
There is no moral, that's the point of it,

20

30

40

No moral. But I'm glad of this panache
That sparkles, as from flint, from us and steel,
True to no crown nor presidential sash

Nor flag nor fame. Let others mourn and feel
He died for nothing: nothings have their place.
While thus the kind and civilised conceal

This spring of unsuspected inward grace
And look on death as equals, I am filled
With queer affection for the human race.

Dorothy Auchterlonie
The Tree

He watched them as they walked towards the tree,
Through the green garden when the leaves stood still,
He saw his scarlet fruit hang tremulously:
He whispered, 'Eat it if you will.'

Knowing as yet they had no will but his,
Were as his hand, his foot, his braided hair,
His own face mocked him from his own abyss:
He whispered, 'Eat it if you dare!'

Without him they could neither will nor dare;
Courage and will yet slumbered in the fruit,
Desire forbore, they still were unaware
That doubt was set to feed the root.

God held his breath: If they should miss it now,
Standing within the shadow of the tree....
Always the I, never to know the Thou
Imprisoned in my own eternity.

'Death sits within the fruit, you'll surely die!'
He scarcely formed the words upon a breath;
'O liberating seed! Eat, then, and I
For this release will die your every death.

'Thus time shall be confounded till you come
Full-circle to this garden where we stand,
From the dark maze of knowledge, with the sum
Of good and evil in your hand.

'Then you will shed the journey you have made,
See millenniums fall about your feet,
Behold the light that flares within each blade
Of grass, the visible paraclete.'

The harsh Word stirred the leaves, the fruit glowed red,
30 Adam's foot struck against the root;
He saw his naked doubt and raised his head:
Eve stretched her hand and plucked the fruit.

Harold Stewart
Orpheus and the Wild Beasts

Orpheus startles from the strings
Arpeggios on rising wings
To wake the Muses; then he sings,
And from creative night is born
The shining strophe of the dawn.

The darker passions on the prowl
Like wolves incarnate, cease to howl;
The bearish moods no longer growl;
And wrath, the lion, dare not roar
10 Proud of his discord, as before.

Those ever-rutting goats of lust,
The body's shameless hungers, must
Turn from excesses in disgust;
Nor are the gorging habits loth
To leave behind their stye of sloth.

A flight of chords across the lyre,
A hymn to purify desire:
The instincts as a herd retire,
And round the poet in a ring
20 Lie pacified with listening.

For poetry and music can
Lay on barbarous deeds a ban,
And tame the animals in man;
And then those bestial powers inspire
The lucid measures of the lyre.

Anne Elder
Farmer Goes Berserk

Perhaps she said, lively at first but once
too often in that softly stubborn voice:
'What kind of a country d'ye call this!'—or
'Pity I can't send for a wee drop of rain
from Home'—and that would be Ballachulish
on Loch Lynne (for the nine hundredth time).
Here, water is khaki and each day a battle
with mouths. Seven, born quick as roses but grown
slowly insupportable with their throats
and itches and grizzles. Two farmed out
(a shame, that) and one in a home,
returned maybe for Christmas and Easter
a frightfully quiet stranger. They kept,
just, the four little girls.
                              Would that be enough?
Rain at last, too much; the spuds
to be got in, tractor on the blink, more
work than feasible for one man with fear
waiting in unopened bills and no rest.
No rest ever from her soft worrying tongue
and that ultimate gnawed bone, no rest within
except in the grog (money ill spent) but oh
the beautiful glad spurt of the grog
                              so that he said
'Shut your trap, woman!' Astoundingly.
With the rabbiting gun. And she slumped
open-mouthed all over the bed and then
the four of them, easy! Sleeping easy
in their bright blood *and* the bloody dog
                              and the excitement
of no fear for the crowning achievement
Him Self . . .
                  By Cripes, we can share it
for one day's wonder in the Stop Press, local.
Was he brute or victim, this assassin?
Or were they simply muddlers, no-hopers
who bred and scrapped together?—who eked out
a widowhood from life behind a veil of gums
in a crazy dump with a cracked iron roof
too remote to be even called infamous.
Now in the darkening puddles of their blood,
briefly limelit, they become neighbours.

Did you ever! He went berserk!
                    Unto Everyman,
according to his worth, acclaim for his labours.

Oodgeroo Noonuccal
We Are Going

For Grannie Coolwell

They came in to the little town
A semi-naked band subdued and silent,
All that remained of their tribe.
They came here to the place of their old bora ground
Where now the many white men hurry about like ants.
Notice of estate agent reads: 'Rubbish May Be Tipped
        Here'.
Now it half covers the traces of the old bora ring.
They sit and are confused, they cannot say their thoughts:
'We are as strangers here now, but the white tribe are the
        strangers.
We belong here, we are of the old ways.
We are the corroboree and the bora ground,
We are the old sacred ceremonies, the laws of the elders.
We are the wonder tales of Dream Time, the tribal legends
        told.
We are the past, the hunts and the laughing games, the
        wandering camp fires.
We are the lightning-bolt over Gaphembah Hill
Quick and terrible,
And the Thunder after him, that loud fellow.
We are the quiet daybreak paling the dark lagoon.
We are the shadow-ghosts creeping back as the camp fires
        burn low.
We are nature and the past, all the old ways
Gone now and scattered.
The scrubs are gone, the hunting and the laughter.
The eagle is gone, the emu and the kangaroo are gone from
        this place.
The bora ring is gone.
The corroboree is gone.
And we are going.'

Max Harris
The Tantanoola Tiger

There in the bracken was the ominous spoor mark,
Huge, splayed, deadly, and quiet as breath,
And all around lay bloodied and dying,
Staring dumbly into their several eternities,
The rams that Mr. Morphett loved as sons.

Not only Tantanoola, but at Mount Schanck
The claw welts patterned the saplings
With mysteries terrible as Egypt's demons,
More evil than the blueness of the Lakes,
10   And less than a mile from the homestead, too.

Sheep died more rapidly than the years
Which the tiger ruled in tooth and talk,
And it padded from Beachport to the Border,
While blood streamed down the minds of the folk
Of Mount Gambier, Tantanoola, of Casterton.

Oh this tiger was seen all right, grinning,
Yellow and gleaming with satin stripes:
Its body arched and undulated through the tea-tree;
In this land of dead volcanoes it was a flame,
20   It was a brightness, it was the glory of death,

It was fine, this tiger, a sweet shudder
In the heath and everlastings of the Border,
A roc bird up the ghostly ring-barked gums
Of Mingbool Swamp, a roaring fate
Descending on the mindless backs of grazing things.

Childhoods burned with its burning eyes,
Tantanoola was a magic playground word,
It rushed through young dreams like a river
And it had lovers in Mr. Morphett and Mr. Marks
30   For the ten long hunting unbelieving years.

Troopers and blacks made safari, Africa-fashion,
Pastoral Quixotes swayed on their ambling mounts,
Lost in invisible trails. The red-faced
Young Lindsay Gordons of the Mount
Tormented their heartbeats in the rustling nights

While the tiger grew bigger and clear as an axe.
'A circus once abandoned a tiger cub.'
This was the creed of the hunters and poets.
'A dingo that's got itself too far south'
40   The grey old cynics thundered in their beers,

And blows were swapped and friendships broken,
Beauty burst on a loveless and dreary people,
And their moneyed minds broke into singing
A myth; these soured and tasteless settlers
Were Greeks and Trojans, billabong troubadours,

Plucking their themes at the picnic races
Around the kegs in the flapping canvas booths.
On the waist-coats shark's teeth swung in time,
And old eyes, sharply seamed and squinting,
50   Opened mysteriously in misty musical surprise,

Until the day Jack Heffernan made camp
By a mob of sheep on the far slope of Mt. Schanck
And woke to find the tiger on its haunches,
Bigger than a mountain, love, or imagination,
Grinning lazily down on a dying ewe,

And he drew a bead and shot it through the head.
Look down, oh mourners of history, poets,
Look down on the black and breeding volcanic soil,
Lean on your fork in this potato country,
60   Regard the yellowed fangs and quivering claws

Of a mangy and dying Siberian wolf.
It came as a fable or a natural image
To pace the bars of these sunless minds,
A small and unimpressive common wolf
In desperately poor and cold condition.

It howled to the wattle when it swam ashore
From the wreck of the foundered Helena,
Smelt death and black snakes and tight lips
On every fence-post and slip-rail.
70   It was three foot six from head to tail.

Centuries will die like swatted blowflies
Before word or wolf will work a tremor
Of tenderness in the crusty knuckles
Around the glasses in the Tantanoola pub
Where its red bead eyes now stare towards the sun.

Dimitris Tsaloumas
Autumn Supper

Only this table by the draughty window
bare since the beginning of time:

a knife, black olives, a hunk of bread.
The bottle glows dark in the late

autumn light, and in the glass,
against the wind and the raging seas,

the one rose of the difficult year.
All my life long I've hankered

after simplicity. When night falls
don't come to light the candles and pour

the wine. There's not enough for two;
I cannot share my hunger.

Dorothy Hewett
Anniversary

Death is in the air—

today is the anniversary of his death in October
(he would have been thirty-one)
I went home to High Street
& couldn't feed the new baby
my milk had dried up
so I sat holding him numbly
looking for the soft spot on the top of his head
while they fed me three more librium
you're only crying for yourself he said
but I kept on saying *It's the waste I can't bear.*

All that winter we lived
in the longest street in the world
he used to walk to work in the dark
on the opposite side of the street
somebody always walked with him but they never met

he could only hear the boots
& when he stopped they stopped.

The new baby swayed in a canvas cot lacing his fingers
I worried in case he got curvature of the spine
Truby King said a baby needed firm support
he was a very big bright baby
the cleaner at the Queen Vic. said every morning
you mark my words that kid's been here before.

The house was bare & cold with a false gable
we had no furniture only a double mattress
on the floor a big table & two deal chairs
every morning I dressed the baby in a shrunken jacket
& caught the bus home to my mother's to nurse the child
who was dying the house had bay windows
hidden under fir trees smothered in yellow roses
the child sat dwarfed at the end of the polished table
pale as death in the light of his four candles
singing *Little Boy Blue.*

I pushed the pram to the telephone box
I'm losing my milk I told her *I want to bring him
home to die Home* she said *you left
home a long time ago to go with that man.*

I pushed them both through the park
over the dropped leaves (his legs were crippled)
a magpie swooped down black out of the sky
& pecked his forehead a drop of blood splashed on
his wrist   he started to cry

It took five months & everybody was angry
because the new baby was alive & cried for attention
pollen sprinkled his cheeks under the yellow roses.

When he died it was like everybody else
in the public ward with the screens around him
the big bruises spreading on his skin
his hand came up out of the sheets *don't cry*
he said *don't be sad*

I sat there overweight in my Woolworth's dress
not telling anybody in case they kept him alive
with another transfusion—

Afterwards I sat by the gas fire
in my old dressing gown turning over the photographs
wondering why I'd drunk all that stout
& massaged my breasts every morning to be
        a good mother.

R.A. Simpson
Captain Oates, 1912

Each sentence and each pause grew black.
Men hunched like snow against the night.
He rose, inferred that he'd be back,

Then walked toward the reasoned white
That was his last reply. And what
Would I have done? Consider light

Within my window, ease and wit
To keep this room just warm with flame:
I think I would have waited, sat

10   Until the storm defaced my name.
But heroes make men think of them,
Defy the snow we cannot blame.

Yet left upon a cliff, a rim,
I do not know what mouthless voice
Would speak in me. Though white and grim,

Oblivion becomes a choice
When blizzards blow across the mind,
And heroes, cowards wait for peace,

For miracles as days grow blind.
20   So lovers turn, compelled, afraid,
Like every creature that's profound,
And dread the death that they have made.

Ethel

She stood, arm raised, beside the table,
And quickly metronomed the flies away
Though children said, 'There are no flies.'

My mother's sister, Ethel, married young,
Lived in a corrugated silence
Of tin until the desert supplanted reason;
And she came home. Children were exiled
Lest we frighten her, or be afraid.

10 The finest secret we had as children
Was Ethel, and in darkest rooms
We could intone her name to friends at last:
'Tomorrow they'll take her away
And put a lid on all those madder flies.'

Tomorrow came. Children were banished.
I think of passageways in pyramids
Where the dead walk as if alive.

David Lake
To Horace

'How sweet and fit, for fatherland to die—'
Your bland official voice,
Horace, charms half-truth to a double lie
That still bemuses boys.

It's not (to start with) pure self-sacrifice
That's laid down in the drill:
In Father Caesar's service that's a vice—
True Virtue means to kill.

And, come to that, it's never sweet to fall
With metal in your guts:
It smells, and hurts—sweeter far from it all
To tumble girls in huts;

For fathering the country, fitter too,
Since Nature made that wound

And tooled the weapon fittingly, as you,
Friend Horace, must have found

After you dropped all causes with your shield
And sensibly kept warm
With loyal odes far from Philippi's field
On your snug Sabine farm

Where you sincerely celebrated wine,
Love, fireside—as to war,
You praised the patriotic death divine
And broached another jar.

Philip Martin
Reading the Lines

She reads my palm. 'You've got the Writer's Fork.'
So Fate made me a poet! 'No,' she answers,
'It may have been your will that drew the sign.'
At any rate it's there. The Writer's Fork.

'And now,' she says, 'let's see if you're to die
In a Foreign Country. Oh, the lines aren't clear.'
Another sign? Australia gave me flesh,
Europe runs in my veins from childhood on.
Which is my own, which is the Foreign Country?

Christmas Ghosts

This first Australian Christmas
You welcome me, and yet my northern blood
Is troubled: where are the ghosts?

Centuries before Christ
My Danish ancestors buried their dead
In the house floor. No separation. So

My English family still expect their ghosts.
Kindly all, they step in from the cold,
Sit down with us at table.

Even the earliest dead may brush a sleeve.
At vision's edge, all lift a fork, a glass,
Their eyes glint in the firelight.

In your country I find
All ghosts are laid. And too few places laid.
Bring in your dead.

Vivian Smith
Deathbed Sketch

For an unnamed portrait, signed

At last a page is turning. Change of scene.
That once young poet's power's failing fast
and I must jot down quickly what occurred
before his name's a footnote in the past.

His first book made him known to a small band;
it passed in the antipodes for Art,
with verses full of God and sex and wars.
It proved he had no ear and far less heart.

And yet it was encouraged as things go:
the sturdy thinness of our cultural scene
makes anything that's literate appear
a contribution to the might-have-been

which still defines our future and our past.
But let's attack the few who really matter—
those without talent, art's sly parasites,
these we caress, cajole, and slowly flatter.

The early ideal, the true poet's vision,
the search to find a language and a voice
was hardly his to lapse from or regret;

a certain cunning had defined his choice.

Art itself, Art as he understood it,
Art was a way to conquer and impress;
he'd long known that his favourite type of woman
enjoyed an artist's hand beneath her dress . . .

And men too showed an interest in his skills.
One said, 'I just love everything he writes',
but later he confessed he most preferred
the fluent figure in its swimming tights.

In time our poet found his public role;
opinion-making offers sure returns
as those who trade in reputations find—
theirs is the first the careless goddess spurns.

Appeared as poet-critic on TV:
'Poets are good at stirring others up.'
Increasing dangers of complacency
followed by *Comments on the Melbourne Cup*.

He stood amazed to see his small part growing,
an invitation here, addresses there;
'When all I want is to be with the Muse
my social conscience leads me to despair'—

It was a way to keep conviction flowing,
though like the most successful he'd soon learned
contempt for others and their slow goodwill:
a certain arrogance is never spurned.

He always found the crowd that needed him
to tell them what to think, to set their fashion
in Art and comment: 'The whole country needs
my kind of person's tragic sense of mission.'

He kept his name in print with book reviews,
his verse appeared in his own magazine:
'It gives a wider vista to my views.
Here in a land where Judith Wright is queen

of lady poets and poor Alec Hope
has let the team down badly with his verse,
I must turn critic, speak aloud the truth.
Without my voice things would be even worse.'

He chose publicity. He chose display.
Rage for success at all costs drove him on;
but like a dancer who's outlived his prime,
knew he could now be neither prince nor swan

30

40

50

60

nor merely someone watching from the wings.
'I can't keep up as every writer must . . .
Torn between TV and my Lit Fund Lectures,
why poetry—it's just—a sort of lust.'

'I'll never write again,' he used to smile,
'This country's done my talent too much harm';
and saw within the mirror how the leaks
were slowly spreading through his schoolboy charm.

And yet from time to time a verse appeared
70   saying how big men are compared with birds;
and these were one day gathered in a second
book that was merely ideas set to words.

Of course we all agreed we would be kind,
haunted by our own sense of deeper failure.
It's human not to keep your standards high.
We need his type of person in Australia.

Twenty Years of Sydney

It's twenty years of Sydney to the month
I came here first out of my fog-bound south
to frangipani trees in old backyards,
and late at night the moon distorting palms.

Even then the Cross was crumby, out of touch.
I was too timid for Bohemia as a style
or living long in rooms in dark Rose Bay hotels.
All one night a storm flogged herds of Moreton Bays,
for days the esplanade was stuck with purple figs.
10   The flying boat circled for hours and couldn't land.

That was the week I met Slessor alone
walking down Phillip Street smoking his cigar,
his pink scrubbed skin never touched by the sun.
Fastidious, bow tie, he smiled like the Cheshire cat:
'If you change your city you are sure to change your style.'
A kind man, he always praised the young.

Jennifer Strauss
Migrant Woman
on a Melbourne Tram

Impossibly black
Amid the impudence of summer thighs
Long arms and painted toenails
And the voices
Impossibly obscure
She hunches sweltering
Twists in sweating hands
A scrap of paper—address, destination,
Clue to the labyrinth
10 Where voices not understood
Echo
Confusing directions.

(There was a time
They sent them out of Greece
In black-sailed ships
To feed the minotaur.
Whose is the blind beast now
Laired in Collingwood,
Abbotsford, Richmond,
20 Eating up men?)

Street-names in the glare
Leap ungraspably from sight
Formless collisions of letters
Impossibly dark
She is forlorn in foreign words and voices,
Remembering a village
Where poverty was white as bone
And the great silences of sea and sky
Parted at dusk for voices coming home
30 Calling names
Impossibly departed.

Fay Zwicky
Kaddish

For My Father
Born 1903, Died at Sea, 1967

Lord of the divided, heal!

Father, old ocean's skull making storm calm and the
    waves to sleep,
Visits his first-born, humming in dreams, hiding the
    pearls that were
Behind *Argus*, defunct Melbourne rag. The wireless
    shouts declarations of

War. 'Father,' says the first-born first time around (and
    nine years dead),
10   Weeping incurable for all his hidden skills. His country's
    Medical Journal
Laid him out amid Sigmoid Volvulus, Light on Gastric
    Problems, Health Services

For Young Children Yesterday Today and Tomorrow
    which is now and now and now and
Never spoke his name which is Father a war having
    happened between her birth, his
Death: Yisborach, v'yistabach, v'yispoar, v'yisroman,
    v'yisnaseh—Hitler is

20   Dead. The Japanese are different. Let us talk of now. The
    war is ended.
Strangers found you first. Bearing love back, your
    first-born bears their praise
Into the sun-filled room, hospitals you tended, city roofs
    and yards, ethereal rumours.

Gray's Inn Road, Golden Square, St. George's,
    Birmingham, Vienna's General, the

Ancient Alfred in Commercial Road where, tearing paper
in controlled strips, your
First-born waited restless and autistic, shredding life,
lives, ours. 'Have to

See a patient. Wait for me,' healing knife ready as the
first-born, girt to kill,
Waited, echoes of letters from Darwin, Borneo, Moratai,
Brunei ('We thought him
Dead but the little Jap sat up with gun in hand and took a
shot at us',) the heat

A pressing fist, swamps, insect life ('A wonderful war'
said his wife who also
Waited) but wait for me wait understand O wait between
the lines unread.
Your first-born did not. Tested instead the knife's
weight.   *   *   *

Let in the strangers first: 'Apart from his high degree of
medical skill he
Possessed warmth' (enough to make broken grass live?
rock burst into flower?
Then why was your first-born cold?) But listen again: 'It
was impossible for

Him to be rude, rough, abrupt.' Shy virgin bearing gifts
to the proud first and
Only born wife, black virgin mother. Night must have
come terrible to such a
Kingdom. All lampless creatures sighing in their beds,
stones wailing as the

Mated flew apart in sorrow. Near, apart, fluttered, fell
apart as feathered
Hopes trembled to earth shaken from the boughs of
heaven. By day the heart
Was silent, shook in its box of bone, alone fathered three
black dancing imps,

The wicked, the wise and the simple to jump in the house
that Jack built: This

Is the priest all shaven and shorn who married the man all
    tattered and torn
Who kissed the maiden all forlorn who slaughtered the ox
    who drank the water

Who put out the fire who burnt the staff who smote the
    dog who bit the cat who
70   Ate the kid my father bought from the angel of death:
    'Never heard to complain,
Response to inquiry about his health invariably brought a
    retort causing laughter.'

Laughter in the shadow of the fountain, laughter in the
    dying fire, laughter
Shaking in the box of bone, laughter fastened in the silent
    night, laughter
While the children danced from room to room in the
    empty air.

80   What ailed the sea that it fled? What ailed the mountains,
    the romping lambs
Bought with blood? Tremble, earth, before the Lord of
    the Crow and the Dove
Who turned flint into fountain, created the fruit of the
    vine devoured by the

Fox who bit the dog that worried the cat that killed the
    rat that ate up Jack
Who built the house: Yisgaddal v'yiskaddash sh'meh
    rabbo—miracle of seed,
90   Mystery of rain, the ripening sun and the failing flesh,
    courses of stars,

Stress from Sinai:

Let (roared God)

    Great big Babylon
    Be eaten up by Persia
    Be eaten up by Greece
    Be eaten up by Rome
    Be eaten up by Ottoman
    Be eaten up by Edom
100   Be eaten by Australia
    Where Jack's house shook.

Be (said Jack's Dad)

Submissive to an elder
Courteous to the young
Receive all men with
Cheerfulness and
Hold your tongue.

Strangers, remember Jack who did as he was told.

*   *   *

To the goddess the blood of all creatures is due for she
110 gave it,
Temple and slaughterhouse, maker of curses like
  worm-eaten peas:

As the thunder vanishes, so shall the woman drive them
  away
As wax melts before flame, so let the ungodly perish
  before her:

She is mother of thunder, mother of trees, mother of
  lakes,
Secret springs, gate to the underworld, vessel of
120 darkness,

Bearer, transformer, dark nourisher, shelterer, container
  of
Living and dead, coffin of Osiris, dark-egg devourer,
  engenderer,

Nurturer, nurse of the world, many-armed goddess
  girdled by cobras,
Flame-spewer, tiger-tongued queen of the dead and the
  violent dancers.

Mother of songs, dancer of granite, giver of stone—
130 Let his wife speak:

'Honour thy father and thy mother'
So have I done and done and done—no marriage shall
  ever

Consume the black maidenhead—my parents are heaven
Bound. I shall rejoin them;

Bodies of men shall rejoin severed souls
At the ultimate blast of invisible grace.

Below, I burn,
Naomi of the long brown hair, skull in a Juliet cap.

140   Do the dead rot? Then rot as I rot as they rot.
'Honour thy Father' sing Armistice bells, *espressivo*.

The stumbling fingers are groping
To pitch of perfection.

I am that pitch
I am that perfection.

Papa's a civilian again, mother is coiled in a corset,
Dispenses perfection with:

Castor oil
Tapestry
150   Tablecloths (white)
Rectal thermometers
Czerny and prunes
Sonatinas of Hummel
The white meat of chicken
The white meat of fish
The maids and the lost silver.

Lord, I am good for nothing, shall never know want.
Blinded, I burn, am led not into temptation.

The home is the centre of power.
160   There I reign
Childless. Three daughters, all whores, all—

Should be devoured by the fires of Gehenna
Should be dissolved in the womb that bore tham
Should wander the wastelands forever.

Instead, they dance.

Whole towns condemn me. Flames from the roofs
Form my father's fiery image. He waves, laughs,

Cools his head among stars, leaves me shorn,
Without sons, unsanctified, biting on

170   Bread of affliction. Naked, I burn,
Orphaned again in a war.

The world is a different oyster:
Mine.

His defection will not be forgotten.

                    *   *   *

Blessed be He whose law speaks of the three different
        characters of children whom
we are to instruct on this occasion:

        What says the wicked one?

'What do you all mean by this?'
180   This thou shalt ask not, and thou hast transgressed, using
        you and excluding thyself.

Thou shalt not exclude thyself from:

The collective body of the family
The collective body of the race
The collective body of the nation

Therefore repeat after me:

'This is done because of what the Eternal did
For me when I came forth from Egypt.'

The wicked wants always the last word (for all the good
190   It does): 'Had I been there, I would still not be worth

My redemption.' Nothing more may be eaten, a beating
        will
Take place in the laundry. Naked.

'Honour thy father and thy mother'

        What says the wise one?

'The testimonies, statutes, the judgments delivered by
	God
I accept.'

Nonetheless, though thou are wise,
200	After the paschal offering there shall be no dessert.

'Honour thy father and thy mother'

What says the simple one?

Asks merely: 'What is this?'
Is told: 'With might of hand

Did our God bring us forth out of Egypt
From the mansion of bondage.'

Any more questions? Ask away and be damned.

'Honour thy father and thy mother'

*	*	*

Yisborach, v'yistabach, v'yispoar, v'yisroman,
210	v'yisnaseh, v'yishaddor,
v'yisalleh, v'yishallol, sh'meh d'kudsho, b'rich hu

Praise death who is our God
Live for death who is our God
Die for death who is our God
Blessed be your failure which is our God

Oseh sholom bim'romov, hu yaaseh sholom, olenu v'al
	kol yisroel, v'imru Omen.

*	*	*

And he who was never born and cannot inquire shall say:

There is a time to speak
220	and a time to be silent
There is a time to forgive
and a time in which to be
Forgiven.
After forgiveness,

Silence.

Chris Wallace-Crabbe
Melbourne

Not on the ocean, on a muted bay
Where the broad rays drift slowly over mud
And flathead loll on sand, a city bloats
Between the plains of water and of loam.
If surf beats, it is faint and far away;
If slogans blow around, we stay at home.

And, like the bay, our blood flows easily,
Not warm, not cold (in all things moderate),
Following our familiar tides. Elsewhere
Victims are bleeding, sun is beating down
On patriot, guerrilla, refugee.
We see the newsreels when we dine in town.

Ideas are grown in other gardens while
This chocolate soil throws up its harvest of
Imported and deciduous platitudes,
None of them flowering boldly or for long;
And we, the gardeners, securely smile
Humming a bar or two of rusty song.

Old tunes are good enough if sing we must;
Old images, re-vamped *ad nauseam*,
Will sate the burgher's eye and keep him quiet
As the great wheels run on, and should he seek
Variety, there's wind, there's heat, there's frost
To feed his conversation all the week.

Highway by highway the remorseless cars
Strangle the city, put it out of pain,
Its limbs still kicking feebly on the hills.
Nobody cares. The artists sail at dawn
For brisker ports, or rot in public bars.
Though much has died here, little has been born.

David Malouf
Suburban

Safe behind shady carports, sleeping under
the stars of the commonwealth and nylon gauze . . .

Asia is far off, its sheer white mountain-peaks, its millions
of hands; and shy bush-creatures in our headlamps

prop and swerve, small grass under the sprinklers
dreams itself ten feet tall as bull-ants lumber

between its stems—pushing
towards Sunday morning and the motor-blades . . .

Safe behind lawns and blondwood doors, in houses
10   of glass. No one throws stones. The moon dredges

a window square. Chrome faucets in the bathroom
hold back the tadpole-life that swarms in dams, a
        Kelvinator

preserves us from hook-worm. But there are days,
after drinks at the Marina, when dull headaches

like harbour fog roll in, black cats give off
blackness, children writhe out of our grip;

and only the cotton-wool in medicine-bottles stands
        between us
20   and the capsules whose cool metallic colours

lift us to the stars. In sleep we drift
barefoot to the edge of town, pale moondust flares
        between our toes,

ghosts on a rotary-hoist fly in the wind . . .
under cold white snow-peaks tucked to the chin, we stare

at an empty shoe like Monday . . .
Sunlight arranges itself beyond our hands.

Antigone Kefala
Freedom Fighter

A freedom fighter, she said
lighting the gas stove.
In the mountains we fought
great days . . .
the words stubborn
weary in the shabby kitchen
with the yellowed fridge
and the tinted photograph
of the dead husband.
10   The house full of morose
rooms suffocated with rugs.

We came out on the low verandah
her heavy stockings pitch black
the rough spun dress the
indigo blue of some wild flower
the Sunday neighbourhood still asleep.
Come again, she said indifferently
watching the windy street
and the Town Hall squatting
20   on its elephant legs,
come again.

Randolph Stow
The Utopia of Lord Mayor Howard

'Lord Mayor Howard . . . said that the
trees on the corner had grown so tall
that they had lost their attraction.
Neat rose gardens would be much more
attractive.' *The West Australian.*

His delicate fingers, moving among the roses,
became a symbol. His words, a battle-cry.
'Nothing shall be taller than Lord Mayor Howard
but insurance buildings.'

A fanatical army, wild with Cromwellian zeal,
laid waste Kings Park, denuded Darlington.
Guerillas of Pemberton fried alive in their forests,
as mile on mile, that the giant unattractive karri
had once encumbered, fell thrall to triumphant Peace.

10   And not Peace alone, but also Dame Edith Helen,
Comtesse Vandal, and even a brand new strain:
Mrs Lord Mayor Howard.

Only you and I, my subversive and admirable brethren,
did not join in the celebrations. A malicious rumour
that some of us had been seen to spit on roses
obliged us to fly the land.

On Kerguelen, New Amsterdam and such friendly islands
pitching our tents, and on each one planting one karri,
under the name of Yggdrasil we worshipped them.
20   —Tenderly, humbly, as became the last plants on earth
that were taller than Lord Mayor Howard.

And although the news of our ruthless persecution
of every breed of rose caused shudders in Guildford,
and although our faith, known as anti-Rosaceanism,
was condemned in the United Nations and *The Times*,

the remembrance of our trees so sighs in their sleep
that the immigrants have been more than we can handle.
And in truth, we half expect to see Lord Mayor Howard.

The Singing Bones

Out there, beyond the boundary fence, beyond
the scrub-dark flat horizon that the crows
returned from, evenings, days of rusty wind
raised from the bones a stiff lament, whose sound
netted my childhood round, and even here still blows.

My country's heart is ash in the market-place,
is aftermath of martyrdom. Out there

its sand-enshrined lay saints lie piece by piece,
Leichhardt by Gibson, stealing the wind's voice,
10   and Lawson's tramps, by choice made mummia and air.

No pilgrims leave, no holy-days are kept
for these who died of landscape. Who can find,
even, the camp-sites where the saints last slept?
Out there their place is, where the charts are gapped,
unreachable, unmapped, and mainly in the mind.

They were all poets, so the poets said,
who kept their end in mind in all they wrote
and hymned their bones, and joined them. Gordon died
happy, one surf-loud dawn, shot through the head,
20   and Boake astonished, dead, his stockwhip round his throat.

Time, time and time again, when the inland wind
beats over myall from the dunes, I hear
the singing bones, their glum Victorian strain.
A ritual manliness, embracing pain
to know; to taste terrain their heirs need not draw near.

Judith Rodriguez
Eskimo Occasion

I am in my Eskimo-hunting-song mood,
Aha!
The lawn is tundra   the car will not start
the sunlight is an avalanche   we are avalanche-struck at our
      breakfast
struck with sunlight through glass   me and my spoonfed
      daughters
out of this world in our kitchen.

I will sing the song of my daughter-hunting,
10   Oho!
The waves lay down   the ice grew strong
I sang the song   of dark water under ice
the song of winter fishing   the magic for seal rising
among the ancestor-masks.

I waited by water to dream new spirits,
Hoo!

The water spoke   the ice shouted
the sea opened   the sun made young shadows
they breathed my breathing   I took them from deep water
20   I brought them fur-warmed home.

I am dancing the years of the two great hunts,
Ya-hay!
It was I who waited   cold in the wind-break
I stamp like the bear   I call like the wind of the thaw
I leap like the sea spring-running.   My sunstruck daughters
        splutter
and chuckle and bang their spoons:

Mummy is singing at breakfast and dancing!
So big!

Mudrooroo Narogin
Under an Aboriginal Tree

Under an Aboriginal tree,
Scrawny and willowy
Just like me, naturally,
I thought—
Where do those thick fellows come from?

Next to a kangaroo—
Ever tried getting close
To one of those fellows?—
You have to look like a brother,
10   I thought:
This one'll taste good in the cooking pot.

Next to my white brother—
I thought: Brother?
Got legs and arms
And things like that—
Been out of the sun though—
And my brother turned to me,
Said: 'You want Australia.'
And I said: 'Right on, Jack,'
20   And walked away.
If they think like that,
We'll take back Australia,
And send 'em all back home.

Geoffrey Lehmann
Five Days Late

Late, five days late. At night in sleep they fumble
To feel the cool gold ring which is not there,
The space beside them which is sometimes man,
The single girls who laughed and ran from Daddy.
The wind-chimes stir. From their high rented rooms
The city is a wave of black stars breaking
In violet abysses, clouds of gasoline.
Pads of rouge, scent bottles, eyelash brushes
Are mummified in the dressing table mirror.
10   They travel nightmare elevators up
And down with flimsy shift fanned by ozone,
In an empty building, buttons pressed by no one.
Memories of kisses hang around their necks
Like stones, dolls fall from burning aeroplanes,
And ghosts of children crawl in moonlit playpens,
Clamber and strain for milk from dormant breasts,
Breasts which have never existed, dangling playthings
Craving the press of life, the tug of lips,
Anguished wombs twisting, curving to be filled
20   With Baby and his big blind head of bread,
The bawling nightmare spilling porridge on floors,
The handful of tears blowing a paper trumpet,
The bib daubed with chocolate kissing the stars goodbye.
In rented rooms the coffee cups are cold,
And single girls toss in their night of doubt.
When morning wakes with blood, they weep, are safe.

Andrew Taylor
Developing a Wife

In the one cool room in the house
he held her face two inches under the water
rocking it ever so gently
ever so gently. Her smile
of two hours earlier came back to him
dimly at first through the water, then with more
boldness and more clarity.
The world is too much with us

on a hot day (he thought); better
10 this kind of drowning into a new degree,
a fraction of a second infinitely
protracted into purity. Her smile
free now of chemical and the perverse
alchemy of heat dust and destroying wind
free from the irritation, the tears
and the anger that had finally driven him
down to this moment,
was perfect, was
irreversible, a new reality.
20 Is it, he thought, that there is truth
here which she imperfectly embodies?
Or is it I that I'm developing here—
my dream, my vision of her,
my sleight of hand?
Perhaps, he thought, our marriage is like this?—
flimsy, unreal, but in its own way real:
a moment, a perfection glimpsed, then gone, gone
        utterly,
yet caught all the same, our axis, stationary,
30 the other side of drowning?
                                He bore
her smile out in the heat to her, as a gift.

Geoff Page
Smalltown Memorials

No matter how small
Every town has one;
Maybe just the obelisk,
A few names inlaid;
More often full-scale granite,
Marble digger (arms reversed),
Long descending lists of dead:
Sometimes not even a town,
A thickening of houses
10 Or a few unlikely trees
Glimpsed on a back road
Will have one.

1919, 1920:
All over the country;
Maybe a band, slow march;
Mayors, shire councils;
Relatives for whom
Print was already
Only print; mates,
20   Come back, moving
Into unexpected days;

A ring of Fords and sulkies;
The toned-down bit
Of Billy Hughes from an
Ex-recruiting sergeant.
Unveiled;
Then seen each day—
Noticed once a year;
And then not always,
30   Everywhere.

The next bequeathed us
Parks and pools

But something in that first
Demanded stone.

Kate Llewellyn
Eve

Let's face it
Eden was a bore
nothing to do
but walk naked in the sun
make love
and talk
but no one had any problems
to speak of
nothing to read
10   a swim
or lunch might seem special
even afternoon tea wasn't invented
nor wine

a nap might be a highlight
no radio
perhaps they sang a bit
but as yet no one had made up
many songs

and after the honeymoon
wouldn't they be bored
walking and talking

with never a worry in the world
they didn't need to invent an atom
or prove the existence of God
no it had to end
Eve showed she was the bright one
bored witless by Adam
no work
and eternal bliss
she saw her chance
they say the snake tempted her to it
don't believe it
she bit because she hungered
to know
the clever thing
she wasn't kicked out
she walked out

Roger McDonald
1915

Up they go, yawning,
the crack of knuckles dropped
to smooth the heaving
in their legs, while some,
ashamed, split bile
between their teeth,
and hum to drown their stomachs.

Others touch their lips
on splintered wood
to reach for home—
'a bloke's a mug'

thinks one (who sees
a ringbarked hill)
another hisses drily
(leaping burrs).

All dreaming,
when the whistle
splits the pea, as up
they scramble, pockets fat
20   with Champion Flake
in battered tins,
and letters wadded thick
from Mum (who says
'always keep
some warm clothes on . . .')

Up from slits in dirt
they rise, and here they stop.
A cold long light swings over.

Hard like ice
30   it cracks their shins—
they feel a drill and mallet
climb their bones, then cold
then warmth as blood spills out from pockets,
chests, and mouths.
No mother comes to help, although
a metal voice is whining
'boys, relax', as one
by one they totter to their knees.

Robert Gray
'In the early hours . . .'

In the early hours, I have come out to lean in the empty
corridor of the train, as it's crashing and lurching through the
night.
    A liquified dark scrub. And those paddocks where
silverish-grey mist is rising, slowly as a stirred moon dust.
    The orange moon, like a basketball fumbled over waste
ground, is bouncing among the tops of a dark forest.
    In the frosty, thick night a single farmhouse light floats
wetly as a flare.

10   I have lain awake in such a bed, and it has seemed to me,
also, it would be sufficient to be one of those carried within
this wind-borne sound . . .

      (And I can remember, too, the Mail train: a fine chain of
lights as I stood in the paddocks of a wintry dusk. Its sound
was that of wind through the swamp oaks.)

Mark O'Connor
Letter from the Barrier Reef

Here, by this shore of the Pacific ocean
I think of that less-coralled sea,
the wine-dark midland lake of Homer's skiffs,
that *mare nostrum* where our verse began
and poets return.

The wonder is that Shakespeare never travelled,
for England's verse has never stayed at home;
and if her wealth was borrowed from the East,
almost as much, her soul was nourished by the Fleet.

10   Wordsworth and Coleridge, it is true,
though travelled far, might seem to probe the rule.
But Keats and Byron sought the sun. Their
tongue was English, but the South was home.
They went abroad to live and feel and write
in that perspicuous Southern light
which Shelley found in the 'intenser day'
round marble mansions drowned in Baiae's bay.

Browning might pen his *Home Thoughts from Abroad*
but Italy was where his spirit soared.
20   And so from Milton on to Pound
the universal exodus is found.

Lines penned in furious exaltation
and some more frankly 'In Dejection'.
Strange scrappy chattings with the Muse
(who having in those parts seen better days
was glad to thrill the young with classic lays)
mixed with sombre reflections on the news

or detailed comments on friends' views.
Ephemeral stuff, but from a brighter world
whose flag might soon be everywhere unfurled.

And when they died, schoolmasters took their rhymes,
re-graded them and dated them like wines;
then taught the young to praise that verbal skill
which only a distant climate could fulfill.

Rhyll McMaster
The Journey

The ground mist moves towards us
in silent puffs
rearing at the headlights
grabbing each way at the windshield.

On each side a field
stands in the wings
waiting like an actor for his cue.
(I knew
those stone-pretending toads wouldn't play chicken
with our rolling, squashing wheels.)
The road seems to quicken its threading race beneath us.
We do not move in our softly roaring bubble.
The stagehands prove
how clever they are at shifting scenery;
though lulled into belief
we really know the bush is rope-jerked greenery.

We find relief
in corners—
slowing down, catching our emotions before the next act.
The toads hunch waiting in the hollows;
Road fawners—
then catapult like spotted chewing gum.
We kill some.

Caught up in our make-believe world
we want to travel alone, together, forever.
We want to be eternally hurled into darkness.

Gary Catalano
Australia

I breathe the air of another country
when I walk among these people.
How terrible it is!

Generations have yearned for the new life
and it comes to this!
What will hold them upright

when their dreams are repossessed
and sold again at a discount?
But give me the smell of used nails

10 rusting in tins, and the dreams
that were swaddled in hessian.
I want the scene before it changed—

the blackberry-choked creeks,
the roads going nowhere, the shyness
of youth. Let me see again

the glitter of galvanized iron,
the scatter of farms and chicken-sheds,
and pictures like this:

in an afternoon of its own
20 a tortoise makes its slow way
across a road of blue metal and tar.

It pulls in its head at the sound
of an approaching car, whose driver stops,
gets out, then moves it into the tall grass

at the side of the road,
where a creek has begun to unthread itself
from a soak, and etch its straggly line

across the adjoining paddock,
whose wall of trees closes off the scene
30 from all the other countries in the world.

Peter Kocan
Barbecue

Which of us will one day sit alone
In that last isolation nothing mends,
Remembering a long-lost afternoon
And a casual gathering of friends?

The women, milky-breasted, beautiful,
Watching their children toddle on the grass . . .
The men, skylarking with a bat and ball
Until the Sunday sun begins to pass . . .

Decades on, this sun will re-emerge
10   With aching clarity in someone's mind,
To shake and grieve them in their senile age
And shine the brighter when the eyes are blind.

For one amongst us will outlive the rest
And weep to think, perhaps at ninety-five,
About this knife-edged brilliance of the past
When all of us were happy and alive.

And so, my friends, let's cling together now
Against the future that we cannot see.
Let's love each other, for we cannot know
20   Who the condemned survivor is to be.

Michael Dransfield
Like This for Years

In the cold weather
the cold city the cold
heart of something as pitiless as apathy
to be a poet in Australia
is the ultimate commitment.

When you've been thrown out of the last car
for speaking truthfully or mumbling poems
and the emptiness is not these stranded
endless plains but knowing that you are completely
10   alone in a desert full of strangers

and when the waves cast you up who sought
to dive so deep and come up with
more than water in your hands
and the water itself is sand is air is something
unholdable

you realise that what you taste now in the mornings
is not so much blood as the failure of language
and no good comes of singing or of silence
the trees wont hold you you reject rejection
20   and the ultimate commitment
is survival

Alan Wearne
St Bartholomew Remembers Jesus Christ as an Athlete

Always in training. Yet helping with his work
was, partly boring, sometimes even nasty.
Still, even when I felt he'd gone too far,
think: here we go again, out came the logic
smooth as a circle, Roman-disciplined.
Brilliant. Yes. Yet never near to God.

Only when he ran.
Only when I saw him striding.
(He'd leap and throw his arms above his head.)
10   It really was a case of 'run with me'.
I did. And often we came down the mountains,
(jogging loosely—never with a cramp).
My running partner—heading for Jerusalem—
appeared as if his feet were next to God.

This too was a feat,—running for a month,
(as rumour had it).
        Sprinting in the temple
was nothing less than perfect. Tables knocked,
Whips raised and money lost,
20   He charged them twice.

Of course revenge was needed, and his arms
were raised once more; his feet, however, broken;
sort of enforced retirement. Still,
he made a comeback, to end all comebacks:
                                        Once
there were ten, and I half-walking, pacing,
(my room mates seated, limbered-up in thought).
We stopped the noise and movement; standing still
I heard the footsteps pounding up the stairs.

Kevin Hart
A Dream of France

Restless at night and during storms
my father tore me from my heavy sleep

like a picture from a thick black book—
and walked me through his dream,

the nightmare streets of 1944
that stuck him to the past.

He groped about my room, barefoot,
unearthly, gasping as shells

unleashed their violet energy
about his hugeness, then

quietly curled up on my bed
one eye half-open, waiting

for the dark to come upon him
as a picture when the page is turned.

The Old

You cannot forget the old.
They become part of you.
They take you for themselves.

I have watched them in the city.
They stack themselves up
against the walls like chairs.

They always seem to be waiting
for something to happen.
It never does.

Or if it does I'm never there.
I do not trust them.
They aren't satisfied with death.

They keep on coming back.
Someone old will be inside your flesh
not long from now—

taking you over completely
going about your business
sleeping with your wife.

I know the one who wants me.
Sometimes I think I know his thoughts.
He will know me very well.

But still we won't get on.
He will walk for miles
just thinking of me.

It will be very much like love.
He will leaf through old books
where I have written silly things.

He will search out photograph albums
and stare at pictures of me—
adjusting old white corners

smelling the gum.

INDEX OF POETS

INDEX OF TITLES
AND FIRST LINES

ACKNOWLEDGEMENTS

The editors and publisher would like to thank the following for granting permission to publish copyright material. In cases where there is a discrepancy between a title mentioned in the Author's Notes and the title credited in these Acknowledgements, the latter indicates later publication of the poem(s) in a more recent collection.

Angus & Robertson Publishers for: three poems from *Collected Verse* by A.B. Paterson; seven poems by John Shaw Neilson from *The Collected Poems of Shaw Neilson*; ten poems from *Collected Poems 1930–1970*, 'Magpies' from *Antechinus* and 'Hay Fever' from *A Late Picking* by A.D. Hope; thirteen poems from *Collected Poems 1942–1970* by Judith Wright; eight poems from *Selected Poems* and 'Bellbirds' from *Death and Pretty Cousins* by David Campbell; ten poems from *Collected Poems* by James McAuley; seven poems from *Selected Poems* by Rosemary Dobson; five poems from *Selected Poems* and 'Mother Who Gave Me Life' from *The Lion's Bride* by Gwen Harwood; four poems from *Collected Poems* by Francis Webb; four poems from *Letters to Live Poets* and 'The Entertainer' from *Selected Poems* by Bruce Beaver; six poems by Les A. Murray from *The Vernacular Republic: Poems 1961–1981;* 'Old Botany Bay' from *The Passionate Heart and Other Poems* and 'Nationality' from *Selected Verse* by Mary Gilmore; 'Said Hanrahan' by John O'Brien from *Around the Boree Log and Other Verses;* three poems by Lesbia Harford from *The Poems of Lesbia Harford;* 'The Wind at Your Door' from *Forty Years' Poems* and 'Song in Autumn' from *This Night's Orbit* by R.D. FitzGerald; 'Love Me and Never Leave Me' and 'The Passionate Clerk to His Love' from *Quod Ronald McCuaig* by Ronald McCuaig; 'Space' from *Selected Poems 1936–1984* by William Hart-Smith; 'A Sailor's Grave' and 'Death of a Whale' from *A Beachcomber's Diary* by John Blight; 'Terra Australis' and 'B Flat' from *Collected Poems 1936–1967* by Douglas Stewart; 'The Children Go' and 'An Old Inmate' by Kenneth MacKenzie from *Selected Poems*; 'Orpheus and the Wild Beasts' from *Orpheus and Other Poems* by Harold Stewart; 'Farmer Goes Berserk' from *Crazy Woman and Other Poems* by Anne Elder; 'Deathbed Sketch' from *An Island South* and 'Twenty Years of Sydney' from *Tide Country* by Vivian Smith; 'Five Days Late' from *Selected Poems* by Geoffrey Lehmann; and 'In the early hours . . .' from *The Skylight* by Robert Gray.

Australian National University Press for 'The Tree' by Dorothy Auchterlonie from *The Dolphin*.

Vincent Buckley for the complete sequence 'Stroke' from *Arcady and Other Places*.

Gary Catalano for his poem 'Australia'.

Curtis Brown (Australia) for: 'My Country' by Dorothea Mackellar from *The Closed Door*; and 'Suburban' by David Malouf from *Neighbours in a Thicket*.

Hale & Iremonger for 'Letter from the Barrier Reef' by Mark O'Connor from *The Fiesta of Men*.

Max Harris for his poem 'The Tantanoola Tiger' from *A Window at Night*.

Dorothy Hewett for her poem 'Anniversary' from *Rapunzel in Suburbia*.

Hyland House for 'Under an Aboriginal Tree' from *The Song Cycle of Jacky and Other Poems* by Mudrooroo Narogin.

Jacaranda Wiley for 'We Are Going' by Oodgeroo Noonuccal from *My People*.

Peter Kocan for his poem 'Barbecue'.

David Lake for his poem 'To Horace'.

Kate Llewellyn and Women's Redress Press for 'Eve' from '*Luxury*'.

Longman Cheshire Company Pty Ltd for: six poems by Bruce Dawe from *Sometimes Gladness: Collected Poems 1954–1982*; and two poems by Philip Martin from *A Flag for the Wind*.

Lothian Publishing Company for 'Australia' by Bernard O'Dowd from *Collected Poems of Bernard O'Dowd*.

R. Mudie for 'They'll Tell You About Me' by Ian Mudie from *The Blue Crane*.

Oxford University Press for six poems by Peter Porter from *Collected Poems*.

R.A. Simpson for his poem 'Captain Oates, 1912'.

Richard Scott Simon Ltd for 'The Utopia of Lord Mayor Howard' from *The Outsider* and 'The Singing Bones' from *A Counterfeit Silence* by Randolph Stow.

Sisters Publishing for: 'Migrant Woman on a Melbourne Tram' from *Winter Driving* by Jennifer Strauss; and 'Freedom Fighter' from *Mrs Noah and the Minoan Queen* by Antigone Kefala.

University of Queensland Press for: 'The Tomb of Lt. John Learmonth, A.I.F.' from *Collected Verse* by John Manifold; 'Autumn Supper' from *Falcon Drinking* by Dimitris Tsaloumas; 'Ethel' from *Selected Poems* by R.A. Simpson; 'Kaddish' from *Kaddish and Other Poems* by Fay Zwicky; 'Eskimo Occasion' from *Water Life* by Judith Rodriguez; 'Developing a Wife' from *The Cool Change* by Andrew Taylor; 'Smalltown Memorials' from *Smalltown Memorials* by Geoff Page; '1915' from *Airship* by Roger McDonald; 'The Journey' from *The Brineshrimp* by Rhyll McMaster; 'Like This For Years' from *Streets of the Long Voyage* by Michael Dransfield; and 'A Dream of France' and 'The Old' from *The Departure* by Kevin Hart.

Chris Wallace-Crabbe for his poem 'Melbourne' from *Selected Poems*.

Alan Wearne for his poem 'St Bartholomew Remembers Jesus Christ as an Athlete' from *Public Relations*.

Every effort has been made to trace and contact copyright holders. Should any error or omission have ocurred the editors and publishers would be pleased to receive enquiries from any persons who believe they hold copyright to material used in this book.